I0461689

The Church Through the Tribulation

A Comprehensive Presentation of Biblical Eschatology

Gordon Griffo

Watchful Servant Publishing
Snowflake, Arizona

All Scripture quotations taken from the King James Version.

Watchful Servant Publishing
P.O. Box 865
Snowflake, AZ 85937
www.watchfulservant.com

Contents

Introduction

The reason for writing this book can be found in one brief prophecy given by the Lord Jesus: "And then shall many be offended" (Matt. 24:10). He spoke these words to four of his apostles just days before his crucifixion while informing them of the signs that will precede his Second Coming.

He spoke of a great tribulation that will precede his return and will be the worst that has ever befallen humanity. The persecutions and spiritual deceptions that will occur during this time will be the cause of many people being offended.

Who are these people that he is referring to? And what does being "offended" mean? The people are Christians, those who will be alive during the great tribulation, and being offended means departing from the faith.

A large segment of believers today is being taught that this prophecy is speaking of a different group of Christians. Ones that will be converted by the preaching of a group of evangelical Jews after all those alive before the tribulation are taken into heaven by the Lord in a pretribulation rapture. According to this doctrine, believers alive today have nothing to be concerned about or prepare for since we will be spectators of these prophesied events, removed from the earth before any of the trouble begins.

Contrary to this view, this book will show that God's faithful remnant of the Jews will enter into this time in unbelief and will be tried, tested, and purged by the tribulation, only to become believers in Christ on the last day. It will also be shown that the church is in a terrible state of apostasy and will go through the great tribulation for the same reasons as the Jews, to be tried and purged, only to be raptured on the last day. This last day is Christ's Second Coming, referred to throughout the Bible as the Day of the Lord. It is also referred to in the New Testament as the believer's blessed hope.

It will be shown that the signs that will precede the Lord's Second Coming have been given to us—believers—so that we can be fully

1

prepared at his arrival and not be among those who have fallen away from the faith during the persecutions and judgments of the great tribulation. This is exactly what the believer is called to do, remain in the faith and the truth to the end. Those who do so will be rewarded with eternal life.

To establish these points, this book sets forth a comprehensive presentation of biblical eschatology. The first section is a series of studies on the prophecies of Daniel and is followed by a series of general studies. The final section is a series of studies on Revelation. The purpose is to examine the totality of God's teachings on the subject of eschatology and present the consistent message that is taught throughout Scripture.

One final point must be addressed in these studies. The greatest obstacle to a proper understanding of Revelation is the consecutive treatment of the judgments. This interpretation considers the trumpet judgments to follow the seal judgments and the vial judgments to follow the trumpets.

Instead, it will be shown that God uses a prophetic delivery method that can best be described as "multiple prophecies with concurrent fulfillment and a common endpoint," or simply stated—prophetic layering. It should also be understood that this is not "recapitulation" since recapitulation means "to say again." What will be demonstrated is that the separate prophecies are describing different events and different participants in the great tribulation.

This will be shown to be the way that the prophecies of Daniel have been delivered and how the Lord taught the apostles in the Olivet Discourse. It will also be shown that when this understanding is applied to the prophecies of Revelation, all of the details fall right into place, and there will be no "loose threads" that need to be explained. Things that simply can't be explained with the consecutive-fulfillment model will now make perfect sense.

There is a companion study chart to this book available as a free digital download. It depicts all of the prophetic chapters of Revelation and is titled *The Time of the End*. Please go to the publisher's website, www.watchfulservant.com, for a free download.

1

The Times of the Gentiles

Two Prophecies

There is a phrase that is used on only one occasion in the Bible, "the times of the Gentiles": "And they shall fall by the edge of the sword, and shall be led away captive into all nations: and Jerusalem shall be trodden down of the Gentiles, until the times of the Gentiles be fulfilled" (Luke 21:24). Most commentators agree that this period began with the overthrow of the southern kingdom by Nebuchadnezzar in 586 B.C and will end at a future date with the triumphant return of Christ.

From the time of the Babylonian captivity, Israel has ceased to be a sovereign nation under God. It has been a time of Gentile rule over the people of Israel, and Luke 21:24 is a prophecy of the destruction of Jerusalem in 70 A.D. by the Romans and the subsequent dispersion of the Jews throughout the world.

In our first study, we will examine two prophecies in the book of Daniel that cover this entire period. The first was delivered to Nebuchadnezzar by way of a dream and interpreted by Daniel in Daniel 2. And the second was delivered to Daniel by way of a vision and interpreted by an angel in Daniel 7.

Historical Setting (Dan. 1)

The book of Daniel opens at the time of the first siege of Jerusalem in 605 B.C. God had given over the southern kingdom of Judah to Nebuchadnezzar, king of Babylon, as a judgment for their sins, just as he had given over the northern kingdom to Assyria some 117 years earlier. The king ordered a limited number of captives to be taken, among whom were Daniel and his three companions. Daniel and his companions were to be trained for three years in preparation to serve in the king's court. To prepare Daniel and his companions for their prophetic calling, "God gave them knowledge and skill in all learning and wisdom: and Daniel had understanding in all visions and dreams" (Dan. 1:17).

Nebuchadnezzar's Dream (Dan. 2)

Introduction (vv. 1–13)

Daniel 2 opens in the second year of Nebuchadnezzar, 604–603 B.C. The king had a dream that troubled him greatly, and he sought the meaning of the dream from his magicians, astrologers, sorcerers, and other occult practitioners ("wise men"). These sorts of practitioners have been led by the same power throughout all time. From Egypt to Babylon until the present, that power has been Satan and his fallen angels—demons. Their objectives are always at odds with those of God.

The king informed his wise men that he had forgotten the dream (Dan. 2:5) and commanded them to tell him the dream first under penalty of death. Since if they were able to do this, he would know that their interpretation would be correct (Dan. 2: 9). None were able to do so, and the decree went forth that they all should be slain (Dan. 2:12–13).

Dream Revealed to Daniel (vv. 14–30)

When Daniel and his companions were sought for death, Daniel made an appeal to the captain of the king's guard to be given the opportunity to tell the king's dream and its interpretation. Daniel and his companions prayed to God, and the secret was revealed to Daniel in a night vision (Dan. 2:19). Daniel gave thanks to God and was brought before the king. Daniel informed the king that where his wise men had failed, the God of heaven was able to provide what the king sought (Dan. 2:27–28).

The Dream and Interpretation (vv. 31–45)

What follows is important for us to understand. Daniel first provided the dream (vv. 31–35) and then continued with the interpretation (vv. 37–45). We see this pattern often; we are given a prophecy which contains much symbolic imagery, then the interpretation follows to inform us of what the symbolism is teaching. In this process, we will learn not only the prophecies delivered but also the specific meanings of the symbols. This will be vital for our understanding of later prophecies, including those in the book of Revelation. Daniel continued as follows:

> [31]Thou, O king, sawest, and behold a great image. This great image, whose brightness was excellent, stood before thee; and the form thereof was terrible. [32]This image's head was of fine gold, his breast and his arms of silver, his belly and his thighs of brass, [33]His legs of iron, his feet part of iron and part of clay. [34]Thou sawest till that a stone was cut out without hands, which smote the image upon his feet that were of iron and clay, and brake them to pieces. [35]Then was the iron, the clay, the brass, the silver, and the gold, broken to pieces together, and became like the chaff of the summer threshingfloors; and the wind carried them away, that no place was found for them: and the stone that smote the image became a great mountain, and filled the whole earth. [36]This is the dream; and we will tell the interpretation thereof before the king. [37]Thou, O king, art a king of kings: for the God of heaven hath given thee a kingdom, power, and strength, and glory. [38]And wheresoever the children of men dwell, the beasts of the field and the fowls of the heaven hath he given into thine hand, and hath made thee ruler over them all. Thou art this head of gold. [39]And after thee shall arise another kingdom inferior to thee, and another third kingdom of brass, which shall bear rule over all the earth. [40]And the fourth kingdom shall be strong as iron: forasmuch as iron breaketh in pieces and subdueth all things: and as iron that breaketh all these, shall it break in pieces and bruise. [41]And whereas thou sawest the feet and toes, part of potters' clay, and part of iron, the kingdom shall be divided; but there shall be in it of the strength of the iron, forasmuch as thou sawest the iron mixed with miry clay. [42]And as the toes of the feet were part of iron, and part of clay, so the kingdom shall be partly strong, and partly broken. [43]And whereas thou sawest iron mixed with miry

clay, they shall mingle themselves with the seed of men: but they shall not cleave one to another, even as iron is not mixed with clay. [44]And in the days of these kings shall the God of heaven set up a kingdom, which shall never be destroyed: and the kingdom shall not be left to other people, but it shall break in pieces and consume all these kingdoms, and it shall stand for ever. [45]Forasmuch as thou sawest that the stone was cut out of the mountain without hands, and that it brake in pieces the iron, the brass, the clay, the silver, and the gold; the great God hath made known to the king what shall come to pass hereafter: and the dream is certain, and the interpretation thereof sure. (Dan. 2:31–45)

Daniel described the great image in the king's dream as a man having a head of gold, breast and arms of silver, belly and thighs of brass, legs of iron, and feet part of iron and part of clay. He told the king that the head of gold represents the king and his kingdom. The silver represents a kingdom that will follow his. The brass is the kingdom that follows that one, and then finally, the legs of iron follow this third kingdom.

He described each kingdom as being successively inferior to the one before, and we see this shown in the metals becoming baser as they go down the image. We also see that by the fourth kingdom, the metal is the basest and also the most destructive. An important thing to note here is that in Daniel's interpretation, he specifically states that there are only four kingdoms (v. 40), even though it initially seems that the feet may well be a fifth (v. 33). Clearly, we are being told that the feet and toes are a part of the fourth kingdom. This becomes extremely important when we get to Revelation 17 and have to discern the sixth and seventh kingdoms presented to us there. These kingdoms are also consecutive, one arising after the other. And they are man's kingdoms, which is conveyed by the form of the image itself being that of a man. The four kingdoms described here are Babylon, Medo-Persia, Greece, and Rome.

Daniel continued to describe a stone that was cut out "without hands" (v. 34) that struck the image on the feet and destroyed them and the entire image. This stone then "became a great mountain, and filled the whole earth" (v. 35). In the interpretation, Daniel told the king that the God of heaven will "set up a kingdom" that will destroy these kingdoms, and his kingdom shall stand for ever (v. 44). The "great mountain" is a symbolic representation of the kingdom of God, and the "stone" that struck the feet of the image is a symbolic representation of Christ's Second Coming in destructive judgment upon the Gentile kingdoms of the world.

Daniel also gave a detailed description of the feet and toes (vv. 41–43). This kingdom will be a divided kingdom, partly strong and partly broken, as represented by the iron and clay. Here "divided" and "partly strong, and partly broken" are referring to a lack of cohesion within the kingdom and its ten kings, depicted by the ten toes. "They shall mingle themselves with the seed of men: but they shall not cleave to one another" may well be referring to political leaders mingling with the people of the world in the form of representative government,[1] iron being the strength of imperial rule, clay being the populist element.

Keep in mind, the word "divided" refers to the character of this final kingdom, not how it will come to an end. The way this Gentile kingdom will come to an end is by the sudden, destructive impact of the stone. We see that this will happen "in the days of these kings" (v. 44). This is referring to the ten kings represented by the ten toes of the image. The feet and toes are the kingdom (v. 41), and the toes themselves are the kings (v. 44). The important thing to note here is that these ten kings are contemporaneous, ruling over the world at the same time as opposed to the four consecutive kingdoms we saw represented earlier by the parts of the great image.

The King's Reaction (vv. 46–49)

The king was so amazed at what Daniel was able to tell him that he fell before him and worshipped him: "Of a truth it is, that your God is a God of gods, and a Lord of kings, and a revealer of secrets, seeing thou couldest reveal this secret" (Dan. 2:47). He made Daniel ruler over the whole province of Babylon and chief of the governors over all of the wise men.

---

1 West, *Daniel's Great Prophecy*, 38–39.

Important Lessons

We have already noted that there are only four Gentile kingdoms that are represented by the image, and the fifth is the kingdom of God, which succeeds them. An interesting thing happens between the time of the legs of iron and the feet of iron and clay. We know this because we have not yet seen this ten-ruler manifestation of the Roman Empire that is represented by the ten toes, and we have not yet seen the return of Christ to destroy these kingdoms and establish the kingdom of God on earth.

What is happening here is referred to as prophetic foreshortening, a way of saying that a great span of time passes from one verse of prophecy to the next with no apparent clue in the text. This will be a feature of prophecy that we will encounter very often, and it is up to us to make the determination of which parts of a prophecy are past and which parts are still to come in the future. In this case, the fourth kingdom—Rome—has both a historic manifestation that came to an end in 476 A.D. and a future manifestation that has yet to be realized.

This prophecy forms the foundation for all of the subsequent prophecies of Daniel. It foretells the entire period from Daniel to the Second Coming of Christ—the times of the Gentiles—and shows what will follow, the kingdom of God on earth. All of the subsequent prophecies will layer more information on the framework established here. The future is far too complex to cover in simply one vision, so God uses multiple prophecies to provide the additional details and create a composite picture of the future.[2] This is important for us to understand since this same pattern of showing an entire period first, in lesser detail, and then returning to fill in additional information is also how the prophecies of Revelation are delivered.

Daniel's Night Vision (Dan. 7)

Introduction (v. 1)

> [1]In the first year of Belshazzar king of Babylon Daniel had a dream and visions of his head upon his bed: then he wrote the dream, and told the sum of the matters. (Dan. 7:1)

---

2   West, *Daniel's Great Prophecy*, 37.

Daniel 7 opens some 50 years after the events of Daniel 2. Babylon is now under the reign of Belshazzar, who began his reign in 553 B.C. as co-regent with his father, Nabonidus.[3] Nebuchadnezzar died in 562 B.C., and with his death the glory of Babylon also began to fade. Belshazzar reigned until 539 B.C., when the kingdom fell to Medo-Persia, events we see chronicled in Daniel 5. This second prophecy of the times of the Gentiles is delivered to Daniel in a "dream and visions" (v. 1) in the year 553 B.C.

Overview

Daniel 7 is an overlay of Daniel 2 and provides a tremendous wealth of additional prophecy in symbolic form. We also see a repeat of the pattern of a prophecy being delivered, then followed by the interpretation, this time provided by an angel. We see the same four kingdoms: Babylon, Medo-Persia, Greece, and Rome. But this time, they are represented by "beasts," whose characteristics correspond to attributes of the individual kingdoms. We also see the destruction of the Gentile world powers and the establishment of the kingdom of God on earth at Christ's Second Coming. Not as a stone crushing the feet and toes as before, but now as the Son of Man coming in the clouds to establish his everlasting kingdom. We also get a much more detailed description of the fourth kingdom, particularly the final "ten toes" future stage. This time, the final ten kings are represented by the ten horns on the fourth beast. We are also introduced to yet one more character in these events, the "little horn" (vv. 8, 20–21). We will learn that this little horn is the Antichrist, whom the Lord will destroy at his Second Coming (vv. 11, 26; c.f. Rev. 19).

Please be aware that as the prophecies narrow their focus on one participant or period, we must update our understanding of previous prophecies to incorporate these new revelations. So, what we saw very generally as ten toes being crushed by the great stone in Daniel 2 is now being fleshed out with far greater detail to provide additional information and clarity. It also bears mention that these prophecies, while delivered in very symbolic imagery, are conveying very specific, literal details of what the future holds.

---

3   Miller, *New American Commentary: Daniel*, 44, 194.

In addition to using "beasts" to symbolize Gentile kingdoms, we are introduced to the use of "waters" to represent peoples or nations of the world (v. 2), the phrase "four winds of heaven" to refer to events coming from all directions of the compass (v. 2), "heads" to represent rulers (v. 6), "horns" to refer to kings or seats of power (vv. 7, 8), and "thrones" to represent judgment (v. 9). We also see the personification of symbols in the example of the little horn being given "eyes of a man" and a "mouth speaking great things" (v. 8)—blasphemies against God (v. 25)—to teach us that this little horn represents a final world leader. We see that a beast can refer to a kingdom (v. 23) and to a man (v. 11) and that the terms "king" and "kingdom" are often used interchangeably (vv. 17, 23). We are introduced to a figurative way of describing a specific period of time: "a time and times and the dividing of time" is used to mean a three-and-one-half-year period (v. 25). The use of the word "time" to represent a year is first seen in Daniel 4 when describing the humiliation of Nebuchadnezzar (Dan. 4:16, 23, 25, 32). Also, the title "Ancient of Days" refers to God the Father (v. 9) and "Son of Man" refers to Jesus Christ (v. 13). Finally, we must be alert to indicators of prophetic foreshortening to determine which portion of the prophecy pertains to historic Rome and which pertains to future Rome.

Vision Introduced (vv. 2–3)

> ²Daniel spake and said, I saw in my vision by night, and, behold, the four winds of the heaven strove upon the great sea. ³And four great beasts came up from the sea, diverse one from another. (Dan. 7:2–3)

The vision is introduced in vv. 2–3. It is referred to as a "night vision," in which Daniel saw the "four winds of heaven" striving upon the "great sea" and four "beasts" arising from the "sea." Waters are often a symbolic reference to the peoples or nations of the world since they portray an image of instability, constant change, and variability. The "beast" symbol is interpreted by the angel and means a kingdom (v. 23). We can well interpret this passage to depict worldwide turmoil (winds from all directions), from which four Gentile kingdoms arise.

We should, however, not get dogmatic about the interpretation of the four winds striving upon the sea. Language like this is highly figurative and can well have several very reasonable interpretations. What is important is that we should not consider all of the remainder of the symbolism in the prophecy to be equally subject to interpretation since it is much more specific in its content and we often have the interpretation provided in the text. Where the interpretation is not provided for us, we should use other Bible texts to determine the proper meaning. Where we can get into trouble is when we have similarly symbolic prophecy given to us, as in Revelation, and don't have the interpretation of the angel. Then we must remember what we have learned in these early prophecies concerning the proper interpretation of the symbols.

Historic Portion of the Prophecy (vv. 4-7)

> [4]The first was like a lion, and had eagle's wings: I beheld till the wings thereof were plucked, and it was lifted up from the earth, and made stand upon the feet as a man, and a man's heart was given to it. [5]And behold another beast, a second, like to a bear, and it raised up itself on one side, and it had three ribs in the mouth of it between the teeth of it: and they said thus unto it, Arise, devour much flesh. [6]After this I beheld, and lo another, like a leopard, which had upon the back of it four wings of a fowl; the beast had also four heads; and dominion was given to it. [7]After this I saw in the night visions, and behold a fourth beast, dreadful and terrible, and strong exceedingly; and it had great iron teeth: it devoured and brake in pieces, and stamped the residue with the feet of it: and it was diverse from all the beasts that were before it; and it had ten horns. (Dan. 7:4–7)

Daniel begins by describing the first beast arising from the sea as being like a lion and having eagle's wings. He watched until he saw its wings plucked off. After which, it was lifted up from the earth, made to stand upon its feet as a man, and given a man's heart (v. 4). These all provide figurative descriptions of Babylon and its primary king Nebuchadnezzar. The lion refers to ferocity, and eagle's wings depict swiftness in battle. "Wings plucked off" is speaking of a transformation from this winged lion to a man with a man's heart. This probably refers to the king's humiliation in Daniel 4, where he was caused to live with the animals of the field for seven years as punishment for his unwillingness to humble himself. After the seven years had passed, he was given back his mental faculties and his kingdom. At that time he praised God (Dan. 4:34–37), thus the reference to being given a man's heart.

Similarly, the second beast is likened to a bear, which raised itself up on one side. It had three ribs in its mouth and was told to arise and devour much flesh (v. 5). This is speaking of the Medo-Persian Empire, with its primary king being Cyrus. The bear is another animal known for its ferocity and voracious appetite. "Raised up on one side" shows this two-part kingdom, with the Persian side being the greater, and the "three ribs" are probably a reference to its three major military conquests—Babylon, Lydia, and Egypt.

The third beast is likened to a leopard, having four wings and four heads (v. 6). This is speaking of the Greek Empire, with its primary king being Alexander the Great. The leopard is among the swiftest of predators, and the four wings add to this imagery. This provides an accurate picture of Alexander the Great's lightning-fast conquests. The "four heads" refer to the four generals among whom the kingdom was divided upon Alexander's death in 323 B.C.

Finally, the fourth beast is described as follows: "After this I saw in the night visions, and behold a fourth beast, dreadful and terrible, and strong exceedingly; and it had great iron teeth: it devoured and brake in pieces, and stamped the residue with the feet of it: and it was diverse from all the beasts that were before it; and it had ten horns" (v. 7). Notice this text is lacking a full description of the beast's appearance as we got for the first three beasts. All we are told is that it has great iron teeth and ten horns. Later, we are told that it has nails of brass (v. 19).

Also, at the second colon in the verse, we have a break point in time. The portion before this refers to both historic and future Rome; what follows refers to future Rome exclusively. The words that indicate this transition are that it is "diverse" from the others and has "ten horns." Later, both of these will be explained to be attributes of future Rome (vv. 23–24).

As mentioned earlier, these ten horns are the same contemporaneous kings represented by the ten toes of Nebuchadnezzar's image.

This is the point in the vision where the prophetic foreshortening occurs. The prophecy jumps many centuries from historic Rome to future Rome with no apparent time lapse. As for a full description of the beast, we will eventually get that when we read Revelation 13:1–7.

Future Portion of the Prophecy (vv. 8-28)

The remainder of this chapter pertains entirely to future Rome and its king, the little horn—the Antichrist. Everything that was captured in the first prophecy of Daniel 2 by the stone crushing the feet and toes of the image and becoming a mountain that fills the entire earth is now expounded on in much greater detail.

There is considerable interplay between Daniel and the interpreting angel as well as alternating between the vision and the interpretation. To briefly summarize, vv. 8–14 and 19–22 contain the entire future portion of the vision. In v. 15, we see Daniel's reaction to the vision. In v. 16, Daniel approached one of "them" that was standing near and asked for the interpretation. The most reasonable understanding of whom he was asking is an angel of God. The angel obliged in v. 16 and provided a very condensed interpretation in vv. 17–18. In vv. 19–22, Daniel was still curious about the fourth beast, specifically future Rome, identified as being diverse from all the others. He wanted to know about the ten horns, and in particular, the one that arose from among them—this time referred to as "more stout" than the others. He also provided additional details about the vision that he had just seen. What follows in vv. 23–27 is the angel's detailed interpretation, and in v. 28, we see the effect it had on Daniel. Let's look at Daniel's first pass through the prophecy and his reaction:

> [8]I considered the horns, and, behold, there came up among them another little horn, before whom there were three of the first horns plucked up by the roots: and, behold, in this horn were eyes like the eyes of man, and a mouth speaking great things. [9]I beheld till the thrones were cast down, and the Ancient of days did sit, whose garment was white as snow, and the hair of his head like the pure wool: his throne was like the fiery flame, and his wheels as burning fire. [10]A fiery stream issued and came forth from before him: thousand thousands ministered unto him, and ten thousand

times ten thousand stood before him: the judgment was set, and the books were opened. [11]I beheld then because of the voice of the great words which the horn spake: I beheld even till the beast was slain, and his body destroyed, and given to the burning flame. [12]As concerning the rest of the beasts, they had their dominion taken away: yet their lives were prolonged for a season and time. [13]I saw in the night visions, and, behold, one like the Son of man came with the clouds of heaven, and came to the Ancient of days, and they brought him near before him. [14]And there was given him dominion, and glory, and a kingdom, that all people, nations, and languages, should serve him: his dominion is an everlasting dominion, which shall not pass away, and his kingdom that which shall not be destroyed. [15]I Daniel was grieved in my spirit in the midst of my body, and the visions of my head troubled me. (Dan. 7:8–15)

Daniel provides a rough view of future Rome, its kings, and Christ's Second Coming. Next, Daniel asked one of the angels for the interpretation. The angel's very condensed response follows:

[16]I came near unto one of them that stood by, and asked him the truth of all this. So he told me, and made me know the interpretation of the things. [17]These great beasts, which are four, are four kings, which shall arise out of the earth. [18]But the saints of the most High shall take the kingdom, and possess the kingdom for ever, even for ever and ever. (Dan. 7:16–18)

The angel stated that the beasts are four in number (v. 17), confirming our understanding of the fourth beast as representing both historic Rome and future Rome. The beast symbolism teaches us how God perceives them: wild, unruly, devouring their prey, focused on death and destruction, etc. They are referred to here as kings, showing that the word king can be used to describe a king or a kingdom. This will be very important for us to remember later when we get to Revelation 17.

Arising out of the "earth" (v. 17) is again symbolic, just as we saw that the beasts came up from the "sea" (v. 3). This is not some kind of a contradiction; God doesn't make mistakes like that. If we read something and it doesn't make sense or seems like a contradiction, then the problem is in us, not in the Word of God. So how can this be explained? As stated earlier, "seas" (waters) are often a symbolic reference to peoples or nations of the world. Now we must attempt to determine what the "earth" symbol is referring to.

In the New Testament, the "world" is used to refer to the physical earth, all mankind in general (John 3:16), as well as a system of rebellion against God (John 7:7; 8:23; 14:30; Col. 2:8, 20; James 1:27; 1 John 2:15–17; 4:5). Could it be this system of rebellion against God that the "earth" symbolizes? "Ye adulterers and adulteresses, know ye not that the friendship of the world is enmity with God? whosoever therefore will be a friend of the world is the enemy of God" (James 4:4). If so, it would fit very well in this case, and it may be that these beasts arising out of the "earth" is teaching that they represent this "world system" of rebellion against God. This is also evident in the obvious contrast between these "beasts of the earth" (ungodly kingdoms) and the "saints of the Most High" who take and posses the kingdom just one verse later. This symbolism will show up again in the Revelation studies that follow.

To conclude his very brief interpretation, the angel simply stated that "the saints of the Most High" will take and possess the kingdom for ever. At this point, Daniel still wanted to know more, specifically about the fourth beast with ten horns. He also provided some extra details of the vision:

> [19]Then I would know the truth of the fourth beast, which was diverse from all the others, exceeding dreadful, whose teeth were of iron, and his nails of brass; which devoured, brake in pieces, and stamped the residue with his feet; [20]And of the ten horns that were in his head, and of the other which came up, and before whom three fell; even of that horn that had eyes, and a mouth that spake very great things, whose look was more stout than his fellows. [21]I beheld, and the same horn made war with the saints, and prevailed against them; [22]Until the Ancient of days came, and judgment was given to the saints of the most High; and the time came that the saints possessed the kingdom. (Dan. 7:19–22)

The angel responded with a detailed interpretation, and we see the effect it had on Daniel, that he was greatly troubled to the point of his countenance being affected:

> 23Thus he said, The fourth beast shall be the fourth kingdom upon earth, which shall be diverse from all kingdoms, and shall devour the whole earth, and shall tread it down, and break it in pieces. 24And the ten horns out of this kingdom are ten kings that shall arise: and another shall rise after them; and he shall be diverse from the first, and he shall subdue three kings. 25And he shall speak great words against the most High, and shall wear out the saints of the most High, and think to change times and laws: and they shall be given into his hand until a time and times and the dividing of time. 26But the judgment shall sit, and they shall take away his dominion, to consume and to destroy it unto the end. 27And the kingdom and dominion, and the greatness of the kingdom under the whole heaven, shall be given to the people of the saints of the most High, whose kingdom is an everlasting kingdom, and all dominions shall serve and obey him. 28Hitherto is the end of the matter. As for me Daniel, my cogitations much troubled me, and my countenance changed in me: but I kept the matter in my heart. (Dan. 7:23–28)

Through this process we see the interplay between Daniel and the angel and between the vision and the interpretation. What are we to make of this? For starters, we can determine that Daniel was given a vision of events that are entirely in the future for him. These consist of near term events which precede the first advent of Christ and much more distant events which precede his Second Coming. We see that in God's view, man's kingdoms are likened to beasts and that there are four kingdoms that will rule the world from the time of Daniel to the time of Christ's Second Coming. The fourth kingdom is completely in the future for Daniel, but for us, part of it has passed and part still remains for the future. This future fourth kingdom is initially characterized by a ruling coalition of ten kings, from among whom a stronger ("more stout") one arises and kills ("plucks up," "causes to fall before him," "subdues") three of the original ten. This king will then continue to blaspheme God and make war with the saints, whom he will be allowed to prevail against. The saints will be given over to him for a period of three-and-one-half years—"a time and times and the dividing of time" (v. 25). At that point, Christ will return in victory and destroy the king (v. 11)—the Antichrist—and Gentile rule over the earth (v. 26). He will give judgment to his saints and establish his kingdom of God on earth.

The three-and-one-half-year period is what is known as the great tribulation. Later, we will see that both Christians and Jews will be persecuted by the Antichrist during this period. We see this above in that he will "make war with the saints," "prevail against them," "and shall wear out the saints of the Most High." The statement, "and think to change times and laws," means that he will also change Jewish festival times and ritual laws during this time of intense persecution. This fourth kingdom, and the Antichrist who arises from it, will also have a worldwide dominion. This is conveyed in the phrase, "and shall devour the whole earth."

It must also be noted that depending on the context, the "beast" symbol can be referring to a man (v. 11), a kingdom (v. 7), or both (v. 17). This is something we will see again in Revelation. The beast that is destroyed and thrown into the burning flame (v. 11) is the Antichrist; this is the same event that is shown in much greater detail in Revelation 19:11–21.

Also, the reason for the phrase "a time and times and the dividing of time" being interpreted as meaning three-and-one-half years is as follows: the first "time" is one year, the "times" that follow are two more years, and the "dividing of time" is a half-year, for a total of three-and-one-half years. Later references to this period (Dan. 12:7; Rev. 11:2, 3; 12:6, 14; 13:5) confirm this understanding.

Concluding Thoughts
The Saints of the Most High

We see the saints of the Most High referred to in the prophecy and interpretation on six occasions. Of them it is said, they will take and possess the kingdom for ever and ever (vv. 18, 22), the little horn will make war and prevail (for a limited time) against them (v. 21), judgment will be given to them (v. 22), they will be worn out and given

17

into the hands of the little horn for three-and-one-half years (v. 25), and they will be given an everlasting kingdom where they will serve and obey the Most High (v. 27). As we continue in our studies, it will become apparent that these are the same promises that are made to believers in Christ. After the destruction of the Antichrist and Gentile powers, these promises will initially be fulfilled in a thousand-year (millennial) reign of Christ on earth and then for all eternity in a new heaven and new earth, with God the Father himself present among them.

Worship in Heaven-Preparation for Judgment

In vv. 9–10, we see a beautiful picture of God's majesty, an innumerable host of angels worshipping him, and the opening of the books in preparation for judgment. This picture of the events in heaven provides a stark contrast to the events on earth. God is in control, and there will be a time of worldwide judgment. As we proceed in these studies, we will see that this judgment occurs in two stages. The first is in destructive wrath upon the world kingdoms and unbelievers, which will occur at the end of this world; the second is in eternal judgment of all souls, which will occur at the end of Christ's millennial reign on earth.

The other thing that is so evident from these passages is that we see two of the three persons of the Trinity described. The Ancient of Days (God the Father) and Son of Man (Christ) are clearly and distinctly identified. The title Son of Man is also how Christ refers to himself in the gospels and Olivet Discourse.

Son of Man Coming in the Clouds-the Day of the Lord

We have already noted that Christ's Second Coming is in view in these prophecies. It is depicted as the stone crushing the feet and toes in Nebuchadnezzar's dream and spoken of here as the Son of Man coming in the clouds to take possession of his kingdom for his saints (vv. 13–14, 27). This same event is described here: "And then shall appear the sign of the Son of man in heaven: and then shall all the tribes of the earth mourn, and they shall see the Son of man coming in the clouds of heaven with power and great glory" (Matt. 24:30); and here, "Ye men of Galilee, why stand ye gazing up into heaven? this

18

same Jesus, which is taken up from you into heaven, shall so come in like manner as ye have seen him go into heaven" (Acts 1:11).

In a later study, we see this referred to as the Day of the Lord and learn that multiple decisive events will happen on this day—his Second Coming. This day goes by many other names in the Old and New Testaments, such as "that day," "great and dreadful day of the Lord," "day of wrath," and others. This is spoken of as the time when "the mystery of God should be finished" (Rev. 10:7)—the day when God's redemptive plan for this world will be completed. Believers in Christ will be given their glorified bodies, the Antichrist and Gentile powers will be destroyed, and Christ will establish the kingdom of God on earth. Faithful Jews will have the Holy Spirit poured out on them and come to faith in Christ. They will also be given the promise that was made to them in the Old Testament, a kingdom with Christ sitting on the throne of David. We will see this day and the events that happen in much clearer detail as we progress through these studies. For now, we can say that it will be a day of destructive judgment upon unbelievers and blessings for believers.

Continuity Within the Bible

I have always thought of the book of Revelation as having been delivered to us through the visions of two prophets, separated by some 650 years. The first being Daniel in the sixth century B.C., and the second being John in the late first century A.D. We get so many points of connection between these two books that we must become very well versed in what we are being taught here in Daniel in order to understand Revelation. Obvious connections, such as symbolism using beasts, and well-defined periods, such as the three-and-one-half years, were introduced in this chapter. We also see slightly less obvious connections, such as the missing attributes of the fourth beast, which will eventually be provided for us in Revelation. And still further, the meaning of statements like "their lives were prolonged for a season and time" (v. 12) will become clear as we proceed in our studies.

Things like this make it so obvious that the words that we are studying can be from none other than the God of heaven. Not only that, but the fact that these prophecies of Daniel came in the sixth century B.C. and contain detailed descriptions of events that we can historically verify as having already occurred makes it even more certain that the prophecies that pertain to our future will be fulfilled exactly as described.

Please refer to page 66 for a chart that shows God's prophetic layering of all the prophecies of Daniel. Prophecies are presented by chapter, and the visions and interpretations are distinguished. The numbers under the corresponding periods covered by the prophecies are the verse numbers in the indicated chapter.

2

Antiochus IV–Prefiguring the Antichrist

Introduction (vv. 1–2)

> ¹In the third year of the reign of king Belshazzar a vision appeared unto me, even unto me Daniel, after that which appeared unto me at the first. ²And I saw in a vision; and it came to pass, when I saw, that I was at Shushan in the palace, which is in the province of Elam; and I saw in a vision, and I was by the river of Ulai. (Dan. 8:1–2)

Daniel 8 opens in the third year of Belshazzar, approximately 550 B.C. In this second vision, Daniel saw himself as being in the palace of Shushan (a province of Babylon) by the river Ulai. This is Daniel's second vision; he refers to the vision of the four beasts (Dan. 7) as "the first" (v. 1).

Overview

This vision brings us two additional prophetic tools which God employs. The first is the use of a historic event or personality to prefigure a future one. The second is delivering a vision to a prophet and then instructing him to close it to be revealed to us at a later time. This chapter in Daniel takes a much closer look at the second and third kingdoms presented in Daniel 2 and 7. It then focuses on one ruler of the third kingdom—Antiochus IV Epiphanes (175–163 B.C.)—and uses him to prefigure the eventual Antichrist.

Antiochus was a particularly brutal dictator who oppressed the Jews during his reign. We will see similarities between the things that he did and what the Antichrist will do. Just as the persecutions by Antiochus brought Israel back to God, so will the persecutions by the Antichrist.

This chapter uses the same process as before of providing the details of the vision given to Daniel followed by an interpretation, this time by the angel Gabriel. Once again, we must differentiate between the portions of the prophecy that pertain to the past and those that pertain to the future.

Daniel was given two visions in this chapter. The first is recorded in vv. 3–12; the second was given at the appearance of the angel Gabriel (v. 17) and was "shut up" (not presented to us in the text) at Gabriel's instruction (v. 26). The first vision shows the Medo-Persian and Greek empires up to the fourfold division of Alexander's empire (vv. 3–8). Prophetic foreshortening occurs at this point, and v. 9 jumps ahead by nearly 150 years to the arrival of Antiochus IV Epiphanes on the scene. The vision ends at v. 12, and in vv. 13–14, we hear two angels referring to this vision and providing additional pertinent information about it.

After this, Daniel sought greater understanding (vv. 15–16), and the angel Gabriel appeared in the form of a man to provide it. Verses 17–19 take an interesting twist; before providing the interpretation of the vision that Daniel had just received, Gabriel delivered another vision to him between v. 17 and v. 18. This second vision pertains to "the time of the end" (v. 17).

Gabriel continued by providing interpretation of the visions (vv. 20–25). Up through v. 22, he was describing historic Medo-Persia and Greece. Verse 23 begins a transition from Antiochus to the Antichrist, containing elements that can apply to both. After this, he was speaking of the Antichrist.

Gabriel gave Daniel the instructions "shut thou up the vision" (conceal, keep hidden), and we see Daniel's reaction to this vision (vv. 26–27). This second vision is described as being of "the evening and the morning," a reference to the Day of the Lord—Christ's Second Coming.

The Vision Concerning the Daily Sacrifice–Antiochus (vv. 3–14; 20–22)

> ³Then I lifted up mine eyes, and saw, and, behold, there stood before the river a ram which had two horns: and the two horns were high; but one was higher than the other, and the higher came up last. ⁴I saw the ram pushing westward, and northward, and southward; so that no beasts might stand before him, neither was there any that could deliver out of his hand; but he did according to his will, and became great. ⁵And as I was considering, behold, an he goat came from the west on the face of the whole earth, and touched not the ground: and the goat had a notable horn between his eyes. ⁶And he came to the ram that had two horns, which I had seen standing before the river, and ran unto him in the fury of his power. ⁷And I saw him come close unto the ram, and he as moved with choler against him, and smote the ram, and brake his two horns: and there was no power in the ram to stand before him, but he cast him down to the ground, and stamped upon him: and there was none that could deliver the ram out of his hand. ⁸Therefore the he goat waxed very great: and when he was strong, the great horn was broken; and for it came up four notable ones toward the four winds of heaven. (Dan. 8:3–8)

Here we have Gabriel's interpretation:

> ²⁰The ram which thou sawest having two horns are the kings of Media and Persia. ²¹And the rough goat is the king of Grecia: and the great horn that is between his eyes is the first king. ²²Now that being broken, whereas four stood up for it, four kingdoms shall stand up out of the nation, but not in his power. (Dan. 8:20–22)

The vision begins in v. 3 with a ram that has two horns pushing westward, northward, and southward—the Medo-Persian Empire. One of the two horns was higher and came up later, representing Persia. In v. 5, a goat came from the west—Greece—and did not even touch the ground, speaking of Alexander's lightning-fast conquests. Its notable horn represents Alexander. In vv. 6–7, the goat moved in on the ram "with choler against him, and smote the ram, and brake his two horns . . ." This is the conquest of Medo-Persia by Alexander, which was completed in 331 B.C.[1] In v. 8, the goat "waxed great" and "when he was strong" the "great horn was broken," describing Alexander's untimely death, at the age of 32, when he was at the peak of his career.[2] Four notable horns came up in his place "toward the four winds of heaven," describing the partitioning of his empire among his four generals.[3] Of concern to us will be Ptolemy in Egypt and Seleucus in Syria. Gabriel confirmed this interpretation in vv. 20–22.

In v. 9, we move ahead some 150 years and eight generations of the Seleucid dynasty to a notorious figure in history—Antiochus IV Epiphanes—who usurped the Syrian throne in 175 B.C.[4]

> [9]And out of one of them came forth a little horn, which waxed exceeding great, toward the south, and toward the east, and toward the pleasant land. [10]And it waxed great, even to the host of heaven; and it cast down some of the host and of the stars to the ground, and stamped upon them. [11]Yea, he magnified himself even to the prince of the host, and by him the daily sacrifice was taken away, and the place of his sanctuary was cast down. [12]And an host was given him against the daily sacrifice by reason of transgression, and it cast down the truth to the ground; and it practised, and prospered. (Dan. 8:9–12)

There is general agreement among commentators that this "little horn," spoken of in v. 9, is Antiochus IV Epiphanes. "Epiphanes" means "god manifest." However, his exploits earned him the name "Epimanes"—the mad. It is important to note that the little horn in this chapter is referring to someone other than the little horn in Daniel 7. His military campaigns to the south (Egypt), east (Persia), and the pleasant land (Israel) are identified (v. 9). "And it waxed great, even to the host of heaven; and it cast down some of the host and of the stars to the ground, and stamped upon them" (v. 10), is referring to his perse-cutions of the Jews, their religious leaders, and practices. He "magni-

---

1   Miller, *New American Commentary: Daniel*, 223.
2   Miller, *New American Commentary: Daniel*, 224.
3   Tregelles, *Daniel*, 79; Miller, *New American Commentary: Daniel*, 200.
4   West, *Daniel's Great Prophecy*, 94.

fied himself even to the prince of the host" (v. 11) by having the high priest Onias III assassinated in the fall of 170 B.C.[5] Later, he outlawed the morning and evening ("daily") services at the altar. He was "given" a "host" against the daily sacrifice by "reason of transgression" (v. 12). This means that Antiochus was a judgment of God upon Israel for their national sins of idolatry and pursuing false gods. He slaughtered tens of thousands of Jewish men, women, and children; and desecrated the temple by erecting a pagan altar to Zeus, sacrificing swine on it,[6] and erecting a statue of Zeus.[7] What follows is the interpretation of two angels:

> [13]Then I heard one saint speaking, and another saint said unto that certain saint which spake, How long shall be the vision concerning the daily sacrifice, and the transgression of desolation, to give both the sanctuary and the host to be trodden under foot? [14]And he said unto me, Unto two thousand and three hundred days; then shall the sanctuary be cleansed. (Dan. 8:13–14)

The angels spoke of the duration of this "transgression of desolation" as 2,300 days. This coincides with the time from the assassination of Onias III, in the fall of 170 B.C., to the cleansing and rededication of the temple in December of 164 B.C., after the Maccabean revolt.[8]

The Vision of the Evening and the Morning–the Antichrist (vv. 15–19; 23–25)

> [15]And it came to pass, when I, even I Daniel, had seen the vision, and sought for the meaning, then, behold, there stood before me as the appearance of a man. [16]And I heard a man's voice between the banks of Ulai, which called, and said, Gabriel, make this man to understand the vision. [17]So he came near where I stood: and when he came, I was afraid, and fell upon my face: but he said unto me, Understand, O son of man: for at the time of the end shall

---

5   Miller, *New American Commentary: Daniel*, 226.
6   Miller, *New American Commentary: Daniel*, 226.
7   Wenham, *New Bible Commentary*, 758.
8   Miller, *New American Commentary: Daniel*, 229–230.

be the vision. [18]Now as he was speaking with me, I was in a deep sleep on my face toward the ground: but he touched me, and set me upright. [19]And he said, Behold, I will make thee know what shall be in the last end of the indignation: for at the time appointed the end shall be. (Dan. 8:15–19)

After this, Daniel sought greater understanding of what he had just seen and heard (v. 15). Gabriel appeared before him, and instead of giving him further interpretation, gave him another vision (vv. 16–17). This second vision was said to pertain to "the time of the end" (v. 17), which is a description that cannot be applied to the vision we just studied since it pertains to events in the second century B.C. After receiving this second vision, we see Daniel's visceral reaction of being in a deep sleep on his face toward the ground (v. 18). He also needed Gabriel's touch to be set upright again. Gabriel confirms our understanding that he gave Daniel a vision of the end of this world by informing Daniel that he will tell him about the "last end of the indignation" and that "at the time appointed the end shall be" (v. 19).

The "indignation" here is God's righteous anger toward Israel for their ongoing sin. The "last end of the indignation" is speaking of Israel's national redemption at the Second Coming of Christ, referred to here as "the time appointed." This means that there will be no more of God's indignation for Israel. Thus, it is not possible for this to be referring to the indignation under Antiochus because that was by no means "the last." Many passages in the Bible speak of this future day; the following is a beautiful description:

[24]For I will take you from among the heathen, and gather you out of all countries, and will bring you into your own land. [25]Then will I sprinkle clean water upon you, and ye shall be clean: from all your filthiness, and from all your idols, will I cleanse you. [26]A new heart also will I give you, and a new spirit will I put within you: and I will take away the stony heart out of your flesh, and I will give you an heart of flesh. [27]And I will put my spirit within you, and cause you to walk in my statutes, and ye shall keep my judgments, and do them. [28]And ye shall dwell in the land that I gave to your fathers; and ye shall be my people, and I will be your God. (Ezek. 36:24–28)

The remaining two prophecies in Daniel also make specific references to this national redemption of Israel. It is shown to occur at the end of a "seventy week" period (Dan. 9:24). At that time, Daniel's people will "be delivered" (Dan. 12:1), and Old Testament saints will be given their immortal bodies (Dan. 12:2–3). These events will all happen at Christ's Second Coming.

Gabriel's references to the end (vv. 17, 19) make it clear that there was another vision given to Daniel at this point. Notice, however, that we didn't get the description of the vision. Instead, Gabriel went straight into an interpretation (vv. 20–25). His interpretation provides three verses pertaining to historic Medo-Persia and Greece (vv. 20–22) and then transitions to the vision that he had just given Daniel about the Antichrist and "the time of the end." So we aren't given the vision (yet), but we do have Gabriel's interpretation.

We have already seen Gabriel's interpretation of the first vision (vv. 20–22). Now let's look at the remainder of his interpretation:

> 23And in the latter time of their kingdom, when the transgressors are come to the full, a king of fierce countenance, and understanding dark sentences, shall stand up. 24And his power shall be mighty, but not by his own power: and he shall destroy wonderfully, and shall prosper, and practise, and shall destroy the mighty and the holy people. 25And through his policy also he shall cause craft to prosper in his hand; and he shall magnify himself in his heart, and by peace shall destroy many: he shall also stand up against the Prince of princes; but he shall be broken without hand. (Dan. 8:23–25)

The statement "when the transgressors are come to the full" (v. 23) is our indicator that Gabriel's interpretation is transitioning to "the time of the end." As vile as Antiochus was and as horrendous as his transgressions were, they will be greatly overshadowed by those of the Antichrist: "For then shall be great tribulation, such as was not since the beginning of the world to this time, no, nor ever shall be" (Matt. 24:21).

The Antichrist is referred to as the "king of fierce countenance" (v. 23). Further indicators that Gabriel is describing the Antichrist are that "his power shall be mighty, but not by his own power" (v. 24), a reference to being empowered by Satan (Rev. 13:2, 4; 2 Thess. 2:9). And, "He shall also stand up against the Prince of Princes" (v. 25), a description we saw earlier of the Antichrist ("he shall speak great words against the Most High" [Dan. 7: 25] and "he opened his mouth in blasphemy against God" [Rev. 13:6]). The Antichrist's blasphemies reach as high as demanding and receiving worship: "And they worshipped the beast" (Rev. 13:4).

Also, note that the one he stands up against is given the messianic title "Prince of Princes" (v. 25)—Jesus Christ. This is different from the title given to the high priest in the first vision, "prince of the host" (v. 11), indicating two separate visions with two distinct transgressors —Antiochus and the Antichrist. Antiochus' transgressions were against the "prince of the host," the high priest Onias III in 170 B.C. The Antichrist will "stand up" against the "Prince of Princes," Jesus Christ (c.f. Rev. 17:14; 19:19).

Finally, "he shall be broken without hand" is a reference to an action by God, just as we saw the stone that was cut out "without hands" (Dan. 2:34). The Antichrist will be defeated by Christ himself at his Second Coming and thrown alive into the "lake of fire" (Rev. 19:20).

Other characteristics of the Antichrist are the ability to "prosper" and to "destroy the mighty and the holy people" (v. 24), something we saw in the previous chapter where the saints were "given into his hand" for three-and-one-half years (Dan. 7:25; c.f. Dan. 12:7). "Craft" (v. 25), i.e., deceit, will be one of his primary weapons. He will lie and manipulate his way to political prominence. We also have the lessons of Christ in the Olivet Discourse, warning us on four occasions not to be deceived. The future "time of the end" will be characterized by widespread spiritual deceptions and demonically empowered signs and wonders being used to deceive many (Rev. 13:14). He will destroy many "by peace" (v. 25), something we will see in the image of a counterfeit savior—false christ—arriving on a white horse (Rev. 6:1). He will also "magnify himself in his heart" (v. 25), a description that we will see expanded on in Daniel 11:36, and understand "dark sentences" (v. 23), possibly referring to using occult means of gaining knowledge. These provide additional layers of revelation about the future and specifically the Antichrist.

Final Instructions (vv. 26–27)

> [26]And the vision of the evening and the morning which was told is true: wherefore shut thou up the vision; for it shall be for many days. [27]And I Daniel fainted, and was sick certain days; afterward I rose up, and did the king's business; and I was astonished at the vision, but none understood it. (Dan. 8:26–27)

Gabriel called this the vision of "the evening and the morning" (v. 26), a clear reference to the last day—the Day of the Lord. The Hebrew words *'ereb* (evening) and *bôqer* (morning) are used here. These are the same two words used throughout the creation account of Genesis 1: "And the evening and the morning were the first day" (Gen. 1:5). We see the first day and the last day described as "the evening and the morning."

Daniel was also told "shut thou up the vision; for it shall be for many days" (v. 26). Not the near term for Daniel, as was the first vision, but a far more distant future. The word rendered "shut up," *sâtham,*[9] means to conceal or keep secret. We see Daniel's reaction to the vision of fainting and being sick for several days (v. 27) and that he was "astonished" and unable to understand the vision.

Concluding Thoughts

Prefiguring in Prophecy

These two oppressors of God's people—Antiochus and the Antichrist—have so much in common that the former is being used to prefigure (foreshadow) the latter. In prophecy of this sort, the prefiguring event/person is always the lesser and results in an incomplete fulfillment; whereas the latter—the Antichrist—is the greater (more extreme persecution and destruction) and is the complete, final fulfillment of the prophecy. We will need to be able to separate when God is blending together two prophecies, like this, and differentiate between the two. An example that we will study later is the Olivet Discourse in Luke 21, blending the prophecies of the destruction of Jerusalem in 70 A.D. and the Second Coming of Christ. Through this prophetic tool, God uses similarities of the two events/personalities to have the earlier

---

9   Strong, *Concordance*, H5640.

one foreshadow and teach us about the latter. We also have absolute assurance that the latter will happen just as prophesied since we have history to look back at and see that the earlier has already occurred as was foretold.

The Evening and the Morning

Some Bible translations render Daniel 8:26 in the plural, "the vision of the evenings and the mornings." I believe the reason they do this is because these same two Hebrew words ('ereb and bôqer) are used in v. 14 to refer to the 2,300 days of desolation under Antiochus. In v. 14, the plural is appropriate since the words are preceded by a number; in the KJV they are translated "days." However, that is not the case in v. 26.

I believe what may have happened is that since these same two words were used earlier in the chapter, these translators may have assumed that they were referring to the earlier vision and used the plural. The problem that occurs with using the plural in v. 26 is that it points us back to the earlier vision and obscures the fact that a second vision, of the Day of the Lord, was provided to Daniel.

If we fail to recognize that a second vision was provided, we are forced to attribute all of the references to "the time of the end" and Israel's national redemption to events that have happened in the second century B.C. We must also come up with some other definition of "shut thou up" since the vision pertaining to Antiochus was given to us (vv. 9–12) and clearly has not been concealed or kept secret.

Further, we will fail to recognize that we have been given a description of the Antichrist, his activities, and how he will come to his end (vv. 23–25) and erroneously attribute Gabriel's interpretation exclusively to Antiochus. The most egregious example of which would be to apply "he shall also stand up against the Prince of Princes; but he shall be broken without hand" to Antiochus when it is completely consistent with what we are taught about the Antichrist (Dan. 2:34; 7:11, 25–26; 9:27; 11:45; c.f. Rev. 17:14; 19:19–20).

Most importantly, this reference to "the evening and the morning" provides solid evidence for the assertion that the Day of the Lord should be understood to be one day, the final day of this world, when the Lord will return in glory.

Why Close the Vision?

The reason we are given for closing the second vision is its distant fulfillment, "for it shall be for many days" (v. 26), and presumably, that it is intended for a different audience than readers of Daniel's time. Though unstated, I see yet another reason—to create an even more incredible link between the prophecies of Daniel and those given to John in Revelation. Most readers have probably already read the book of Revelation and wondered about the contents of the little book that John was given to eat by an angel:

> [9]And I went unto the angel, and said unto him, Give me the little book. And he said unto me, Take it, and eat it up; and it shall make thy belly bitter, but it shall be in thy mouth sweet as honey. [10]And I took the little book out of the angel's hand, and ate it up; and it was in my mouth sweet as honey: and as soon as I had eaten it, my belly was bitter. (Rev. 10:9–10)

There is much speculation among commentators what this book may be. However, I think that if we realize there was a vision given to Daniel that was intended for a later time, which was closed by Daniel, then the explanation becomes quite obvious. It is very reasonable to consider that it was this closed vision of Daniel that was open in the hand of the angel (Rev. 10:2) and given to John to eat, thereby delivering the vision to the intended audience—church-age believers.

Consider this as well, the little book that John was given was sweet as honey in his mouth but bitter in his belly. This would be exactly how one would expect him to describe the resurrection of dead and the "gathering together"—rapture—of living believers in Christ (2 Thess. 2:1), followed by the pouring out of the "wrath of the Lamb" (Rev. 6:16–17) upon unbelievers. It would also explain why Daniel was not able to understand it (v. 27), while it would be much more understandable to John. We will see a much clearer picture of this "evening and morning" in Revelation 19.

The only place where this particular prophetic delivery tool is used in the Bible is in the book of Daniel. It serves to separate the interpretation from the vision. Here in Daniel, we have the interpretation; later in Revelation, we have the vision. However, so we don't think that it's a fluke or something that we're reading too much into, God does the same thing again in the final vision given to Daniel.

Israel Redeemed, Antichrist Destroyed-the Day of the Lord

Every one of the prophecies in Daniel gives us a glimpse into the events of the Second Coming of Christ—the Day of the Lord. In this chapter, we see the redemption of Israel referenced in the phrase "the last end of the indignation." There is also the reference to how the Antichrist will come to his end, "being broken without hand." The remaining two prophecies in Daniel will continue to reveal additional details of the events that will be transpiring at this most glorious return of Christ.

God's Indignation-Only for Israel?

Even though the Day of the Lord will be a time of God's indignation being poured out on all of humanity, earlier it was stated that "the last end of the indignation" was specifically referring to God's indignation with Israel. This narrower application of the term was chosen instead of the broader indignation with the whole world for several reasons.

"The last end of the indignation" under the Antichrist is foreshadowed by the "indignation" under Antiochus. Antiochus was a means of dispensing God's anger toward Israel. Later, it will be the Antichrist who will perform this same function (Rev. 12:6, 13). God will use the chastening by the Antichrist to "refine" his people: "And I will bring the third part through the fire, and will refine them as silver is refined, and will try them as gold is tried: they shall call on my name, and I will hear them: I will say, It is my people: and they shall say, The LORD is my God" (Zech. 13:9). God uses godless kings and nations to fulfill his will in this way (c.f. Isa. 10:5–6). The word "indignation," when used in this way, refers to God's righteous wrath being poured out.

We also see that once the Antichrist has served his purpose, God will put an end to his reign of terror: "And the king shall do according to his will; and he shall exalt himself, and magnify himself above every god, and shall speak marvellous things against the God of gods, and shall prosper till the indignation be accomplished: for that that is determined shall be done" (Dan. 11:36). He will only be allowed to prosper until the "indignation be accomplished," after which the Jews will be "delivered" (Dan. 12:1).

This is not to say that God's indignation will not also be poured out upon an unbelieving world during the great tribulation as well— because it will be: "Therefore wait ye upon me, saith the LORD, until the day that I rise up to the prey: for my determination is to gather the nations, that I may assemble the kingdoms, to pour upon them mine indignation, even all my fierce anger: for all the earth shall be devoured with the fire of my jealousy" (Zeph. 3:8). However, since this prophecy in Daniel is specifically teaching of God's indignation with Israel and the remaining two prophecies in Daniel both point to the events of Israel's national redemption (Dan. 9:24; 12:1), I think that the narrower view of the "last end of the indignation," referring to a completion of God's redemptive plan for Israel, is appropriate.

Please refer to the prophetic timeline on page 66 to see how the prophecies of this chapter are adding additional details to the frame-work of the times of the Gentiles established earlier.

3

The Seventieth Week–the Prince That Shall Come

Introduction (vv. 1–2)

Daniel 9 opens in the first year of Darius, approximately 538 B.C. Cyrus, king of Persia, had just overthrown Babylon in the fall of 539 B.C. and had appointed Darius, the Mede, governor over Babylon while he continued in his conquests.[1] Cyrus took the sole reign of Babylon upon the death of Darius in 536 B.C. Daniel had been reading the prophecies of Jeremiah (Jer. 25:11–12; 29:10) and knew that Judah's seventy years of captivity in Babylon would soon come to an end.

Daniel's Prayer (vv. 3–19)

What follows is a beautiful prayer consisting of a confession of sins and trespasses (vv. 5–6) and an understanding that the people of Judah and Jerusalem had been driven out for this reason (v. 7). Daniel repeated this pattern of confession and acknowledgment of God's righteous judgment upon Israel as a consequence of their breaking God's covenant with Moses (vv. 11–13). He besought God for his anger to be turned away and the reproach against Jerusalem to be lifted (vv. 14–19).

Gabriel Appears to Daniel (vv. 20–23)

²⁰And whiles I was speaking, and praying, and confessing my sin and the sin of my people Israel, and presenting my

---

1   West, *Daniel's Great Prophecy*, 107, 135.

> supplication before the LORD my God for the holy mountain of my God; [21]Yea, whiles I was speaking in prayer, even the man Gabriel, whom I had seen in the vision at the beginning, being caused to fly swiftly, touched me about the time of the evening oblation. [22]And he informed me, and talked with me, and said, O Daniel, I am now come forth to give thee skill and understanding. [23]At the beginning of thy supplications the commandment came forth, and I am come to shew thee; for thou art greatly beloved: therefore understand the matter, and consider the vision. (Dan. 9:20-23)

While he was still praying, the angel Gabriel appeared to Daniel about the time of the evening offering (v. 21). Daniel knew his name and identified him as the one whom he had seen in the vision "at the beginning." This is a reference to the first vision given to Daniel in 553 B.C., the vision of the four beasts (Dan. 7), and informs us that it was Gabriel who provided the interpretation of that vision. The word translated "at the beginning" is the same that is translated "at the first" in Daniel 8:1, which Daniel used to refer to that first vision as well. Gabriel told Daniel that he has come to give him "skill and understanding" (v. 22) and that from the beginning of Daniel's prayer and supplication, the command was given for him to come because Daniel is "greatly beloved" (v. 23).

What follows is very interesting. Gabriel stated, "Therefore understand the matter, and consider the vision" (v. 23). Gabriel must be referring to the first vision given to Daniel, some fifteen years earlier, since there is no vision presented in this chapter. At the end of that vision, Daniel stated that he was troubled (Dan. 7:28). Now, it appears that Gabriel has arrived to provide greater clarity to what Daniel had previously seen. And by doing so, he provides another layer of prophecy pertaining to the times of the Gentiles. We have just been introduced to another prophetic delivery tool used by God. That is having an angel provide additional interpretation ("skill and understanding") to a previously delivered vision.

The interpretation provided along with the vision of the four beasts had a primary focus on the beasts and Christ's Second Coming to destroy the Antichrist and hand the kingdom of God over to the saints.

The interpretation presented in this chapter has a primary focus on the first advent of Christ and the redemption of Israel at his Second Coming. It also provides much more detail about the activities of the Antichrist during the great tribulation.

Daniel had been praying for the forgiveness of sins that had led to the captivity in Babylon and for a return to Jerusalem. However, Gabriel did not come to answer that prayer. Instead, he came to give Daniel knowledge of the time when Israel's national sin will be forgiven—"the last end of the indignation"—which will occur at "the time of the end."

The Seventy Weeks (vv. 24–27)

Gabriel stated the following sixfold promise that will accompany the closing out of a "seventy-week" period, which God has "determined" upon Israel:

> 24Seventy weeks are determined upon thy people and upon thy holy city, to finish the transgression, and to make an end of sins, and to make reconciliation for iniquity, and to bring in everlasting righteousness, and to seal up the vision and prophecy, and to anoint the most Holy. (Dan. 9:24)

These six events constitute a complete reversal of the state that Israel was in at the time of Daniel's prayer and continues to be in to this day: "For I would not, brethren, that ye should be ignorant of this mystery, lest ye should be wise in your own conceits; that blindness in part is happened to Israel, until the fulness of the Gentiles be come in" (Rom. 11:25). Further, "According as it is written, God hath given them the spirit of slumber, eyes that they should not see, and ears that they should not hear; unto this day" (Rom. 11:8; c.f. 2 Cor. 3:14–17).

There is a time coming when Israel will be redeemed from this blindness and God will "pour out" the Holy Spirit upon them (Zech. 12:10). He will deliver them from their "sins and uncleanness" (Zech. 13:1), and they will "look upon the one that they pierced and mourn for him" (Zech. 12:10). Christ will "destroy all the nations that come against Jerusalem" (Zech. 12:9), and "in that day there shall be one Lord" and "the Lord shall be king over all the earth" (Zech. 14:9). This is the event that we have been seeing gradually revealed to us in the previous three prophecies in Daniel—the Day of the Lord.

Likewise, this redemption is spoken of here: "And I will cleanse them from all their iniquity, whereby they have sinned against me; and I will pardon all their iniquities, whereby they have sinned, and whereby they have transgressed against me" (Jer. 33:8); "And it shall come to pass, that whosoever shall call on the name of the LORD shall be delivered: for in mount Zion and in Jerusalem shall be deliverance, as the LORD hath said, and in the remnant whom the LORD shall call" (Joel 2:32).

This brief recitation of other Old Testament prophecies corroborates what is taught in Daniel 9:24. At the end of this seventy-week period, the Jews and Jerusalem will be saved (c.f. Joel 2:32; Zech. 12:9). The "transgression" will be "finished" (c.f. Jer. 33:8) and there will be an "end" of Israel's "sins" (c.f. Zech. 13:1). God will "pardon their iniquity" (c.f. Jer. 33:8; Zech. 12:10) and "bring in everlasting righteousness" (c.f. Zech. 14:9). The "Most Holy" that will be anointed is Christ as king over the entire world (Dan. 7:14, 27): the "stone" crushing the "feet and toes" of Daniel 2, the Son of Man coming in the clouds of Daniel 7, and the "Prince of Princes" who will break the Antichrist "without hand" in Daniel 8.

In this revelation to Daniel, Gabriel referred to the seventy weeks as having been "determined" for the Jews and Jerusalem "to seal up the vision and the prophecy" (v. 24), meaning that everything that has been revealed to Daniel will be fulfilled at the end of this period. The vision being referred to is the vision of the four beasts (Dan. 7), which covers the times of the Gentiles, and the prophecy is that of the seventy weeks. This means that the seventy weeks span the entire times of the Gentiles. The end of this seventy weeks will mark "the last end of the indignation" (Dan. 8:19)—Israel's national redemption. Please note this day also coincides with the arrival of the "fulness of the Gentiles" (Rom. 11:25)—the end of this world. The references to this redemption of Israel at the "time appointed" (Dan. 8:19) and "determined" (v. 24) mean that this is all in God's hands and will transpire when he has decided.

The word "week" means an interval of seven, and there is a general consensus among commentators that the period spelled out here is seventy intervals of seven years or 490 years. Gabriel continued by revealing to Daniel when to start counting these years and certain events that will occur during this time:

> 25Know therefore and understand, that from the going forth of the commandment to restore and to build Jerusalem unto the Messiah the Prince shall be seven weeks, and threescore and two weeks: the street shall be built again, and the wall, even in troublous times. 26And after threescore and two weeks shall Messiah be cut off, but not for himself: and the people of the prince that shall come shall destroy the city and the sanctuary; and the end thereof shall be with a flood, and unto the end of the war desolations are determined. 27And he shall confirm the covenant with many for one week: and in the midst of the week he shall cause the sacrifice and the oblation to cease, and for the overspreading of abominations he shall make it desolate, even until the consummation, and that determined shall be poured upon the desolate. (Dan. 9:25–27)

In v. 25, Gabriel told Daniel that from the time of the commandment to restore and build Jerusalem up to the "Messiah the Prince" there will be a total of sixty-nine weeks (483 years). This period is spelled out as the sum of seven and sixty-two weeks. This is followed by mention of the streets and wall being built in troublous times. It is quite reasonable to infer that this is telling us the first seven weeks (49 years) will mark the completion of the rebuilding of Jerusalem, and the next sixty-two weeks (434 years) will mark the arrival of the Messiah —the first advent of Jesus Christ.

Please note the different title for Christ in this passage than that used in v. 24. Here we see the first advent of Christ in sight, and he is referred to with the title "Messiah the Prince"; in the previous passage, the Second Coming is in sight, and he is referred to as the "Most Holy."

After the sixty-two weeks, Christ will be "cut off"—crucified—but "not for himself" (v. 26), not for any sins of his own but for the sins of all those who will believe. The "prince that shall come" is referring to the Antichrist. Since he will come from future Rome, "the people of the prince that shall come" are the Romans. So, v. 26 foretells the destruction of Jerusalem and the temple in 70 A.D. by the Romans as well as the horrific nature of the assault—"the end thereof shall be with a flood." "Flood" imagery is often used to describe an over-whelming military conquest. "And unto the end of the war desolations are determined" speaks of the dispersion of the Jews throughout the world after the destruction of Jerusalem and likens it to a war.

In these two verses (vv. 25–26), we have just seen the foretelling of the first advent of Christ, his crucifixion, the destruction of Jerusalem, and the Jewish dispersion throughout the world. Between v. 26 and v. 27, there is a considerable period of prophetic foreshortening. The first sixty-nine weeks are all in the past for us, and the final "week," seven-year period, is in the future. The sixfold promises of v. 24 will not occur until the end of this world at Christ's Second Coming, which will mark the end of the seventy weeks.

Gabriel followed by saying, "And he shall confirm the covenant with many for one week" (v. 27). The "he" referred to here is the "prince that shall come"—the Antichrist. He will "confirm the covenant" (some sort of treaty), "with many" (Israel and many other nations), "for one week" (a seven-year period). This final seven year period is referred to as the Seventieth Week. Earlier, we saw that he will destroy many "by peace" (Dan. 8:25), making it a very reasonable assumption that the covenant that will be confirmed will be a multina-tional peace treaty. This tells us the event that will initiate the Seven-tieth Week—the confirmation of a covenant.

Gabriel continued, "And in the midst of the week he shall cause the sacrifice and the oblation to cease" (v. 27). The Antichrist will break the covenant at the midpoint of the seven-year period; the "oblation" is the grain offering. This begins the final three-and-one-half-years we saw spelled out previously, "a time and times and the dividing of time" (Dan. 7:25). We also have identified this as the great tribulation.

At that time, the Antichrist will put an end to temple services and sacrifices just as we saw foreshadowed by Antiochus IV (Dan. 8:11–14). This will necessitate the rebuilding of the temple in Jerusalem and reestablishment of the services there. Earlier, we saw one of many prophecies of the regathering of the Jews to Israel before their redemp-tion (Ezek. 36:24). That has already occurred, and in this verse, we see an implicit prophecy that they will have a rebuilt temple and services again in Jerusalem before the great tribulation.

Gabriel concluded by saying, "And for the overspreading of abominations he shall make it desolate, even until the consummation, and that determined shall be poured upon the desolate" (v. 27). The "overspreading of abominations" creates a figurative image of a bird of prey spreading its wings to describe the all-encompassing extent of the Antichrist's atrocities (c.f. Isa. 8:7–8). It will be the temple in Jerusalem that will be "desolated" (c.f. Rev. 11:2). These abominations will be allowed to continue for three-and-one-half years (Dan. 7:25), forty-two months (Rev. 13:5), "until the consummation," at which time Christ will put an end to it. "That determined shall be poured upon the desolate" speaks of Christ's return in judgment to pour out his wrath on the Antichrist, referred here to as "the desolate." This "desolation event" at the midpoint of the Seventieth Week, performed by the Antichrist, is what Christ refers to as the "abomination of desolation" in the Olivet Discourse (Matt. 24:15).

Now, all that remains is to determine the appropriate starting point for counting the sixty-nine weeks (seven plus sixty-two) and we will know exactly when Christ was prophesied to arrive as the Messiah. Notice this is the one event that has been prophesied to occur at a definite time. The other two events of v. 26, his crucifixion and destruction of Jerusalem, will happen after this, as will the beginning of the final Seventieth Week (v. 27).

The Commandment to Restore and Build Jerusalem

Gabriel stated that the sixty-nine weeks will begin with the "going forth of the commandment to restore and to build Jerusalem" (v. 25). There are several possible options for when this may have occurred. To determine the correct starting point, we must examine the process by which the Jews returned to Israel. There were three groups of exiles from Babylon that returned to Jerusalem after the seventy years in captivity. The first was led by Zerubbabel in the first year of Cyrus, 536 B.C. (Ezra 1:1–3); the second, led by Ezra in the seventh year of Artaxerxes, 457 B.C. (Ezra 7:1–7); and the third, led by Nehemiah in the twentieth year of Artaxerxes, 444 B.C. (Neh. 2:1–8).[2]

The decree made by Cyrus (536 B.C.) was very specific: "Who is there among you of all his people? his God be with him, and let him go

---

2   Rose, *Book of Bible Charts*, Foldout Timeline.

up to Jerusalem, which is in Judah, and build the house of the LORD God of Israel, (he is the God,) which is in Jerusalem" (Ezra 1:3). It was to rebuild the temple, not the city. This was later confirmed by Darius in 521 B.C. when he searched the records and found Cyrus' written decree (Ezra 6:1–5). For these reasons, it can be ruled out as the starting point for the prophecy.

Some commentators have used the decree made by Artaxerxes to Nehemiah (444 B.C.) as the starting point of the prophecy since it was in response to Nehemiah's request to be allowed to return to Jerusalem to "build it" (Neh. 2:5). However, Nehemiah's request to be allowed to return to Jerusalem to rebuild it does not preclude the possibility of a previously stated decree to rebuild the city, and there is no other evidence that Artaxerxes specifically authorized the rebuilding at that time. Considering this lack of evidence for the later date (444 B.C.) and the strong evidence in favor of using the first decree of Artaxerxes to Ezra in 457 B.C., I believe that to be the correct starting point.

Before we examine the details, we must first recognize that the entire return to Jerusalem and rebuilding of the temple and city was a very difficult process, and the returning exiles faced great opposition from the neighboring nations. Ezra was a scribe and a priest, and he has recorded much of the detail for us, from the first return under Cyrus to his return under Artaxerxes and even thereafter. The book of Nehemiah records his return and the period that followed. We have nearly 100 years of history between the two.

Ezra 4 records the opposition that they faced from their "adversaries" (Ezra 4:1) under Cyrus, Darius, Ahasuerus, and Artaxerxes (Ezra 4:4–7). We get a picture of extended strife during the rebuilding process, referred to as "troublous times" (v. 25). In Ezra 4:7–16, we see the opposition that Ezra faced after he had returned to Jerusalem in 457 B.C. The nations around Jerusalem had accused the Jews of rebuilding the city in a letter sent to Artaxerxes (Ezra 4:12). In response to this, the king made a search of the records and sent back the order that the rebuilding of the city should cease until he sends another decree (Ezra 4:21).

While it is not sufficient to rely solely on the accusations of Jerusalem's enemies, we see that Ezra prayed in thanks to God for being allowed to rebuild the wall in Judah and Jerusalem (Ezra 9:9).

He was also given a letter from the king authorizing him to do whatever he saw fit (Ezra 7:18, 21). Further, we also see that Ezra encountered a grave situation upon his arrival (Ezra 9:1). The people of Israel were involved in the abominations of all the surrounding nations. Consequently, he focused his attention on that problem, and it is understandable that thirteen years later, at the time of Nehemiah's request, the work had not yet been completed.

Unto the Messiah the Prince

Based on this historic evidence, we should be able to use the year 457 B.C. as the staring point of the seventy weeks prophecy. Thus, the rebuilding of the city would have been completed after forty-nine years, in 408 B.C., and the Messiah would have arrived after another 434 years—27 A.D. Since most scholars agree that Jesus was born about 4 B.C., this would exactly coincide with the start of his ministry at the baptism in the Jordan River. Following this, the prophecy foretells his death and the destruction of Jerusalem in that order. Since these are in the past for us, all that remains to be fulfilled of this prophecy is the initiation of the Seventieth Week with the confirmation of a covenant with the Antichrist (Dan. 9:27).

Concluding Thoughts

In this chapter, we have been introduced to yet one more significant period of time—the Seventieth Week—a yet-to-be-fulfilled prophecy. We have also seen that the great tribulation of three-and-one-half years has been identified as starting at the midpoint of this period ("in the midst of the week") with the abomination of desolation. I feel comfortable saying that "the time of the end" from Daniel 8 is referring to the entire seven-year period.

Still further, we see the incredible fulfillment of the arrival of the Messiah exactly as foretold by this prophecy. Not only that he would arrive but the exact timing of the arrival as well. This means that the Jewish religious leaders were without excuse for their rejection of the Lord Jesus. Further, this informs us that we should expect every detail of the prophecies that pertain to our future to be fulfilled in this same precise manner. There should be no question that they will occur exactly as foretold by the prophets.

We also see the continued use of the prophetic tool of giving Daniel details of near-term events, the first advent of Christ and destruction of Jerusalem and the temple, followed by much more distant events, the Seventieth Week and the activities of the Antichrist. In this prophecy, the siege and destruction of Jerusalem serve to foreshadow the great tribulation, just as Antiochus foreshadowed the Antichrist. However, on the Day of the Lord, Jesus will return and crush the world powers arrayed against the city and redeem faithful Jews.

Finally, referring to the covenant of the Antichrist, the word translated "confirm" (v. 27) means to strengthen. So, it appears that there will be an existing covenant in place, and the Antichrist will act in some way to further strengthen it. Please refer to page 66 to see the layering of these prophecies.

4

The Great Vision–the Self-Exalted King

Introduction (Dan. 10)

Daniel's fourth prophecy spans chapters 10 through 12. Daniel 10 opens in the third year of Cyrus, king of Persia, approximately 534 B.C. In the first verse, we are told that the "thing was true," that Daniel "understood" it, that "the time appointed was long," and that there was a "vision" involved. This last point is quite important in arriving at a proper understanding of these chapters.

> [1]In the third year of Cyrus king of Persia a thing was revealed unto Daniel, whose name was called Belteshazzar; and the thing was true, but the time appointed was long: and he understood the thing, and had understanding of the vision. [2]In those days I Daniel was mourning three full weeks. [3]I ate no pleasant bread, neither came flesh nor wine in my mouth, neither did I anoint myself at all, till three whole weeks were fulfilled. [4]And in the four and twentieth day of the first month, as I was by the side of the great river, which is Hiddekel; [5]Then I lifted up mine eyes, and looked, and behold a certain man clothed in linen, whose loins were girded with fine gold of Uphaz: [6]His body also was like the beryl, and his face as the appearance of lightning, and his eyes as lamps of fire, and his arms and his feet like in colour to polished brass, and the voice of his words like the voice of a multitude. [7]And I Daniel alone saw the vision: for the men that were with me saw not the vision; but a great quaking fell upon them, so that they fled to hide themselves. [8]Therefore I was left alone, and saw this

> great vision, and there remained no strength in me: for my comeliness was turned in me into corruption, and I retained no strength. (Dan. 10:1–8)

Daniel was fasting and mourning for three full weeks and was by the side of the Tigris (Hiddekel) River when a mighty angel appeared to him and delivered a prophetic vision. The angel's appearance is provided in vv. 5–6 and is nothing short of amazing. Daniel was the only one to see this amazing "vision" because the men who were with him had a "great quaking" (terror) fall upon them, and they fled (v. 7). Daniel reiterates that he was left alone "and saw this great vision," and as a consequence, all his strength left him (v. 8).

At this point, Daniel has referred to two events: a "certain man clothed in linen" that appeared before him (v. 5) and a "great vision" (vv. 1, 7, 8). Before we proceed further in this analysis, we must determine whether they are a single, or two separate events. The reason for this is that many commentators look at the intensity of the reactions that Daniel had, and continues to have throughout this chapter, and note the similarity between the description of this "man in linen" and that of Christ when he appeared to John on the island of Patmos (Rev. 1:11–20) and conclude that Daniel has witnessed a christophany, a pre-incarnate vision of the Lord Jesus. These interpreters tend to believe that "the vision" that has been referred to on these four occasions and on three subsequent occasions is the sight of the Lord himself. And they attribute the intensity of Daniel's reactions solely to being in the presence of the Lord.

Still others see this "man in linen" as a mighty angel who has appeared to deliver the interpretation of a vision given to Daniel. To resolve this issue, we will address two related questions: Is the "man in linen" Christ or an angel? And, was there a separate vision given to Daniel, or was this "man in linen" the extent of what he saw? The reason for making these determinations will become evident shortly.

Christophany or an Angel?

> [9]Yet heard I the voice of his words: and when I heard the voice of his words, then was I in a deep sleep on my face, and my face toward the ground. [10]And, behold, an hand touched me, which set me upon my knees and upon the

palms of my hands. [11]And he said unto me, O Daniel, a man greatly beloved, understand the words that I speak unto thee, and stand upright: for unto thee am I now sent. And when he had spoken this word unto me, I stood trembling. [12]Then said he unto me, Fear not, Daniel: for from the first day that thou didst set thine heart to understand, and to chasten thyself before thy God, thy words were heard, and I am come for thy words. [13]But the prince of the kingdom of Persia withstood me one and twenty days: but, lo, Michael, one of the chief princes, came to help me; and I remained there with the kings of Persia. [14]Now I am come to make thee understand what shall befall thy people in the latter days: for yet the vision is for many days. [15]And when he had spoken such words unto me, I set my face toward the ground, and I became dumb. [16]And, behold, one like the similitude of the sons of men touched my lips: then I opened my mouth, and spake, and said unto him that stood before me, O my lord, by the vision my sorrows are turned upon me, and I have retained no strength. [17]For how can the servant of this my lord talk with this my lord? for as for me, straightway there remained no strength in me, neither is there breath left in me. [18]Then there came again and touched me one like the appearance of a man, and he strengthened me, [19]And said, O man greatly beloved, fear not: peace be unto thee, be strong, yea, be strong. And when he had spoken unto me, I was strengthened, and said, Let my lord speak; for thou hast strengthened me. [20]Then said he, Knowest thou wherefore I come unto thee? and now will I return to fight with the prince of Persia: and when I am gone forth, lo, the prince of Grecia shall come. [21]But I will shew thee that which is noted in the scripture of truth: and there is none that holdeth with me in these things, but Michael your prince. (Dan. 10:9–21)

Commentators that see this as a christophany admit that there is a problem with this view since the one speaking to Daniel "was sent" to him (v. 11), informed him that the "prince of the kingdom of Persia" impeded him for three weeks (v. 13), needed the help of the archangel Michael (v. 13), and restrained the demonic forces over Persia with

Michael (v. 21). Since these statements cannot be describing Christ, they contend that at the first "comforting" of Daniel (v. 10), an angel has stepped in and has become the primary person interacting with Daniel.

However, when we get to Chapter 12, Daniel says that "other two" (angels) appeared and that one of them spoke to the "man clothed in linen" (Dan. 12:5–6), making it sound very much like it was the "man in linen" who was there all along speaking with Daniel. After this, the "man clothed in linen" raised his hands to heaven and swore by him that "liveth for ever" (Dan. 12:7), exactly as the angel that spoke with John did (Rev. 10:5–6), once again, not sounding like what Christ would do.

Further, when Christ did appear to John, he referred to himself as "Alpha and Omega" (Rev. 1:11), and the text provides the messianic title Son of Man (Rev. 1:13). Here we have no such references. In view of these issues, I contend that the "man in linen" was an angel sent to Daniel, just like the one who appeared to John (Rev. 10:1–3), and was the primary person involved in the dialog throughout the entire interaction. The significance of this determination is that Daniel's extreme reactions cannot be solely attributed to being in the presence of Christ.

Vision Delivered or Just an Interpretation?

By v. 8, Daniel has already referenced "the vision" on four occasions and indicated that there was no strength left in him as a consequence of seeing it. In v. 9, he heard the voice of this mighty angel, after which he was in a deep sleep upon his face. This is the same reaction that he had in Daniel 8 after Gabriel appeared to him and delivered the second vision, which pertained to "the time of the end" (Dan. 8:18).

Further evidence that there was a vision delivered to Daniel is that the man in linen referred to "the vision" (v. 14) and told Daniel that it is "for many days." Daniel also informed the angel that "the vision" has caused him great sorrow and to have no strength (v. 16). Finally, when providing the interpretation of the vision (Dan. 11:14), the angel informed Daniel that "the robbers of thy people" (the violent men of the Jews) will rise up against the "king of the south" (Egypt) in order to "establish" (confirm) the vision. This means that there was a vision in which certain Jews were to rise up against Egypt and that their rebellion would serve to confirm the vision.

Conversation like this makes it evident that there was a vision given to Daniel, which we don't have provided to us in the text. This is consistent with the instructions given to Daniel to "shut up" and to "seal" the "book" (Dan. 12:4). It is further confirmed to him by the angel that the words are "closed up" and "sealed" (Dan. 12:9) until "the time of the end." This evidence of a vision being given to Daniel, which was subsequently closed and sealed for a later time, combined with the evidence that it was not Christ who gave him the vision, indicates that it was the horrific nature of what he saw in this vision that made him fall to the ground and be powerless. This final vision in Daniel is the second time that God used the prophetic tool of providing a vision to one prophet and then having him close it to be passed on to another prophet at a later date.

Interaction With the Angels

In Daniel 10, there are at least two angels present: the one that first appeared to him, the "man in linen," of whom we have the full description; and another who revived him and gave him strength on three occasions (vv. 10, 16, 18),[1] the "comforting angel." Daniel referred to the man in linen as the one that "stood before" him (v. 16) and "my lord" (vv. 16, 19).

Daniel's interactions with the comforting angel were as follows: he was helped up to his knees and palms after seeing the vision by the touch of a hand (v. 10), his ability to speak was restored (v. 16), and he was again strengthened (v. 18). He was briefly spoken to by this comforting angel (v. 19), to whom he said, "Let my lord speak; for thou hast strengthened me." With the brief exception of this interaction with the "comforting angel," it appears that all of the dialog is with the man in linen.

More interesting than the details of the interactions are the specifics of what the man in linen told Daniel. He informed Daniel that he had been "withstood" by the "prince of the kingdom of Persia" (v. 13). The

---

1   It is a very reasonable assertion that the first "comforting" (v. 10) was performed by the "man in linen" and the subsequent two by the "other" angel. In the interest of brevity, I have attributed all three "comfortings" to the "other" angel since it does not alter the interpretation and avoids unnecessary complexity.

most reasonable conclusion is that this "prince" is a demon over the Persian Empire since he was in opposition to one of God's angels. And Michael, "one of the chief princes," came to assist the man in linen, and he remained there for three weeks with the "kings" of Persia. Since the demon that he was fighting is referred to as the "prince," it is quite reasonable to infer that these "kings" are the human kings over Persia. This angel also informed Daniel that he "stood to confirm and strengthen" Darius the Mede in his first year (Dan. 11:1) and that upon leaving Daniel he will return to "fight with the prince of Persia" (v. 20). Daniel 10 concludes with the man in linen stating that Michael is the only one that restrains ("holdeth") these forces of evil with him and that after he returns, the "prince of Grecia" will come (vv. 20–21). This means that his conflict will soon be with the demon of Greece.

Even though we are not specifically told the name of this angel, it is not unreasonable to assume that it is Gabriel. What we know of him is that he has provided the interpretation in the previous three prophecies given to Daniel and that he stands "in the presence of God" (Luke 1:19). Previously, he appeared to Daniel as a man (Dan. 7:16; 8:15; 9:21), and if this is Gabriel, his appearance this time is much more fitting for one who holds such a high honor.

This chapter provides a unique understanding of an unseen battle that is raging in the heavenly arena. It is also a very interesting preface to what follows, which is a prophecy of raging conflict on earth. The reasonable inference is that these forces of good and evil, and the heavenly warfare in which they are involved, are influencing what is happening on earth among men.

The Angel's Interpretation and Instructions (Dan. 11–12)

Overview

What follows in Daniel 11 and 12 is an interpretation of the great vision given to Daniel by the man in linen and some final instructions. The historic portion of the interpretation (Dan. 11:1–35) begins with a brief prophecy of the next four kings of the Medo-Persian Empire (v. 2); continues by describing the rise, fall, and partitioning of Alexander's empire (vv. 3–4); and concludes with an incredibly detailed prophecy of some 140 years of Syrian wars between Ptolemaic Egypt and Seleucid Syria (vv. 5–30). Antiochus IV Epiphanes is the "vile person" introduced in v. 21 and is again used to prefigure the Antichrist.

Verse 35 provides a transition to the future portion of the prophecy (vv. 36–45), in which the focus is exclusively on the Antichrist. The destruction of the Antichrist is given in v. 45. Daniel 12 transitions to the redemption of Israel and the resurrection of the dead. Also, Daniel is given some final instructions and some important periods of time pertaining to these prophecies.

Historic Portion of the Prophecy (Dan. 11:1-35)

In the biblical text, the Seleucid king is referred to as the "king of the north" and the Ptolemaic king as the "king of the south." The details of their exploits are so perfectly aligned with the historic record that many have attributed these writings to someone who recorded the details after the fact, rather than admit the perfect foreknowledge of God regarding the events on this earth. For us, this is more confirmation that the prophecies that pertain to our future will occur exactly as stated.

For the purposes of our studies, we will not go through every verse of the historic portion of the prophecy.[2] Instead, we will examine several events that occurred under Antiochus IV, which serve to foreshadow what will occur under the Antichrist, and then move on to the future portion of the prophecy.

Antiochus is introduced to us in v. 21 as a "vile person," and the entirety of the prophecy from that point to v. 35 pertains to him. When the prophecy transitions to him, it no longer refers to him as the "king of the north" as it did previously with earlier Seleucid kings (vv. 6, 7, 8, 11, 13, 15). Instead, the personal pronouns "he/his" are used when referring to him. The reason for noting this now will soon become evident.

His early military campaigns are detailed in vv. 21–30. Most notable is his use of deceit (v. 23) and treachery (v. 27), as well as his hatred for the Jews and their religion (v. 28). Historical details of the

---

2   A search for information on the Syrian wars will provide the details of these prophecies. Also see West, *Daniel's Great Prophecy*, 149–166 and Miller, *New American Commentary: Daniel*, 290–304 for a full accounting.

horrors he wrought can be found in the books of the Maccabees. The man in linen provides additional details about Antiochus as follows:

> [31]And arms shall stand on his part, and they shall pollute the sanctuary of strength, and shall take away the daily sacrifice, and they shall place the abomination that maketh desolate. [32]And such as do wickedly against the covenant shall he corrupt by flatteries: but the people that do know their God shall be strong, and do exploits. [33]And they that understand among the people shall instruct many: yet they shall fall by the sword, and by flame, by captivity, and by spoil, many days. [34]Now when they shall fall, they shall be holpen with a little help: but many shall cleave to them with flatteries. [35]And some of them of understanding shall fall, to try them, and to purge, and to make them white, even to the time of the end: because it is yet for a time appointed. (Dan. 11:31–35)

In v. 31, we see the same "desolation" of the temple that we studied in Daniel 8. The prophecy speaks of using military force to defile the sanctuary, take away the sacrifices, and set up the "abomination that maketh desolate." This latter offense was done by erecting a pagan altar, sacrificing on it, and erecting a statue of Zeus.[3] This abomination of desolation under Antiochus serves to foreshadow what the Antichrist will do (Dan. 9:27; 12:11). Christ refers to the abomination of desolation under the Antichrist in Matthew 24:15. The Antichrist will even have a statue of himself made, which will be satanically empowered to speak and kill those who will not worship it (Rev. 13:14–15).

Those that "do wickedly against the covenant" are contrasted with "the people that do know their God" (v. 32). This speaks of two kinds of people among the Jews. "The wicked" are of the liberal faction, apostates, who had no problem with the Hellenizing mandates of Antiochus. They were willingly corrupted with "flatteries"—good sounding promises. The unwavering, those who "know their God," resisted these efforts to wipe out the Jewish faith and worship and "instructed" many in God's ways (v. 33). For this, they were perse-

---

3   Wenham, *New Bible Commentary*, 761. I have even seen that this statue of Zeus was made in the likeness of Antiochus himself.

cuted, tortured, and put to death. These people "of understanding" were God's faithful remnant in the days of Antiochus. The purpose of these horrors was to "try" (test), "purge" (separate believers from unbelievers), and to make "them white" (purify).

Verse 35 provides a transition from the times of Antiochus to those of the Antichrist. Just as there were those "of understanding" who fell during the persecutions of Antiochus for their faith, there will be those during the times of the Antichrist who do the same. This verse has a double fulfillment. The first, precursive fulfillment, was under Antiochus; the final fulfillment will be under the Antichrist. Our indicator that these descriptions apply to the future as well as the past is in the phrase "even to the time of the end: because it is yet for a time appointed." Prophetic foreshortening occurs at this point.

Future Portion of the Prophecy (Dan. 11:36–12:3)
His Character

> 36And the king shall do according to his will; and he shall exalt himself, and magnify himself above every god, and shall speak marvellous things against the God of gods, and shall prosper till the indignation be accomplished: for that that is determined shall be done. 37Neither shall he regard the God of his fathers, nor the desire of women, nor regard any god: for he shall magnify himself above all. 38But in his estate shall he honour the God of forces: and a god whom his fathers knew not shall he honour with gold, and silver, and with precious stones, and pleasant things. 39Thus shall he do in the most strong holds with a strange god, whom he shall acknowledge and increase with glory: and he shall cause them to rule over many, and shall divide the land for gain. (Dan. 11:36–39)

The king referred to here is now the Antichrist. The use of the personal pronouns "he/him" that were previously applied to Antiochus now apply to the Antichrist. The text provides an even greater character study on this man. He is described as self-willed and self-exalted, placing himself above every god and blaspheming the God of heaven. He will be allowed to "prosper till the indignation be accomplished: for that that is determined shall be done" (v. 36). This means that God will use him as a chastening tool and allow him to fulfill his purposes and nothing more.

This man will not regard the "God of his fathers," presumably the God of heaven, nor will he seek to be desired by women (v. 37). Everything will take a back seat to his self-exaltation. However, he will honor and worship a "god of forces" and will give reverence to this god in "strongholds" (military fortresses) with material wealth and precious things (vv. 38, 39). This "god of forces" is best understood to be a god of overwhelming military strength and power. We know that he will use military force as never before ("who is able to make war with him?" [Rev. 13:4]) and will reward his enablers in these endeavors with leadership positions (v. 39). He will also "divide the land"—speaking of Israel—as a means of gain for himself (v. 39).

The Wars

[40]And at the time of the end shall the king of the south push at him: and the king of the north shall come against him like a whirlwind, with chariots, and with horsemen, and with many ships; and he shall enter into the countries, and shall overflow and pass over. [41]He shall enter also into the glorious land, and many countries shall be overthrown: but these shall escape out of his hand, even Edom, and Moab, and the chief of the children of Ammon. [42]He shall stretch forth his hand also upon the countries: and the land of Egypt shall not escape. [43]But he shall have power over the treasures of gold and of silver, and over all the precious things of Egypt: and the Libyans and the Ethiopians shall be at his steps. [44]But tidings out of the east and out of the north shall trouble him: therefore he shall go forth with great fury to destroy, and utterly to make away many. [45]And he shall plant the tabernacles of his palace between the seas in the glorious holy mountain; yet he shall come to his end, and none shall help him. (Dan. 11:40–45)

In Daniel 10, the man in linen informed Daniel about the heavenly warfare in which he was involved and his intercessions on behalf of the Jews. The prophecies of the Syrian wars and those of Antiochus show how these heavenly battles have played out on earth among men.

For the remainder of Chapter 11, we see the same kinds of military conflicts taking place under the Antichrist.

The "king of the south" and the "king of the north" will both "push" at "him"—the Antichrist (v. 40). The attack from the north is described as a "whirlwind," meaning great and fast attacks with land and sea forces. The Antichrist will respond with a counterattack, "and he shall enter into the countries, and shall overflow and pass over" (v. 40). The words "overflow" and "pass over" mean that he will bring massive quantities of military assets to bear and have decisive victories. The language here is quite figurative. This is also where we need to keep track of the participants in these wars. Here the "king of the north" is not referring to the Antichrist, who is referred to as "he/him." These exchanges are the reason we noted the use of the pronouns earlier for Antiochus and how that usage carried over to the Antichrist.

The Antichrist will also enter Israel, "the glorious land," and many countries will be overthrown, but the nations to the east and southeast of the Dead Sea will be spared (v. 41). His military victories will stretch into North Africa, and he will take all the wealth of Egypt for his own (vv. 42–43).

Further military threats against him from the east and north will cause him to launch more attacks against those nations with devastating destruction (v. 44). He will also make Jerusalem his headquarters ("he shall plant the tabernacles of his palace between the seas in the glorious holy mountain") and "come to his end" there (v. 45). This final part of the last verse, speaking of his death, is the only part of this prophecy that we can state with certainty how and when it will happen —at Christ's Second Coming (Rev. 19:20–21). We also know that at the midpoint of Daniel's Seventieth Week, he will set up the abomination of desolation and begin his persecution of the Jews (Rev. 12:13–14).

These prophecies pertain to "the time of the end" (v. 40). This means that they will be occurring during the Seventieth Week. The "king of the north" and "king of the south" are no longer specifically referring to Syrian and Egyptian Greeks, although they may be referring to the modern nations occupying those territories. If these attacks occur before the Antichrist enters into Israel, the attacks may come from the north and south of his location. We also have no way of knowing whether he will make his headquarters in Jerusalem after all these military actions, as the placement in the text (v. 45) would indicate, or whether that will have already occurred and is simply being stated at the end of the section on the wars.

The way the prophecy is presented in vv. 40–43, it appears that two nations (one from the north and one from the south) will stage an attack on the Antichrist. He will retaliate with a massive military effort and continue on his conquests by entering Israel and overthrowing the nations of North Africa. Since this includes entering into Israel, the most plausible time for this to occur would be the midpoint of the Seventieth Week. This would also be the most reasonable time to assume that he will establish his military headquarters in Israel. It is also entirely likely that the wars described here will be when the Antichrist kills three of the original ten leaders of future Rome.

There may also be two wars that are being described in this passage, with a period of prophetic foreshortening occurring between vv. 43 and 44. This is because the final two verses (vv. 44–45) bring us up to his destruction at the Second Coming, "yet he shall come to his end, and none shall help him."

The one thing we can say with certainty is that the final seven years will be a time of massive wars that will center on Israel. The man in linen continues with a prophecy of the redemption of Israel.

Israel Redeemed

¹And at that time shall Michael stand up, the great prince which standeth for the children of thy people: and there shall be a time of trouble, such as never was since there was a nation even to that same time: and at that time thy people shall be delivered, every one that shall be found written in the book. ²And many of them that sleep in the dust of the earth shall awake, some to everlasting life, and some to shame and everlasting contempt. ³And they that be wise shall shine as the brightness of the firmament; and they that turn many to righteousness as the stars for ever and ever. (Dan. 12:1–3)

The culmination of the warfare in heaven is now seen here; Michael will "stand up" for the Jews (v. 1). This is shown by him throwing

Satan and his fallen angels out of heaven at the midpoint of the Seventieth Week (Rev. 12:7–9). The result is that Satan will no longer be permitted to make accusations to God against the Jews, or Christians for that matter (Rev. 12:10). Michael is also seen on the Day of the Lord doing battle for Israel: "In that day shall the LORD defend the inhabitants of Jerusalem; and he that is feeble among them at that day shall be as David; and the house of David shall be as God, as the angel of the LORD before them" (Zech. 12:8).

Daniel's people will be "delivered" on this last day and have the Holy Spirit poured out on them; the "book" (v. 1) being referred to here is the "book of life." Faithful Jews will have their eyes opened and see the Lord Jesus and become believers in Christ. This is the event that the entire Seventieth Week has been leading up to.

The resurrection of the dead is also pictured (v. 2). At that time, Old Testament saints will be raised incorruptible in their glorified bodies. Even though this verse includes references to some being raised to "everlasting life" and other to "everlasting contempt," it is not teaching a general resurrection. Later, we learn that these resurrections will be separated by one thousand years (Rev. 20).

The "wise" and those that "turn many to righteousness" (v. 3) are described in their glorified bodies as shining like the "brightness of the firmament" (sky) and as "stars" forever. Now, we see those "of understanding" who instructed many under the persecutions of Antiochus (Dan. 11:33–35) and all other Old Testament saints given their rewards. This is the intended result of God's indignation, the reason for the "trials" and "purging."

Instructions to Daniel and Final Teaching (Dan. 12:4-13)

> [4]But thou, O Daniel, shut up the words, and seal the book, even to the time of the end: many shall run to and fro, and knowledge shall be increased. [5]Then I Daniel looked, and, behold, there stood other two, the one on this side of the bank of the river, and the other on that side of the bank of the river. [6]And one said to the man clothed in linen, which was upon the waters of the river, How long shall it be to the end of these wonders? [7]And I heard the man clothed in linen, which was upon the waters of the river, when he held up his right hand and his left hand unto heaven, and sware

> by him that liveth for ever that it shall be for a time, times, and an half; and when he shall have accomplished to scatter the power of the holy people, all these things shall be finished. (Dan. 12:4–7)

Up to this point, the use of the phrase "the time of the end" has been in the "narrow" sense of the word, meaning the seven-year period—Daniel's Seventieth Week. There are passages that use phrases such as "last days" (2 Tim. 3:1; Heb. 1:2; 2 Pet. 3:3) and "last/latter times" (1 Pet. 1:20; 1 Tim. 4:1; 1 John 2:18; Jude 18) in a much broader sense to refer to the entire church age. Under this "broader" definition, we are currently in "the time of the end." It is up to us to determine which usage is most appropriate based on the context of the passage being evaluated.

After describing the resurrected saints to Daniel, the man in linen gave him the following instructions: "But thou, O Daniel, shut up the words, and seal the book, even to the time of the end: many shall run to and fro, and knowledge shall be increased" (v. 4). This was the same instruction given to Daniel after the vision in Daniel 8, to "shut up" (conceal) the vision. It can only apply to the vision since we have no record of it throughout the entire text of Daniel 10–12 and cannot apply to the interpretation since we do have that. In addition to the instruction to "shut up the words," Daniel was also told to "seal the book."

The "time of the end" in this case must be understood in the broader sense as referring to the entire church age. So, at what point has this vision been delivered to believers? I contend that this vision of "great warfare" is contained in the book with seven seals, shown to John in Revelation 5:1, and that we are given the details of this vision when John describes the seal judgments (Rev. 6:1–17; 8:1–5). The many that "shall run to and fro" is referring to church-age believers searching through the Bible texts and prophecies to increase "knowledge" in these final days.

Following this, Daniel saw two "other" angels (v. 5), one or both of whom may have been providing comfort and strength to him when the vision was delivered (Dan. 10). One spoke to the man in linen, asking how long it will be "to the end of these wonders" (v. 6). The answer was three-and-one-half years—"for a time, times, and an half" (v. 7).

This is the same three-and-one-half-year period described in Daniel 7:25. We know that it will begin in the middle of the Seventieth Week (Dan. 9:27), when the Antichrist breaks his covenant with Israel and sets up the abomination of desolation. Here we see the three-and-one-half-year period described as a "time of trouble" (v. 1)—the great tribulation.

The one referred to as "he" in the second half of v. 7 is the Antichrist. He will be allowed to continue until "he shall have accomplished to scatter the power of the holy people." This means that the Jews will be totally broken and facing certain annihilation, and then "all these things shall be finished." The Antichrist will have accomplished God's intended indignation (c.f. Dan. 11:36), and, at that moment, Israel will be saved (vv. 1–3).

> [8]And I heard, but I understood not: then said I, O my Lord, what shall be the end of these things? [9]And he said, Go thy way, Daniel: for the words are closed up and sealed till the time of the end. [10]Many shall be purified, and made white, and tried; but the wicked shall do wickedly: and none of the wicked shall understand; but the wise shall understand. (Dan. 12:8–10)

Daniel still didn't understand "the end of these things" (v. 8), to which the angel replied that the words are "closed up" and "sealed" until "the time of the end" (broader definition). In contrast, we, at the present time, are at a most incredible time in history and *do* understand. "The end of these things" is the Second Coming of Christ.

The angel continued by stating the intended outcome of the great tribulation: "Many shall be purified, and made white, and tried" (v. 10). This is speaking of God's people and is contrasted with "the wicked," who will not change from their ways or understand. There will be this period of "refinement" during the "time of trouble"—the great tribulation. This purification of God's people was the intended outcome of the persecutions under Antiochus (Dan. 11:35) as it will be under the Antichrist as well. This is the reason for interpreting Daniel 11:35 as a transitional verse, bridging the historic portion of the prophecy to the future portion, applying to Antiochus as well as the Antichrist.

> ¹¹And from the time that the daily sacrifice shall be taken away, and the abomination that maketh desolate set up, there shall be a thousand two hundred and ninety days. ¹²Blessed is he that waiteth, and cometh to the thousand three hundred and five and thirty days. ¹³But go thou thy way till the end be: for thou shalt rest, and stand in thy lot at the end of the days. (Dan. 12:11–13)

At this point, we have seen the three-and-one-half-year great tribulation referred to as "a time and times and the dividing of time" (Dan. 7:25) and a "time, times, and an half" (Dan. 12:7). When we get to Revelation, this same period will also be identified as 1,260 days (Rev. 11:3; 12:6) and forty-two months (Rev. 11:2; 13:5). The Jewish prophetic year consisted of twelve thirty-day months or 360 days, thus the reason for three-and-one-half years being expressed as 1,260 days.

In v. 11 above, we are introduced to two additional periods, both beginning at the midpoint of the Seventieth Week: "From the time that the daily sacrifice shall be taken away, and the abomination that maketh desolate set up." The first will end thirty days after the three-and-one-half-year period and the second will end forty-five days after that. Verse 11 states that the total time includes this extra thirty days (1,290 days), and v. 12 states that he that waits and comes to the 1,335th day will be blessed.

There is no other place in the Bible that these thirty- and forty-five-day periods are specifically referenced. But in both the Old and New Testaments, we have some solid clues as to the nature of events that may transpire. After Christ returns and destroys the armies arrayed against Jerusalem, he will pour out the Holy Spirit upon the Jews, and they will realize what they have done and mourn for him (Zech. 12:10). It is quite reasonable to assume that the thirty-day period is for Israel's national mourning. It is also the same length of time that Israel mourned the death of Moses (Deut. 34:8).

There are also two "re-gatherings" of Israel. The first precedes the Day of the Lord (Ezek. 36:24; 28:25; Jer. 30:3) for the purpose of God pouring out his chastening wrath upon the nation. This regathering has already occurred. The second follows the Day of the Lord and is brought about by the hands of the Gentiles and those who will be gathered against Jerusalem on the Day of the Lord and escape (Isa. 66:19–

20; Zech. 8:20–23; Zeph. 3:19–20). The forty-five-day period is associated with a blessing and may very well be the time of this second regathering, to enter into the blessings associated with the culmination of the Seventieth Week.[4]

In addition to these Old Testament teachings, there are events stated in the New Testament that may also occur during the forty-five-day period. The Lord Jesus refers to the "regeneration" when he will sit on his throne (Matt. 19:28), and Peter speaks of the "times of refreshing" and "restitution of all things" which will occur at "the presence of the Lord" (Act 3:19–21). This "regeneration," "refreshing," and "restitution" may be referring to God's supernatural rebuilding of the earth after the great tribulation and the "day of wrath" (Rom. 2:5) in preparation for Christ's reign on earth (Jer. 30:9; Rev. 20:4). We also know that all believers will appear before the "judgment seat of Christ" (2 Cor. 5:10; Rom. 14:10) and that he will judge the living and the dead at his "appearing" (2 Tim. 4:1). This judgment may also take place during the forty-five-day period.

Verse 13 contains the final instruction to Daniel to go his way until the end and an assurance that he will partake in the resurrection of the dead: "For thou shalt rest, and stand in thy lot at the end of the days."

Concluding Thoughts
Israel in Unbelief

There are many interesting comparisons that can be made between Antiochus and the Antichrist. The similarities are profound and include self-exaltation, denial of the God of heaven, blaspheming the God of heaven, extreme brutality in conquest, and a desire to completely wipe out the Jewish religion and people. In the case of the Antichrist, he will even demand worship of himself. God's reasons to use Antiochus to prefigure the Antichrist are apparent.

There are prefiguring characteristics of Israel in the time of Antiochus that we see in the prophecies of the time of the end as well. Just as Israel brought on God's indignation by Antiochus through their unfaithfulness to him and their persistent idolatry, so will it be at the time of the end. Also, as there were two types of Jews in those days, the highly secular apostates and the faithful, so will it be in the future.

---

4   Tregelles, *Daniel*, 161–162; West, *Daniel's Great Prophecy*, 207.

Israel will enter the Seventieth Week in unbelief since there is only one people of God, those who believe in Jesus Christ. The highly secular will be like those who got along with Antiochus and had no regard for the effects of his Hellenizing mandates on their faith. To these Jesus said, "I am come in my Father's name, and ye receive me not: if another shall come in his own name, him ye will receive" (John 5:43). The faithful will be led to rebuild the temple in Jerusalem and reinstate biblical Jewish laws, worship, and temple practices. This is evidenced by the fact that there will be a temple for the Antichrist to desecrate and sacrifices for him to put an end to at the midpoint of the Seventieth Week (Dan. 9:27; 12:11). To these Jesus said, "For I say unto you, Ye shall not see me henceforth, till ye shall say, Blessed is he that cometh in the name of the Lord" (Matt. 23:39).

We have no way of knowing the details of the covenant that will be confirmed between Israel and the Antichrist until it is signed. However, we can engage in some speculation. Currently, what Israel lacks is both physical security and a temple in Jerusalem. It may be that the covenant will provide for both of these. If so, the Antichrist's rise to power will be facilitated by meeting the needs of both of these groups. By allowing the Antichrist to rise to power, God's plan to refine, chasten, purge, and sanctify Israel will begin. At the end of his plan, there will be Jewish believers in Christ who will step into the promises of the kingdom of God on earth. There will be "one fold" (John 10:16), one people of God (Eph. 2:15–16), and "all Israel shall be saved" (Rom. 11:26–27).

The Refiner's Fire

The vision and interpretation of Daniel 10–12 has had one overarching message—the refinement of Israel preceding a time of great blessings. This refinement is when "many shall be purified, and made white, and tried" (Dan. 12:10) and is accomplished through a "time of trouble"—the great tribulation. God's refining fire can be seen in the following:

> [18]Son of man, the house of Israel is to me become dross: all they are brass, and tin, and iron, and lead, in the midst of the furnace; they are even the dross of silver. [19]Therefore thus saith the Lord GOD; Because ye are all become dross,

behold, therefore I will gather you into the midst of Jerusalem. ²⁰As they gather silver, and brass, and iron, and lead, and tin, into the midst of the furnace, to blow the fire upon it, to melt it; so will I gather you in mine anger and in my fury, and I will leave you there, and melt you. ²¹Yea, I will gather you, and blow upon you in the fire of my wrath, and ye shall be melted in the midst thereof. ²²As silver is melted in the midst of the furnace, so shall ye be melted in the midst thereof; and ye shall know that I the LORD have poured out my fury upon you. (Ezek. 22:18–22)

This is spoken of in Jeremiah as well:

³For, lo, the days come, saith the LORD, that I will bring again the captivity of my people Israel and Judah, saith the LORD: and I will cause them to return to the land that I gave to their fathers, and they shall possess it. ⁴And these are the words that the LORD spake concerning Israel and concerning Judah. ⁵For thus saith the LORD; We have heard a voice of trembling, of fear, and not of peace. ⁶Ask ye now, and see whether a man doth travail with child? wherefore do I see every man with his hands on his loins, as a woman in travail, and all faces are turned into paleness? ⁷Alas! for that day is great, so that none is like it: it is even the time of Jacob's trouble; but he shall be saved out of it. ⁸For it shall come to pass in that day, saith the LORD of hosts, that I will break his yoke from off thy neck, and will burst thy bonds, and strangers shall no more serve themselves of him: ⁹But they shall serve the LORD their God, and David their king, whom I will raise up unto them. (Jer. 30:3–9)

This speaks of the first regathering of the Jews back into Israel, and the "time of trouble" is now called the "time of Jacob's trouble" (v. 7). This "trouble" (vv. 5–6) can be seen as a "voice of trembling, of fear, and not of peace"; and "every man with his hands on his loins, as a woman in travail, and all faces are turned into paleness." It is followed by Israel being "saved out of it" (v. 7) "in that day" (v. 8) when he "will break his yoke from off thy neck" (v. 8), culminating with Christ being their king (v. 9).

This is the same process of regathering, purging, saving, and finally blessing that is depicted in the prophecies of Daniel. The "time of Jacob's trouble" is the three-and-one-half-year great tribulation, and "that day" (v. 8) is the Second Coming of Christ to save his people after the Antichrist "shall have accomplished to scatter the power of the holy people." It is important not to conflate the period of purging (3 ½ years) with the time when Israel will be saved (the last day, the evening and the morning, the Day of the Lord).

Faithful Jews Preserved–Israel's Fall Advances God's Purpose

There will be a faithful remnant of the Jews that will be tried, purged, and refined during the great tribulation (Zech. 13:9). The world will know that Israel went into "captivity" (thrown out of their own country) because of their "iniquity and trespass against God" (Ezek. 39:23) for which he "hid his face from them" (Ezek. 39:23, 24). However, God will clear his name among the many nations, be "sanctified in them" (Ezek. 39:27), and "pour out his spirit upon them" (Ezek. 39:29) on the Day of the Lord.

God spoke to Israel, saying, "Thy bruise is incurable, and thy wound is grievous" (Jer. 30:12); "Why criest thou for thine affliction? thy sorrow is incurable for the multitude of thine iniquity: because thy sins were increased, I have done these things unto thee" (Jer. 30:15). But the promise of redemption remained: "For I am with thee, saith the LORD, to save thee: though I make a full end of all nations whither I have scattered thee, yet will I not make a full end of thee: but I will correct thee in measure, and will not leave thee altogether unpunished" (Jer. 30:11). This is the "mystery" (Rom. 11:25) to which Paul refers: "For if the casting away of them be the reconciling of the world, what shall the receiving of them be, but life from the dead?" (Rom. 11:15).

Through Israel's "fall," "salvation is come unto the Gentiles" (Rom. 11:11). When the "fulness of the Gentiles" (Rom. 11:25) has arrived, then "all Israel shall be saved" (Rom. 11:26). This is stated here as well: "And the Redeemer shall come to Zion, and unto them that turn from transgression in Jacob, saith the LORD" (Isa. 59:20). Notice everything here is pointing to the "last day"—the Day of the Lord. Israel will be redeemed, the faithful dead of Israel will be raised and given their glorified bodies (Dan. 12:2–3), and believers in Christ will be raised on this "last day" as well (John 6:39, 40, 44, 54). This is exactly what Martha said to the Lord Jesus when speaking of Lazarus: "Martha saith unto him, I know that he shall rise again in the resurrection at the last day" (John 11:24).

Since the chastening aspect of the great tribulation is so evident in these passages, it is necessary to take a closer look to see the preservation promises and the mercy of God throughout this process: "And I will bring the third part through the fire, and will refine them as silver is refined" (Zech. 13:9). God's preservation is seen here in his bringing them "through the fire." He will also be with them to save them: "For I am with thee, saith the LORD, to save thee" (Jer 30:11). Truly—he is a merciful God: "Therefore thus saith the Lord GOD; Now will I bring again the captivity of Jacob, and have mercy upon the whole house of Israel, and will be jealous for my holy name" (Ezek. 39:25).

As we progress through these studies, we will see further evidence of God's preservation of his faithful remnant of the Jews through the great tribulation.

Daniel's Visions Delivered in Revelation

As noted earlier, the vision of "the evening and the morning" in Daniel 8 and this vision of "great warfare" have not been presented to us in the text of Daniel. The first was closed up, and the second was closed up and sealed. As stated earlier, I contend that the first is contained in the little book that was given to John to eat in Revelation 10, and the second is what we see in the seal judgments of Revelation. If this is the case, then we have a conclusive refutation of the preterist, historicist, and idealist interpretations of Revelation. The futurist view is the only possible explanation that fits. This also means that the prophecies of Revelation should be considered to be equally literal as those in Daniel and expected to occur in the future. Further, it logically follows that Revelation is a highly detailed prophecy of Daniel's Seventieth Week. The following page shows the layering of all of the prophecies of Daniel.

Daniel Prophetic Timeline

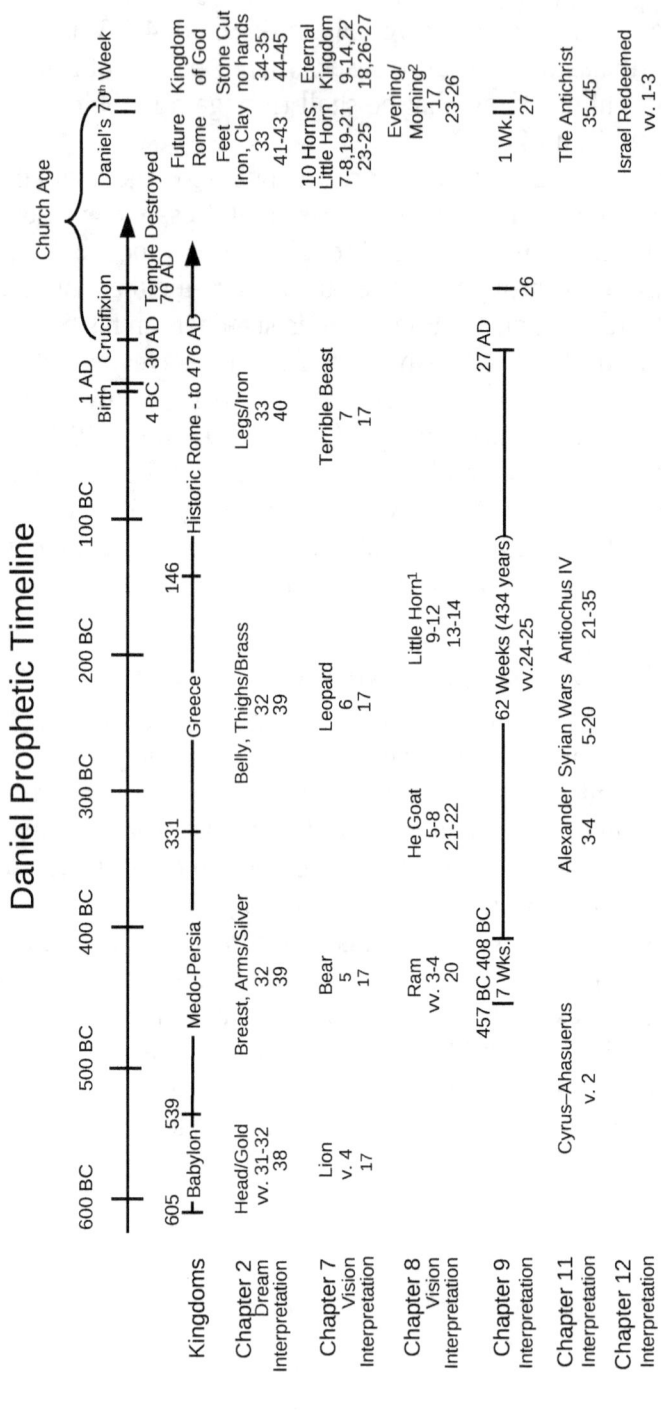

Verse numbers for the visions and interpretations are specified under the corresponding period.

[1]The "little horn" in this prophecy is Antiochus IV, Seleucid ruler (175-163). He persecuted the Jews for 2,300 days (fall 170-Dec 164).

[2]Daniel is given a vision of the Day of the Lord, referred to as the Evening/Morning. He is given a description of the Antichrist, vv. 23-25, but the vision itself is sealed, v.26.

5

The Day of the Lord

Every prophecy in Daniel points to a day in the future that will conclude God's plan for this world. In Nebuchadnezzar's dream, it was the stone crushing the feet and toes of the great image, representing the destruction of Gentile powers. In Daniel's vision of the beasts, it was the Son of Man coming in the clouds, giving the kingdom of God to the saints. In the vision of the evening and the morning, it was the last end of the indignation, a reference to the completion of God's redemptive work with Israel. Also, the king of fierce countenance was shown to be broken without hand, Christ's destruction of the Antichrist. In the prophecy of the seventy weeks, we were again shown the destruction of the Antichrist and the completion of God's redemptive work with Israel. And in the vision of great warfare, it was Daniel's people being "delivered, every one that shall be found written in the book." This day was shown to be preceded by a seven-year period—Daniel's Seventieth Week—the last half of which was referred to as a "time of trouble," also called the great tribulation.

The name of this day in both the Old and New Testaments is the Day of the Lord. With the exception of Christ's crucifixion in atonement for our sins, it will be the most decisive day in world history. When we add other Bible teachings to those of Daniel, it becomes apparent that in broad terms the following events will all take place: (1) the judgment of nations and unbelievers in vengeance, (2) the restoration of Israel, (3) the resurrection of the believing dead (Old and New Testament saints), (4) the rapture of the church, (5) the binding of Satan and his demons in the pit, (6) the restoration of the earth, and (7) the establishment of Christ's kingdom on earth. And it will all start with this sign: "The sun shall be turned into darkness, and the moon into blood, before the great and the terrible day of the LORD come" (Joel 2:31).

Additional Old Testament Teachings

In the Daniel studies alone, we have already seen prophecies of items 1, 2, 3, and 7 on the list shown above. Next, we will briefly examine other Old Testament prophecies, which will corroborate those points as well as establish point 5. Further, we will cover two signs that will precede the Day of the Lord. There will be a sign that begins this day; the sun will be darkened, and the moon will be turned to blood. And there will be a sign that occurs before this, the appearance of Elijah the prophet on the scene. Most importantly, we will also see that the Day of the Lord is literally one day—"the evening and the morning." This will be the final day of the Seventieth Week, which is also the final day of the great tribulation. Before continuing, we must resolve two issues pertaining to the Day of the Lord being a single day.

There are two reasons that there is considerable confusion surrounding the issue of the Day of the Lord being one literal day. The first is that certain events on this day appear to be inconsistent with each other. This is the reason that we spent so much time in the Daniel prophecies, to show that there will be a final day in which the Lord Jesus will return and give blessings to his people (Jews and believers) and render destructive judgment on unbelievers. To many, these events present such a dichotomy that they conclude they must be describing different days. However, nothing could be further from the truth. The prophecies of Daniel taught us that God often gives us only one piece of the total picture in a single prophecy. To understand God's intention, we must put together all of the prophecies to arrive at the composite picture of the totality of events.

Next, there is a series of judgments that will occur during the great tribulation, which must be introduced at this point—the wrath of God. The great tribulation will be a time of God's indignation being poured on an unbelieving world. However, he will use multiple participants during this time to fulfill his indignation. Later, we will see that in addition to the Antichrist being used as a tool of judgment, there will also be judgments rendered by angels, demons, the leaders of political

Rome, Jesus Christ, and God himself. It is the distinction between these latter two that we must establish at this point.

The Day of the Lord refers to Christ's Second Coming on the last day, at which time he will destroy the armies of the world at the battle of Armageddon, which will be centered at Jerusalem. This judgment occurs all on the last day. The wrath of God will consist of a series of seven judgments (Rev. 16) and will occur over a period of time during the great tribulation. The wrath of God will be global, contrasted with the localized events of the battle of Armageddon. They are clearly distinguished as separate actions. The "wrath of God" (Rev. 15:1, 7; 16:1) is shown as judgments poured out of vials; the "wrath of the Lamb" (Rev. 6:16) is the Second Coming of Christ, referred to as the "great day of his wrath" (Rev. 6:17). If this distinction is overlooked, it is very easy to equate the two and consequently conclude incorrectly that the Day of the Lord occurs over a period of time rather than on the last day. It will be shown that the final vial of God's wrath will be poured out on the last day—the Day of the Lord. This will be the point at which these two coincide.

The Judgment of Nations and Unbelievers

The judgment of nations, which was shown symbolically in Daniel, is also taught quite literally in the Old Testament as well:

> [15]Alas for the day! for the day of the LORD is at hand, and as a destruction from the Almighty shall it come. (Joel 1:15)

> [5]The Lord at thy right hand shall strike through kings in the day of his wrath. [6]He shall judge among the heathen, he shall fill the places with the dead bodies; he shall wound the heads over many countries. (Ps. 110:5-6)

> [28]And the destruction of the transgressors and of the sinners shall be together, and they that forsake the LORD shall be consumed. (Isa. 1:28)

> [33]And the slain of the LORD shall be at that day from one end of the earth even unto the other end of the earth: they shall not be lamented, neither gathered, nor buried; they shall be dung upon the ground. (Jer. 25:33)

> ³I have trodden the winepress alone; and of the people there was none with me: for I will tread them in mine anger, and trample them in my fury; and their blood shall be sprinkled upon my garments, and I will stain all my raiment. ⁴For the day of vengeance is in mine heart, and the year of my redeemed is come. (Isa. 63:3–4)

There are numerous passages like these throughout the Old Testament. Notice the different names given to this day: "the great and the terrible day of the LORD," "the day of the Lord," "the day of his wrath," "that day," and "the day of vengeance." These, and all the others like them, speak of the last day of this world—the Second Coming of the Lord Jesus. The clear picture here is that of destructive judgment upon unbelievers. In the following passage, this is seen from the perspective of the prophet Isaiah:

> ⁶Howl ye; for the day of the LORD is at hand; it shall come as a destruction from the Almighty. ⁷Therefore shall all hands be faint, and every man's heart shall melt: ⁸And they shall be afraid: pangs and sorrows shall take hold of them; they shall be in pain as a woman that travaileth: they shall be amazed one at another; their faces shall be as flames. ⁹Behold, the day of the LORD cometh, cruel both with wrath and fierce anger, to lay the land desolate: and he shall destroy the sinners thereof out of it. ¹⁰For the stars of heaven and the constellations thereof shall not give their light: the sun shall be darkened in his going forth, and the moon shall not cause her light to shine. ¹¹And I will punish the world for their evil, and the wicked for their iniquity; and I will cause the arrogancy of the proud to cease, and will lay low the haughtiness of the terrible. ¹²I will make a man more precious than fine gold; even a man than the golden wedge of Ophir. ¹³Therefore I will shake the heavens, and the earth shall remove out of her place, in the wrath of the LORD of hosts, and in the day of his fierce anger. (Isa. 13:6–13)

Again, the immediate signs preceding this day are, "The stars of heaven and the constellations thereof shall not give their light: the sun shall be darkened in his going forth, and the moon shall not cause her light to shine" (v. 10). The destructive judgment shown here is what was represented by the stone crushing the feet and toes of Nebuchadnezzar's image. These passages also blur the distinctions between the final vial of God's wrath and the Second Coming to some extent. These distinctions will be clearly delineated in the Revelation studies to follow.

Events Centered at Jerusalem

The Old Testament also presents prophecies of the localized events at Jerusalem. These serve to corroborate the second point stated earlier, the restoration of Israel.

> ¹For, behold, in those days, and in that time, when I shall bring again the captivity of Judah and Jerusalem, ²I will also gather all nations, and will bring them down into the valley of Jehoshaphat, and will plead with them there for my people and for my heritage Israel, whom they have scattered among the nations, and parted my land. (Joel 3:1–2)

> ⁹Proclaim ye this among the Gentiles; Prepare war, wake up the mighty men, let all the men of war draw near; let them come up: ¹⁰Beat your plowshares into swords, and your pruninghooks into spears: let the weak say, I am strong. ¹¹Assemble yourselves, and come, all ye heathen, and gather yourselves together round about: thither cause thy mighty ones to come down, O LORD. ¹²Let the heathen be wakened, and come up to the valley of Jehoshaphat: for there will I sit to judge all the heathen round about. ¹³Put ye in the sickle, for the harvest is ripe: come, get you down; for the press is full, the fats overflow; for their wickedness is great. ¹⁴Multitudes, multitudes in the valley of decision: for the day of the LORD is near in the valley of decision. ¹⁵The sun and the moon shall be darkened, and the stars shall withdraw their shining. ¹⁶The LORD also shall roar out of Zion, and utter his voice from Jerusalem; and the heavens and the earth shall shake: but the LORD will be the hope of his people, and the strength of the children of Israel. (Joel 3:9–16)

This judgment of the nations will occur in the "valley of Jehoshaphat." Jehoshaphat means "Jehovah Judges." This valley is most likely the Kidron Valley, east of Jerusalem, between the city and the Mount of Olives. It is also referred to as the "valley of decision." There is also the sign which immediately precedes the Day of the Lord, stated again: "The sun and the moon shall be darkened" (v. 15).

It Will Be One Day

God will gather the armies of the world against Jerusalem in this final battle and will allow Jerusalem to fall. At that point, Christ will step foot on the Mount of Olives and defend his people and his city. These events will be shown in greater detail in Revelation. The way for the land armies will be cleared under the sixth vial judgment (Rev. 16:12–16), and the Lord's return will be shown in Revelation 19.

> 2Behold, I will make Jerusalem a cup of trembling unto all the people round about, when they shall be in the siege both against Judah and against Jerusalem. 3And in that day will I make Jerusalem a burdensome stone for all people: all that burden themselves with it shall be cut in pieces, though all the people of the earth be gathered together against it. (Zech. 12:2–3)

> 9And it shall come to pass in that day, that I will seek to destroy all the nations that come against Jerusalem. (Zech. 12:9)

> 1Behold, the day of the LORD cometh, and thy spoil shall be divided in the midst of thee. 2For I will gather all nations against Jerusalem to battle; and the city shall be taken, and the houses rifled, and the women ravished; and half of the city shall go forth into captivity, and the residue of the people shall not be cut off from the city. 3Then shall the LORD go forth, and fight against those nations, as when he fought in the day of battle. 4And his feet shall stand in that day upon the mount of Olives, which is before Jerusalem on the east, and the mount of Olives shall cleave in the midst thereof toward the east and toward the west, and there shall be a very great valley; and half of the mountain shall remove toward the north, and half of it toward the south.

⁵And ye shall flee to the valley of the mountains; for the valley of the mountains shall reach unto Azal: yea, ye shall flee, like as ye fled from before the earthquake in the days of Uzziah king of Judah: and the LORD my God shall come, and all the saints with thee. ⁶And it shall come to pass in that day, that the light shall not be clear, nor dark: ⁷But it shall be one day which shall be known to the LORD, not day, nor night: but it shall come to pass, that at evening time it shall be light. ⁸And it shall be in that day, that living waters shall go out from Jerusalem; half of them toward the former sea, and half of them toward the hinder sea: in summer and in winter shall it be. ⁹And the LORD shall be king over all the earth: in that day shall there be one LORD, and his name one. (Zech. 14:1–9)

Once again, there are references to the signs in the heavens: "And it shall come to pass in that day, that the light shall not be clear, nor dark" (v. 6). What is being referred to is "the day of the Lord" (v. 1), and it is said to be "one day" (v. 7). These events will all happen in one day, and at the evening time, it will be light again (v. 7). This passage also shows the establishment of the Christ's kingdom on this earth (vv. 8, 9). Elsewhere, it is confirmed that the Lord will remove the "iniquity" of Israel in "one day":

⁹For behold the stone that I have laid before Joshua; upon one stone shall be seven eyes: behold, I will engrave the graving thereof, saith the LORD of hosts, and I will remove the iniquity of that land in one day. ¹⁰In that day, saith the LORD of hosts, shall ye call every man his neighbour under the vine and under the fig tree. (Zech. 3:9–10)

This removal of Israel's iniquity is the culmination of Daniel's Seventieth Week—the Day of the Lord.

The Resurrection of the Dead

The cleansing, chastening, and restoration of Israel have been covered in the Daniel Studies. In addition to the resurrection shown in Daniel 12, the Old Testament shows:

¹⁹Thy dead men shall live, together with my dead body shall they arise. Awake and sing, ye that dwell in dust: for thy dew

is as the dew of herbs, and the earth shall cast out the dead. [20]Come, my people, enter thou into thy chambers, and shut thy doors about thee: hide thyself as it were for a little moment, until the indignation be overpast. [21]For, behold, the LORD cometh out of his place to punish the inhabitants of the earth for their iniquity: the earth also shall disclose her blood, and shall no more cover her slain. (Isa. 26:19–21)

Here we see the resurrection of the dead (v. 19), followed by the wrath and destruction of the Day of the Lord (vv. 20–21).

Satan and His Demons Bound in the Pit

[19]The earth is utterly broken down, the earth is clean dissolved, the earth is moved exceedingly. [20]The earth shall reel to and fro like a drunkard, and shall be removed like a cottage; and the transgression thereof shall be heavy upon it; and it shall fall, and not rise again. [21]And it shall come to pass in that day, that the LORD shall punish the host of the high ones that are on high, and the kings of the earth upon the earth. [22]And they shall be gathered together, as prisoners are gathered in the pit, and shall be shut up in the prison, and after many days shall they be visited. [23]Then the moon shall be confounded, and the sun ashamed, when the LORD of hosts shall reign in mount Zion, and in Jerusalem, and before his ancients gloriously. (Isa. 24:19–23)

Satan and his demons will be bound in the pit on that day as well. In this passage, they are referred to as "the host of the high ones that are on high" (v. 21). They will be "shut up" in the pit. We will see more on this in Revelation 20. The signs in the heavens are also referred to: "Then the moon shall be confounded, and the sun ashamed" (v. 23).

Establishment of Christ's Kingdom on Earth

Still other passages in the Old Testament speak of a blessed time that will follow the Day of the Lord when Christ will sit on the throne of David:

[4]But with righteousness shall he judge the poor, and reprove with equity for the meek of the earth: and he shall smite the

earth with the rod of his mouth, and with the breath of his lips shall he slay the wicked. [5]And righteousness shall be the girdle of his loins, and faithfulness the girdle of his reins. [6]The wolf also shall dwell with the lamb, and the leopard shall lie down with the kid; and the calf and the young lion and the fatling together; and a little child shall lead them. [7]And the cow and the bear shall feed; their young ones shall lie down together: and the lion shall eat straw like the ox. [8]And the sucking child shall play on the hole of the asp, and the weaned child shall put his hand on the cockatrice' den. (Isa. 11:4–8)

[17]For, behold, I create new heavens and a new earth: and the former shall not be remembered, nor come into mind. [18]But be ye glad and rejoice for ever in that which I create: for, behold, I create Jerusalem a rejoicing, and her people a joy. [19]And I will rejoice in Jerusalem, and joy in my people: and the voice of weeping shall be no more heard in her, nor the voice of crying. [20]There shall be no more thence an infant of days, nor an old man that hath not filled his days: for the child shall die an hundred years old; but the sinner being an hundred years old shall be accursed. (Isa. 65:17–20)

[22]Therefore will I save my flock, and they shall no more be a prey; and I will judge between cattle and cattle. [23]And I will set up one shepherd over them, and he shall feed them, even my servant David; he shall feed them, and he shall be their shepherd. [24]And I the LORD will be their God, and my servant David a prince among them; I the LORD have spoken it. (Ezek. 34:22–24)

[14]Behold, the days come, saith the LORD, that I will perform that good thing which I have promised unto the house of Israel and to the house of Judah. [15]In those days, and at that time, will I cause the Branch of righteousness to grow up unto David; and he shall execute judgment and righteousness in the land. [16]In those days shall Judah be saved, and Jerusalem shall dwell safely: and this is the name wherewith she shall be called, The LORD our righteousness.

> ¹⁷For thus saith the LORD; David shall never want a man to
> sit upon the throne of the house of Israel; (Jer. 33:14–17)

Jesus Christ is the "one shepherd" (Ezek. 34:23), the "Branch of righteousness" (Jer. 33:15), and the "servant David" (Ezek. 34:23, 24) referred to above. God made the following promise to David: "And thine house and thy kingdom shall be established for ever before thee: thy throne shall be established for ever" (2 Sam. 7:16). Jesus Christ will be the fulfillment of this promise. He will be the one from the lineage of David (Matt. 21:9) who will reign forever on the throne of David (Luke 1:32–33).

Signs Preceding the Day of the Lord

For this day to occur, Israel has to be regathered into its homeland, which has already happened. Another sign that we're waiting for is the arrival of "Elijah the prophet" before the Day of the Lord:

> ¹For, behold, the day cometh, that shall burn as an oven; and
> all the proud, yea, and all that do wickedly, shall be stubble:
> and the day that cometh shall burn them up, saith the
> LORD of hosts, that it shall leave them neither root nor
> branch. ⁵Behold, I will send you Elijah the prophet before
> the coming of the great and dreadful day of the LORD:
> (Mal. 4:1, 5)

This is still in the future, and we will have much more to learn about this in the Revelation 10 and 11 study. Finally, the Day of the Lord has been shown to be one literal day (Zech. 14:7; 3:9), which will begin with the signs of the sun being darkened and the moon turning to blood (Joel 2:31; 3:15; Isa. 13:10; 24:23; Zech. 14:6). These signs will be the final indicator that the last day has begun.

New Testament Teachings

The Day of the Lord continues to be a primary topic in the New Testament as well. Just as there are multiple names for this day in the Old Testament, so are there in the New Testament—namely, "the day of our Lord Jesus Christ" (1 Cor. 1:8), "the day of the Lord Jesus" (2 Cor. 1:14), "the day of Jesus Christ" (Phil. 1:6), "the day of Christ" (Phil 1:10; 2 Thess. 2:2), "the day of wrath" (Rom. 2:5), "the day of redemption" (Eph. 4:30), and "the wrath of the Lamb" (Rev. 6:16).

These are all referring to the same day. It is also referred to as Christ's "coming," "appearing," or "revelation."

Rapture of the Church

This passage uses the word "coming," and we see all of the elements in place that we have studied thus far.

> [29]Immediately after the tribulation of those days shall the sun be darkened, and the moon shall not give her light, and the stars shall fall from heaven, and the powers of the heavens shall be shaken: [30]And then shall appear the sign of the Son of man in heaven: and then shall all the tribes of the earth mourn, and they shall see the Son of man coming in the clouds of heaven with power and great glory. [31]And he shall send his angels with a great sound of a trumpet, and they shall gather together his elect from the four winds, from one end of heaven to the other. (Matt. 24:29–31)

Here we have the words of the Lord Jesus in the Olivet Discourse responding to the question, "Tell us, when shall these things be? and what shall be the sign of thy coming, and of the end of the world?" (Matt. 24:3). The Lord teaches that after the "tribulation of those days"—the great tribulation—"shall the sun be darkened, and the moon shall not give her light" (v. 29). The Lord will appear in the clouds (v. 30), just as in Daniel 7, and at the sound of a trumpet, his angels will gather together his "elect" (v. 31). This is the resurrection of the dead in Christ and the rapture of living believers.

In the New Testament, the "elect" always refers to believers in Christ, and in this case, it also includes Old Testament saints. "The four winds" is idiomatic speech referring to the whole world, and in addition to that, they are gathered from "one end of heaven to the other." The passage in the Gospel of Mark makes this even more clear: "And then shall he send his angels, and shall gather together his elect from the four winds, from the uttermost part of the earth to the uttermost part of heaven" (Mark 13:27).

The ones gathered from heaven are Old Testament saints and church-age believers who have died; the ones from the earth are those alive at the time of Christ's coming. This can be seen in the following passage, which shows the order of the resurrection. Christ was the first to be raised from the dead, and the next resurrection is of those "that are Christ's," which will occur at his "coming":

> [20]But now is Christ risen from the dead, and become the firstfruits of them that slept. [21]For since by man came death, by man came also the resurrection of the dead. [22]For as in Adam all die, even so in Christ shall all be made alive. [23]But every man in his own order: Christ the firstfruits; afterward they that are Christ's at his coming. (1 Cor. 15:20–23)

The word translated "coming" (Matt. 24:3; 1 Cor. 15:23) is the Greek *parousia*. It is also used in this passage, in which Paul allays the concerns of those at the church in Thessalonica about their fellow believers who had already died.

> [13]But I would not have you to be ignorant, brethren, concerning them which are asleep, that ye sorrow not, even as others which have no hope. [14]For if we believe that Jesus died and rose again, even so them also which sleep in Jesus will God bring with him. [15]For this we say unto you by the word of the Lord, that we which are alive and remain unto the coming of the Lord shall not prevent them which are asleep. [16]For the Lord himself shall descend from heaven with a shout, with the voice of the archangel, and with the trump of God: and the dead in Christ shall rise first: [17]Then we which are alive and remain shall be caught up together with them in the clouds, to meet the Lord in the air: and so shall we ever be with the Lord. [18]Wherefore comfort one another with these words. [1]But of the times and the seasons, brethren, ye have no need that I write unto you. [2]For yourselves know perfectly that the day of the Lord so cometh as a thief in the night. (1 Thess. 4:13–5:2)

Please note it is at his "coming" (1 Thess. 4:15) that the dead will rise first and the living will be "caught up together with them in the clouds." It is also quite clear that this coming is referring to "the Day of the Lord" (1 Thess. 5:2). This understanding is again confirmed here:

> [1]Now we beseech you, brethren, by the coming of our Lord Jesus Christ, and by our gathering together unto him, [2]That

ye be not soon shaken in mind, or be troubled, neither by spirit, nor by word, nor by letter as from us, as that the day of Christ is at hand. (2 Thess. 2:1–2)

The Lord's "coming" and our "gathering together" to him will be occurring at the same point in time, identified as the "day of Christ." Elsewhere, the Lord refers to this as the "last day," when he will raise the believer: "This is the will of him that sent me, that every one which seeth the Son, and believeth on him, may have everlasting life: and I will raise him up at the last day" (John 6:40: cf. 6:39, 44, 54).

At the Last Trumpet

Referring back to the Olivet Discourse, Christ said, "He shall send his angels with a great sound of a trumpet, and they shall gather together his elect from the four winds, from one end of heaven to the other" (Matt. 24:31). This passage speaks of a "great sound of a trumpet," as does 1 Thessalonians 4:16 above. We see that here as well:

> [51]Behold, I shew you a mystery; We shall not all sleep, but we shall all be changed, [52]In a moment, in the twinkling of an eye, at the last trump: for the trumpet shall sound, and the dead shall be raised incorruptible, and we shall be changed. [53]For this corruptible must put on incorruption, and this mortal must on immortality. [54]So when this corruptible shall have put on incorruption, and this mortal shall have put on immortality, then shall be brought to pass the saying that is written, Death is swallowed up in victory. [55]O death, where is thy sting? O grave, where is thy victory? (1 Cor. 15:51–55)

This confirms that there will be believers alive at Christ's Second Coming ("we shall not all sleep") who will be "changed, in a moment, in the twinkling of an eye" at the sound of the last trumpet (vv. 51, 52). This change of the living and resurrection of the dead is the moment at which we will be given our immortal bodies. In this passage, it is described as "this corruptible must put on incorruption" and "this mortal shall have put on immortality." The last trumpet that is referred to is the final eschatological trumpet seen in Revelation:

> [7]But in the days of the voice of the seventh angel, when he shall begin to sound, the mystery of God should be finished, as he hath declared to his servants the prophets. (Rev. 10:7)

> [15]And the seventh angel sounded; and there were great voices in heaven, saying, The kingdoms of this world are become the kingdoms of our Lord, and of his Christ; and he shall reign for ever and ever. (Rev. 11:15)

The "mystery of God"—God's redemptive plan for this world—will be finished, and "the kingdoms of this world" will become the "kingdoms of our Lord."

The Blessed Hope

This is precisely the point in time to which the believer's attention is always directed, referred to as the blessed hope: "Looking for that blessed hope, and the glorious appearing of the great God and our Saviour Jesus Christ" (Titus 2:13). Here it is referred to as his "appearing," Greek *epiphaneia*, and here as well: "I charge thee therefore before God, and the Lord Jesus Christ, who shall judge the quick and the dead at his appearing and his kingdom" (2 Tim. 4:1). Peter refers to the same day with the word "revelation," Greek *apokalupsis*: "Wherefore gird up the loins of your mind, be sober, and hope to the end for the grace that is to be brought unto you at the revelation of Jesus Christ" (1 Pet. 1:13). Our hope is always directed to the Second Coming of Christ—"the last day" (John 6:40)—often referred to as his "coming," "appearing," or "revelation."[1] A few examples follow:

> [14]That thou keep this commandment without spot, unrebukeable, until the appearing (*epiphaneia*) of our Lord Jesus Christ: (1 Tim. 6:14)

> [8]Henceforth there is laid up for me a crown of righteousness, which the Lord, the righteous judge, shall give me at that day: and not to me only, but unto all them also that love his appearing (*epiphaneia*). (2 Tim. 4:8)

> [7]That the trial of your faith, being much more precious than of gold that perisheth, though it be tried with fire, might be

---

1   Tregelles, *Second Coming*, 69–73.

found unto praise and honour and glory at the appearing (*apokalupsis*) of Jesus Christ. (1 Pet. 1:7)

[13]But rejoice, inasmuch as ye are partakers of Christ's sufferings; that, when his glory shall be revealed (*apokalupsis*), ye may be glad also with exceeding joy. (1 Pet. 4:13)

[28]And now, little children, abide in him; that, when he shall appear, we may have confidence, and not be ashamed before him at his coming (*parousia*). (1 John 2:28)

[7]So that ye come behind in no gift; waiting for the coming (*apokalupsis*) of our Lord Jesus Christ: (1 Cor. 1:7)

[19]For what is our hope, or joy, or crown of rejoicing? Are not even ye in the presence of our Lord Jesus Christ at his coming (*parousia*)? (1 Thess. 2:19)

But believers are not the only ones that have something to look forward to at Christ's "coming," "appearing," and "revelation." The following passages teach that he will also destroy the Antichrist ("that Wicked") and pour out his wrath on the unbelieving world as well. "Then shall that Wicked be revealed, whom the Lord shall consume with the spirit of his mouth, and shall destroy with the brightness (*epiphaneia*) of his coming (*parousia*)" (2 Thess. 2:8). This will be "the day of wrath and revelation (*apokalupsis*) of the righteous judgment of God" (Rom. 2:5; c.f. 2 Thess. 1:6–10). The last day *really* will be a day of blessings for believers and judgment for unbelievers, just as presented in the prophecies of Daniel.

The Restoration of the Earth

Earlier, we saw Old Testament references to an idyllic time when Christ will reign from Jerusalem on a restored earth. It was also surmised that this restoration may occur during the forty-five-day period that will follow the resurrection (Dan. 12:12). The following passages are looking forward to that same time and show yet one more name for describing Christ's Second Coming, "the presence of the Lord" (Acts 3:19). Also, the resurrection/rapture of believers is referred to as "the manifestation of the sons of God" (Rom. 8:19).

[19]Repent ye therefore, and be converted, that your sins may be blotted out, when the times of refreshing shall come

from the presence of the Lord; [20]And he shall send Jesus Christ, which before was preached unto you: [21]Whom the heaven must receive until the times of restitution of all things, which God hath spoken by the mouth of all his holy prophets since the world began. (Acts 3:19–21)

[18]For I reckon that the sufferings of this present time are not worthy to be compared with the glory which shall be revealed in us. [19]For the earnest expectation of the creature waiteth for the manifestation of the sons of God. [20]For the creature was made subject to vanity, not willingly, but by reason of him who hath subjected the same in hope, [21]Because the creature itself also shall be delivered from the bondage of corruption into the glorious liberty of the children of God. [22]For we know that the whole creation groaneth and travaileth in pain together until now. [23]And not only they, but ourselves also, which have the firstfruits of the Spirit, even we ourselves groan within ourselves, waiting for the adoption, to wit, the redemption of our body. (Rom. 8:18–23)

Succinctly put, the second passage above says that all of creation (referred to as "the creature") is waiting for the resurrection/rapture ("the manifestation of the sons of God," "the adoption," "the redemption of our body") because that is when it will be restored ("delivered from the bondage of corruption"). In the first passage, this restoration of all creation ("the times of refreshing," "the times of restitution of all things") will come at "the presence of the Lord"—the Second Coming. So, if all creation is waiting for the resurrection/rapture to be restored and it will be restored at the Second Coming, then the resurrection/ rapture and the Second Coming must occur at the same time. This is exactly where all of the other passages that we have studied place the resurrection/rapture, at the Second Coming. And this is when the first passage says our sins will be "blotted out." All of creation was put under the curse when Adam and Eve transgressed in the garden of Eden. This tells us that the curse will finally be lifted and the earth restored to its original condition following Christ's return.

The Order of Events

Now that we have seen the events that will transpire on the Day of the Lord, it is time to determine the order in which they will occur. The passages that we studied earlier (Matt. 24:29–31; 1 Thess. 4:13–5:2) shed great light on the subject. This day will start with (1) the sun being darkened and the moon turning red, after which (2) the Lord will appear in the clouds with his angels. (3) His angels will gather the dead and living believers, and (4) we will be transformed into our eternal bodies. (5) Christ will continue on his way down to earth with his angels and all believers, who have just been given their immortal bodies, to (6) judge the nations in wrath.

We have already established points 1 through 4 above; next, we must establish point 5. Notice he will appear in the clouds with his angels (Matt. 24:30–31; 16:27; 2 Thess. 1:7) and will return with all the saints, glorified believers:

> [5]And ye shall flee to the valley of the mountains; for the valley of the mountains shall reach unto Azal: yea, ye shall flee, like as ye fled from before the earthquake in the days of Uzziah king of Judah: and the LORD my God shall come, and all the saints with thee. (Zech. 14:5)

> [4]When Christ, who is our life, shall appear, then shall ye also appear with him in glory. (Col. 3:4)

> [14]And Enoch also, the seventh from Adam, prophesied of these, saying, Behold, the Lord cometh with ten thousands of his saints. (Jude 14)

> [19]For what is our hope, or joy, or crown of rejoicing? Are not even ye in the presence of our Lord Jesus Christ at his coming? (1 Thess. 2:19)

> [13]To the end he may stablish your hearts unblameable in holiness before God, even our Father, at the coming of our Lord Jesus Christ with all his saints. (1 Thess. 3:13)

Now, we return to this passage: "For the Lord himself shall descend from heaven with a shout, with the voice of the archangel, and with the trump of God: and the dead in Christ shall rise first: Then we which are alive and remain shall be caught up together with them in the clouds, to meet the Lord in the air: and so shall we ever be with the Lord" (1 Thess. 4:16–17). The words translated "to meet" (v. 17) are the Greek *eis apantesis*. This points to a practice in Hellenistic times of citizens of a city going out to meet a visiting dignitary and then escorting him back into the city.[2]

It is the same "to meet" that describes the 10 virgins (Matt. 25:1, 6) going out "to meet the bridegroom" and the disciples going out "to meet" Paul as he approached Rome (Acts 28:15). This is exactly what we see in the passages that describe Christ's return with all the saints. We will rise to meet him in the air and return with him.

After the transformation of all believers, Christ will return to earth and defeat the armies that have been arrayed against Jerusalem. The order of events that was started previously now continues with (7) the Jews will see the one that they crucified, (8) he will pour out the Holy Spirit upon them, and (9) they will realize what they have done. (10) The Antichrist and false prophet will be thrown alive into the lake of fire (Rev. 19:20) and (11) Satan and his demons will be bound in the pit for one thousand years (Rev. 20:2–3). (12) Israel's national mourning will begin, (13) the Jews will be regathered into their home-land, (14) the world will be regenerated, and (15) Christ's reign on earth will begin.

Confusion in the Word of God?

To this point, it has been stated that the Day of the Lord is referring to one literal day—the Second Coming of the Lord Jesus. So how can a passage like this be explained?

> [7]But the heavens and the earth, which are now, by the same word are kept in store, reserved unto fire against the day of judgment and perdition of ungodly men. (2 Pet. 3:7)
>
> [10]But the day of the Lord will come as a thief in the night; in the which the heavens shall pass away with a great noise, and the elements shall melt with fervent heat, the earth also and the works that are therein shall be burned up. [11]Seeing then that all these things shall be dissolved, what manner of persons ought ye to be in all holy conversation and godliness, [12]Looking for and hasting unto the coming of the

---

2   Gundry, *Church and Tribulation*, 104.

day of God, wherein the heavens being on fire shall be dissolved, and the elements shall melt with fervent heat? [13]Nevertheless we, according to his promise, look for new heavens and a new earth, wherein dwelleth righteousness. (2 Pet. 3:10–13)

This is not redefining the Day of the Lord to be a nonspecific period or the entire time of Christ's millennial reign. Instead, what is going on is the "blurring of distinctions" between the Day of the Lord at the end of this world and what Peter refers to as "the Day of God" (v. 12), which will occur at the end of the millennial kingdom.

In v. 7, Peter states that the present heavens and earth are "kept in store, reserved unto fire" until "the day of judgment and perdition of ungodly men." This means that the present earth will be preserved by God until it will be burned up with fire at the end of the millennium—the great white throne judgment—when ungodly men will be judged (Rev. 20:11–15).

Verse 10 has prophetic foreshortening at the semicolon. Peter states that the Day of the Lord (end of this world) comes like a thief in the night (cf. 1 Thess. 5:2). Then, he jumps ahead in time to the end of the millennium, when the world will be burned up, for the remainder of the verse. Prophetic foreshortening like this does occur in God's Word. In the following example, Christ's birth is prophesied in the first half of the verse, and at the first colon, it jumps ahead in time to the millennial kingdom and his reign on earth: "For unto us a child is born, unto us a son is given: and the government shall be upon his shoulder: and his name shall be called Wonderful, Counsellor, The mighty God, The everlasting Father, The Prince of Peace" (Isa. 9:6). There is no way to determine the distinction in time without referencing other teachings. This is what we have to do with the 2 Peter passage above.

In the 2 Peter passage, we get a very solid clue, however. Notice he uses the term "Day of God" to juxtapose against the Day of the Lord. Then, he comes back and restates that it is at the Day of God (v. 12) when the "heavens being on fire shall be dissolved, and the elements shall melt with fervent heat." Only with the other teachings that we will be getting in Revelation are we able to make this distinction between the Day of the Lord (at the end of this world) and the Day of God (at the end of the millennium) with certainty.

The primary focus of this passage is not to teach us details about the Day of the Lord or the Day of God but rather to instill the earnest desire in us to live a godly life since all that there is in this world will eventually be burned up. For this reason, our focus should be on the eternal state with God in the new heavens and new earth.

This passage has been used incorrectly to steer people away from the idea that the Day of the Lord is really just one day at the end of this world. For clarity, I should state that this world will end at Christ's Second Coming, at which point he will initiate the millennial kingdom, which will be, however, still on this present earth. Then, at the end of the millennium, this earth will be burned up, and a new heavens and new earth will be formed by God (Rev. 20:11; 21:1), where we will be with him for all eternity.

This same kind of a blurring of distinctions can be seen in the Isaiah passage that we studied earlier, which depicted the idyllic time after Christ's return (Isa. 65:17–20). He speaks of a new heavens and a new earth (v. 17) and then continues to describe a life that is consistent with the millennial kingdom since there is still death and sin (v. 20). This "blurring" of two future periods can only be fully understood after the study of later prophecies. But in each case, the purpose of the earlier prophecies was fulfilled. In Peter, that was to teach holy living, and in Isaiah, to point to a future time of blessing.

A Look Back–a Look Forward

In the prophecies of Daniel, we saw that each time the Day of the Lord was reached, there was only one or maybe two aspects of the total picture presented. As a recap, these were the destruction of Gentile powers (Dan. 2), Christ coming in the clouds, giving the kingdom of God to the saints (Dan. 7), Christ destroying the Antichrist (Dan. 8), the spiritual restoration of Israel and the destruction of the Antichrist (Dan. 9), and the resurrection of the dead (Dan. 12). As we transition into the Revelation studies, we must keep in mind that this is how God presents prophecies.

We are now prepared to look forward to Revelation to establish some endpoints. We see the beginning of the Day of the Lord at the sixth seal with the signs in the heavens: "And I beheld when he had opened the sixth seal, and, lo, there was a great earthquake; and the sun became black as sackcloth of hair, and the moon became as blood" (Rev 6:12). This is the same event that we saw earlier in this chapter, referenced on five occasions by the prophets Joel, Isaiah, and Zechariah. It was also referenced by the Lord Jesus in the Olivet Discourse (Matt. 24:29–31). This identifies the sixth seal as the beginning of the last day (John 6:40), when Christ will raise the dead and rapture the church at his coming (1 Thess. 4:15–17; 2 Thess. 2:1). As the text in Revelation continues, we get further confirmation that this is the initiating point of the Day of the Lord, referred to here as the "wrath of the Lamb":

> [15]And the kings of the earth, and the great men, and the rich men, and the chief captains, and the mighty men, and every bondman, and every free man, hid themselves in the dens and in the rocks of the mountains; [16]And said to the mountains and rocks, Fall on us, and hide us from the face of him that sitteth on the throne, and from the wrath of the Lamb: [17]For the great day of his wrath is come; and who shall be able to stand? (Rev 6:15–17)

This is the same description of the Day of the Lord shown in Isaiah 2:19–21. And if the sixth seal initiates the Day of the Lord, it is quite reasonable to conclude that the seventh is its culmination. We will have confirmation of this later in these studies.

Earlier in this chapter, it was shown that the dead will be raised and living believers will be gathered together with them at the sound of the last trumpet (1 Cor. 15:52). This has identified yet another endpoint as the seventh trumpet judgment of Revelation. It was confirmed for us as follows: "The kingdoms of this world are become the kingdoms of our Lord, and of his Christ; and he shall reign for ever and ever" (Rev. 11:15), teaching the beginning of Christ's millennial reign on this earth immediately after the seventh trumpet.

Yet another endpoint can be seen here at the seventh vial judgment: "And the seventh angel poured out his vial into the air; and there came a great voice out of the temple of heaven, from the throne, saying, It is done" (Rev 16:17). Notice the declaration—"It is done." This is the final culminating event of the judgment of nations and unbelievers that we studied earlier, the final event of "the wrath of God" (Rev. 15:1).

The number seven is generally understood to represent God's perfect completion. And we see the same pattern developing in the judgments of Revelation as we did in Daniel. Each series ends with a different aspect of the Day of the Lord presented. The seventh judgment in each series ends on the last day of this world and represents an endpoint of the perfect completion of God's indignation.

As these studies progress, it will become apparent that there are additional endpoints in Revelation. The purpose, at this point, was to demonstrate the importance of not only discerning what the prophecies teach but *how* they are being framed for us and how they fit together to create a complete picture.

6

And Then Shall Many Be Offended

In this study, we will be looking at two prophecies given by the Lord Jesus himself in the Olivet Discourse and his promise of preservation to those who remain faithful. To set the stage, Jesus had just returned to Jerusalem for the last time, had overthrown the tables of the moneychangers in the temple a day earlier (Matt. 21:12), had called out the hypocrisy of the scribes and Pharisees in the most blistering rebuke of his ministry (Matt. 23), and had now retreated to the Mount of Olives, where he spoke privately with Peter, James, John, and Andrew (Mark 13:3).

What followed was a foretelling of the signs that will precede his Second Coming and warnings to believers. We will devote an entire study to the Olivet Discourse shortly, but for now, will just focus on these two passages:

> ⁹Then shall they deliver you up to be afflicted, and shall kill you: and ye shall be hated of all nations for my name's sake. ¹⁰And then shall many be offended, and shall betray one another, and shall hate one another. (Matt. 24:9–10)

> ¹³But he that shall endure unto the end, the same shall be saved. (Matt. 24:13)

Contained here are the prophecies of persecution of Christians during the great tribulation ("then shall they deliver you up to be afflicted") and the departure from the faith by many ("be offended"). The Greek *skandalizō,* translated above into "offended," means to entrap, trip up, entice to sin and apostasy, or to cause to fall away.[1] The

---

1   Strong, *Concordance,* G4624.

last verse is a promise of preservation to those who stay true to the faith throughout the hardships.

A Word of Caution

There is an interpretive system named dispensationalism, the teachings of which have become thoroughly entrenched within modern Christianity. This system's primary teaching is a pretribulation rapture, the gathering together of believers with Christ before the start of Daniel's Seventieth Week. This claim leads dispensationalists to contend that the Olivet Discourse is not intended for today's Christians since they assert that we won't be on earth during that time. They have rightly determined that the Olivet Discourse is Christ, in his own words, teaching what will occur during the great tribulation. However, since their predetermined belief in a pretribulation rapture precludes the possibility of any church-age believers being in the great tribulation, they have wrongly concluded that the teachings of the Olivet Discourse don't apply to us.

The previous study on the Day of the Lord showed that believers can expect to be on this earth until Christ's Second Coming. And between this study and the one that follows, we will see that there is no evidence within the text of the Olivet Discourse that would lead anyone to believe that it is not intended for church-age Christians. Instead, Christ was speaking to four of his apostles, who would soon be laying the foundation of the church (Eph. 2:20), saying that "you" will be "delivered up to be afflicted," "killed," and "hated" for his name's sake (v. 9)—undeniably referring to Christians.

Some have said that since the apostles were Jews, that means that Christ's message is to the Jews. This non-sequitur can be easily refuted by noting that only a few chapters earlier, Christ said to Peter that his confession is the "rock" on which Christ will build his church (Matt. 16:18). He also spoke figuratively of salvation by referring to the "keys to the kingdom of heaven" and of church decision making, "binding and loosing." No one contends that these statements to Peter are not for the church. Nor does anyone conclude that the writings of the apostles in the New Testament are exclusively for the Jews.

Still others don't give a specific reason for excluding the Olivet Discourse from applicability to today's Christians. Instead, they rely on a misinterpretation of "rightly dividing the word of truth" (2 Tim. 2:15). In their determination, this means that we are to literally cut up God's Word and decide what applies to us and what doesn't. Thus, since they have decided that the pretribulation rapture is a reality, then it follows that the Olivet Discourse must not be speaking to us but rather to Jews enduring the great tribulation.

The problem here is that an honest assessment of "rightly diving the word of truth" would be rightly *discerning* God's Word. Consequently, they use this ill-conceived license to "cut up" God's Word as a means of advancing man's doctrine before God's. Further, it also ignores the fact that great tribulation Jews will not be saved until Christ's Second Coming and will not have any interest in reading the Olivet Discourse.

This is only a small picture of the harm that this doctrine has done. Christ tells us four times that he will raise dead believers on the "last day" (John 6:39, 40, 44, 54). The Holy Spirit, through Paul, tells us that immediately after the dead are raised, living believers will be "caught up together" with them in the clouds (1 Thess. 4:17). Christ confirms precisely this in the following passage:

> 23Jesus saith unto her, Thy brother shall rise again. 24Martha saith unto him, I know that he shall rise again in the resurrection at the last day. 25Jesus said unto her, I am the resurrection, and the life: he that believeth in me, though he were dead, yet shall he live: 26And whosoever liveth and believeth in me shall never die. Believest thou this? (John 11:23–26)

The context above is the "resurrection at the last day" (v. 24); the dead will be raised (v. 25), and the living will be raptured, "shall never die" (v. 26). This makes Christ's return on the last day the only possible time for living believers to be raptured, and there is no possible way to reconcile a pretribulation rapture with these teachings. By adhering to this doctrine, these teachers are directly contradicting both Christ and the Holy Spirit.[2] The following passages that speak of our present time come to mind:

> 1This know also, that in the last days perilous times shall come. (2 Tim. 3:1)

---

2   Tregelles, *Second Coming*, 41–42.

> ³For the time will come when they will not endure sound doctrine; but after their own lusts shall they heap to themselves teachers, having itching ears; ⁴And they shall turn away their ears from the truth, and shall be turned unto fables. (2 Tim. 4:3–4)

We will be studying exactly what God's Word has to say about this apostasy (departure from the truth) of the church in a subsequent study. But since I know how firmly people want to adhere to this doctrine and may decide to stop reading at this point, I must place an admonition here. By claiming that the church will be raptured before the great tribulation, this teaching has added another coming of Christ in addition to his biblically taught Second Coming and has taken the church out of the great tribulation, making this warning to those who "add unto" or "take away from" the Word of God applicable:

> ¹⁸For I testify unto every man that heareth the words of the prophecy of this book, If any man shall add unto these things, God shall add unto him the plagues that are written in this book: ¹⁹And if any man shall take away from the words of the book of this prophecy, God shall take away his part out of the book of life, and out of the holy city, and from the things which are written in this book. (Rev. 22:18–19)

Many very good works have been done that compare dispensational teachings to the Word of God on a point-by-point basis.[3] The purpose of this book is not to repeat those works but rather to make a complete presentation of what God tells us pertaining to the time of the end to clearly show the contrast between God's Word and dispensational teaching.

In this process, it is necessary to make it clear that the church will go through the great tribulation for the same purposes as Israel: purging, chastening, and refining. And just like Israel, believers in Christ are promised preservation by God through the chastening fire. If we are not aware of this, those of us who are present when all the prophesied events begin run the risk of being offended (falling away)

---

3   Gundry, *Church and Tribulation*; Ladd, *Blessed Hope*; Tregelles, *Second Coming*.

as a consequence of the persecutions and spiritual deceptions that will abound.

Then Shall They Deliver You up to Be Afflicted

Christ's prophecy of persecution of Christians is not an isolated teaching in the New Testament. When Paul and Barnabas were preaching the Word in the regions of Galatia, they stated that "we must through much tribulation enter into the kingdom of God" (Acts 14:22). It is also clearly taught that this Christian tribulation can lead the believer to depart from the faith.

> [3]That no man should be moved by these afflictions: for yourselves know that we are appointed thereunto. [4]For verily, when we were with you, we told you before that we should suffer tribulation; even as it came to pass, and ye know. [5]For this cause, when I could no longer forbear, I sent to know your faith, lest by some means the tempter have tempted you, and our labour be in vain. (1 Thess. 3:3–5)

Paul makes it clear that Christians are "appointed" to afflictions and reminded those at Thessalonica that he had told them this previously. The reason for his stating it again is also plain; he needed to know whether they were still in the faith or if Satan—"the tempter"—had caused them to fall away, thereby rendering his labor on them in vain. This is clearly teaching both the certainty of tribulation and that it could well result in a believer departing from the faith, the consequence of which is no longer being saved. Paul even stated how he was comforted to find out from Timothy that they had remained in the faith (1 Thess. 3:6–7) and continued with the following: "For now we live, if ye stand fast in the Lord" (1 Thess. 3:8).

Still further, "In the world ye shall have tribulation" (John 16:33), "All that will live godly in Christ Jesus shall suffer persecution" (2 Tim. 3:12), and "Beloved, think it not strange concerning the fiery trial which is to try you, as though some strange thing happened unto you" (1 Pet. 4:12). These preceding passages show that persecutions are an expected part of a believer's life and are considered "trials," "testings of faith." Christ speaks of these trials metaphorically as believers being "salted with fire": "For every one shall be salted with fire, and every sacrifice shall be salted with salt" (Mark 9:49).

Refining of the Believer

> [2]My brethren, count it all joy when ye fall into divers temptations; [3]Knowing this, that the trying of your faith worketh patience. [4]But let patience have her perfect work, that ye may be perfect and entire, wanting nothing. (James 1:2–4)

> [3]And not only so, but we glory in tribulations also: knowing that tribulation worketh patience; [4]And patience, experience; and experience, hope: [5]And hope maketh not ashamed; because the love of God is shed abroad in our hearts by the Holy Ghost which is given unto us. (Rom 5:3–5)

The reason for these trials is the refining effect on the believer. Further, believers are promised chastening, which should be understood as disciplinary correction: "For whom the Lord loveth he chasteneth, and scourgeth every son whom he receiveth. If ye endure chastening, God dealeth with you as with sons; for what son is he whom the father chasteneth not?" (Heb. 12:6–7). Christ says the same here as well: "As many as I love, I rebuke and chasten: be zealous therefore, and repent" (Rev. 3:19). The following passages show the intended outcome of the trials. Christ gave himself for his church and is now in the process of cleansing it:

> [25]Husbands, love your wives, even as Christ also loved the church, and gave himself for it; [26]That he might sanctify and cleanse it with the washing of water by the word, [27]That he might present it to himself a glorious church, not having spot, or wrinkle, or any such thing; but that it should be holy and without blemish. (Eph. 5:25–27)

> [14]Who gave himself for us, that he might redeem us from all iniquity, and purify unto himself a peculiar people, zealous of good works. (Titus 2:14)

This glorious church, which Christ is in the process of purifying, will be seen at the end of the great tribulation (Rev. 7:14) "not having spot, or wrinkle, or any such thing."

Purging of the Church

Christ's words, "And then shall many be offended" (Matt. 24:10), speak of the effect of the tribulation and spiritual deception on the believer. Many will leave the faith, resulting in a purging effect on the church. This is the burning of the chaff from the wheat. Remember, the chaff is actually part of the wheat, but in the analogy, it is the believer who doesn't stay in the faith when presented with difficulties.

The second "soil" in the parable of the sower (Matt. 13:20–21) expresses this well. The stoney soil heard the word and received it "with joy," but because of "tribulations or persecutions," was "offended"—fell away. Persecutions will not be the only reason for this falling away, however. There will also be tremendous spiritual deception (Matt. 24:4, 5, 11, 24), with the clear teaching that false prophets "shall deceive many" (Matt. 24:11).

The words of Christ are not the only place where it is said that believers will depart from the faith. Here is a very stern warning from Paul to the elders at Ephesus, which contains a prophecy of believers being drawn away by the false prophets.

> [27]For I have not shunned to declare unto you all the counsel of God. [28]Take heed therefore unto yourselves, and to all the flock, over the which the Holy Ghost hath made you overseers, to feed the church of God, which he hath purchased with his own blood. [29]For I know this, that after my departing shall grievous wolves enter in among you, not sparing the flock. [30]Also of your own selves shall men arise, speaking perverse things, to draw away disciples after them. [31]Therefore watch, and remember, that by the space of three years I ceased not to warn every one night and day with tears. [32]And now, brethren, I commend you to God, and to the word of his grace, which is able to build you up, and to give you an inheritance among all them which are sanctified. (Acts 20:27–32)

There is also this prophecy of believers departing from the faith, particularly in these latter times:

> [1]Now the Spirit speaketh expressly, that in the latter times some shall depart from the faith, giving heed to seducing

spirits, and doctrines of devils; ²Speaking lies in hypocrisy; having their conscience seared with a hot iron; (1 Tim. 4:1–2)

Please keep in mind that it is not possible to be "drawn away" or to "depart from" something you don't have. So, these are speaking of believers falling away from the faith.

In this study, we are focused on the individual believer, how we are told of the perils that lie ahead, and the necessity of remaining faithful throughout whatever may come our way. When we turn to a full study of the Olivet Discourse and its parables, it will be clear that Christ is warning us that our faith is the most precious thing we have and that we must guard it at all costs, making sure we do not neglect to have sufficient "oil" like the five "foolish" virgins did.

Christ's Promise of Preservation

In light of these forces drawing the believer away from faith in Christ and the truth, Christ spells out the way to victory: "But he that shall endure unto the end, the same shall be saved" (Matt. 24:13). This should be understood as a promise of preservation spoken to those who "endure unto the end." When Christ says, "The same shall be saved," he means that it is a certainty. This salvation is not necessarily from death or martyrdom but rather preservation "through" the tribulation and being given the eternal life that is promised in Christ.

The word "endure" must be understood to mean remaining in the faith and remaining in the truth. Remaining in the faith needs no further explanation but the "truth" must be understood to mean biblical truth. As we progress in these studies, we will see that the lack of grounding in biblical truth and satanically empowered "signs and wonders" will lead people to believe that a man—the Antichrist—is actually Christ on earth.

Peter speaks of this entire dynamic of chastening trials, God's preservation, and the refinement that it results in:

⁵Who are kept by the power of God through faith unto salvation ready to be revealed in the last time. ⁶Wherein ye greatly rejoice, though now for a season, if need be, ye are in heaviness through manifold temptations: ⁷That the trial of your faith, being much more precious than of gold that

perisheth, though it be tried with fire, might be found unto praise and honour and glory at the appearing of Jesus Christ. (1 Pet. 1:5–7)

Notice the promise is to be "kept" (preserved) by the "power of God through faith." This is key: God "keeps" those who remain in the faith. This is why Christ warns of falling away through the persecutions and warns of deceptions. If we allow ourselves to be deceived or allow the intensity of the persecutions to cause us to renounce our faith, the promise of God's preservation no longer applies.

God also promises that he will not allow us to be tested beyond what we can handle: "There hath no temptation taken you but such as is common to man: but God is faithful, who will not suffer you to be tempted above that ye are able" (1 Cor. 10:13). And by his grace, he will always provide a way out for us: "But will with the temptation also make a way to escape, that ye may be able to bear it" (1 Cor. 10:13; c.f. 2 Pet. 2:9).

Additional promises of preservation follow: "So that ye come behind in no gift; waiting for the coming of our Lord Jesus Christ: Who shall also confirm you unto the end, that ye may be blameless in the day of our Lord Jesus Christ" (1 Cor. 1:7–8); "And the Lord shall deliver me from every evil work, and will preserve me unto his heavenly kingdom" (2 Tim. 4:18). In the first passage, the promise to preserve the believer is seen in the phrase "confirm you unto the end"; in the second, it is stated, "the Lord shall deliver me" and "will preserve me."

We always see that this promise is to those who remain in the faith: "Let that therefore abide in you, which ye have heard from the beginning. If that which ye have heard from the beginning shall remain in you, ye also shall continue in the Son, and in the Father. And this is the promise that he hath promised us, even eternal life" (1 John 2:24–25); and, "To present you holy and unblameable and unreproveable in his sight: If ye continue in the faith grounded and settled, and be not moved away from the hope of the gospel" (Col. 1:22–23). Eternal life is the promise "if that which ye have heard from the beginning shall remain in you" (the truth), and we are promised to be presented "holy and unblameable" "if ye continue in the faith grounded and settled."

In the following, Paul clearly spells out that the believers in Corinth are presently "saved" by the gospel that he has preached to them *if* they do not stray from it, or as he stated, "keep in memory what I preached": "Moreover, brethren, I declare unto you the gospel which I preached unto you, which also ye have received, and wherein ye stand; By which also ye are saved, if ye keep in memory what I preached unto you, unless ye have believed in vain" (1 Cor. 15:1–2).

We can go back to the first verse that we looked at spoken by Paul and Barnabas and see that they gave this same admonition to remain in the faith: "Confirming the souls of the disciples, and exhorting them to continue in the faith, and that we must through much tribulation enter into the kingdom of God" (Acts 14:22; c.f. 2 Thess. 1:4–5). This presents the picture that is consistently portrayed in the New Testament of the believer's promise of security in salvation being conditioned upon remaining in the faith, i.e., "in Christ." Or as the writer of Hebrews stated, "And we desire that every one of you do shew the same diligence to the full assurance of hope unto the end: That ye be not slothful, but followers of them who through faith and patience inherit the promises" (Heb. 6:11–12).

Concluding Thoughts

For the purposes of our studies, it is not necessary to go into any more detail on these topics. The issue at hand is that Christ tells us that believers will be in the great tribulation and will consequently suffer persecutions at the hands of the Antichrist. In future studies, we will see many more examples of believers in the great tribulation and more evidence that it is our continued faith that is called for. We will also see additional admonitions to remain in the faith and promises of God's preservation and protection of believers through the great tribulation.

A secondary purpose of this study was to demonstrate the clear disconnect between what God's Word says and two very pervasive modern teachings. The first, dispensationalism and its doctrine of a pretribulation rapture, has already been addressed. The second is the doctrine of absolute eternal security, otherwise stated as "once saved, always saved" (OSAS). Since it has been shown that Christ tells us that believers will fall away from the faith, as does the Holy Spirit through the prophecies of Paul, it can be simply stated that those who teach this doctrine are directly contradicting the Word of God.

They state that a believer cannot lose their salvation. If that means that God's promise of eternal life will never fail, then they are correct. But it is quite evident that a believer can forfeit their salvation. Paul gives us a very serious warning in the following passage:

> [11]Now all these things happened unto them for ensamples: and they are written for our admonition, upon whom the ends of the world are come. [12]Wherefore let him that thinketh he standeth take heed lest he fall. (1 Cor. 10:11–12)

Here, he uses the example of God taking all Israel out of Egypt to save them. But after being saved, they transgressed God's statutes, and he was forced to destroy many of them in the desert. The warning to believers is this: "Wherefore let him that thinketh he standeth take heed lest he fall." I cannot think of a more plainly stated rebuke of OSAS teaching. The same warning can be found in the epistle to the Romans:

> [20]Well; because of unbelief they were broken off, and thou standest by faith. Be not highminded, but fear: [21]For if God spared not the natural branches, take heed lest he also spare not thee. [22]Behold therefore the goodness and severity of God: on them which fell, severity; but toward thee, goodness, if thou continue in his goodness: otherwise thou also shalt be cut off. (Rom. 11:20–22)

As we continue in these studies, it will be shown that the church is in a terrible state of apostasy and will play an instrumental role in the rise of the Antichrist. Just as Israel is in need of a chastening, so is the church. This is the reason for Christ stating, "For all these things must come to pass" (Matt. 24:6).

I cannot imagine a better way for Satan to get believers to depart from the faith than to teach that we won't be in the great tribulation and that we can't fall away from our salvation. Believers are being taught that there are no signs to watch for and that Christ will rapture us before anything gets really bad. This means that many will be completely unprepared for what is coming since they won't be aware of the biblical warnings to believers. Once they do realize what is going on and understand that they're all in the great tribulation, they may well feel incredible betrayal and despair since what they have been taught about the time of the end has not happened as they expected. Add to this the teaching that you can't forsake your salvation, and people may not realize that taking the "mark of the beast" is a one-way ticket to the lake of fire. This is bound to be a very successful strategy for the devil.

7

Know That It Is Near

Now we are in a position to take a step back and examine the totality of the teaching in the Olivet Discourse from the perspective of this verse: "So likewise ye, when ye shall see all these things, know that it is near, even at the doors" (Matt. 24:33). The Lord Jesus spoke these words after giving a lengthy recitation of the signs that will precede his Second Coming. In Luke, it is stated, "So likewise ye, when ye see these things come to pass, know ye that the kingdom of God is nigh at hand" (Luke. 21:31), and in Mark, "So ye in like manner, when ye shall see these things come to pass, know that it is nigh, even at the doors" (Mark 13:29).

What is being referred to here is the Day of the Lord—Christ's Second Coming. The believer's attention is specifically directed at the signs that precede his Second Coming, which had just been presented to the apostles. Christ gives the believer signs to look for since the exact timing of his Second Coming will be unknown (Matt. 24:36, 42) and its nature will be unexpected: "For in such an hour as ye think not the Son of Man cometh" (Matt. 24:44).

Christ's teaching contains multiple imperatives for the believer to watch for the signs that precede his unexpected arrival. The purpose is to be in a state of preparedness when he comes: "Watch ye therefore: for ye know not when the master of the house cometh, at even, or at midnight, or at the cockcrowing, or in the morning: Lest coming suddenly he find you sleeping. And what I say unto you I say unto all, Watch" (Mark 13:35–37).

Christ's discourse is presented in each of the three synoptic gospels with only slight variations. For our purposes, we will focus on the presentation in Matthew, with brief references to the others. Christ's entire teaching spans Matthew 24 and 25 and is divided into three sections: (1) the prophetic signs of his coming (Matt. 24:3–31), (2) the significance of the signs to the believer (Matt. 24:32–51), and (3) the kingdom parables (Matt. 25:1–46). In the prophetic signs portion, the Lord Jesus parallels the teaching in Daniel 9:26–27, using the Seventieth Week as a framework to add additional details to. And from there, he points the believer to the prophecies in Revelation, specifically the abomination of desolation and the Day of the Lord.

The Signs of His Coming

> [3]And as he sat upon the mount of Olives, the disciples came unto him privately, saying, Tell us, when shall these things be? and what shall be the sign of thy coming, and of the end of the world? [4]And Jesus answered and said unto them, Take heed that no man deceive you. [5]For many shall come in my name, saying, I am Christ; and shall deceive many. [6]And ye shall hear of wars and rumours of wars: see that ye be not troubled: for all these things must come to pass, but the end is not yet. [7]For nation shall rise against nation, and kingdom against kingdom: and there shall be famines, and pestilences, and earthquakes, in divers places. [8]All these are the beginning of sorrows. [9]Then shall they deliver you up to be afflicted, and shall kill you: and ye shall be hated of all nations for my name's sake. [10]And then shall many be offended, and shall betray one another, and shall hate one another. [11]And many false prophets shall rise, and shall deceive many. [12]And because iniquity shall abound, the love of many shall wax cold. [13]But he that shall endure unto the end, the same shall be saved. [14]And this gospel of the kingdom shall be preached in all the world for a witness unto all nations; and then shall the end come.(Matt. 24:3–14)

This passage covers the entire period spelled out by Daniel 9:26–27, the church age, from the crucifixion of Christ to the end of the Seventieth Week in three sections. Verses 4–6 cover the church age up to the beginning of the Seventieth Week. Verses 7–8 cover the first half of the Seventieth Week, now referred to as the "beginning of sorrows." And verses 9–14 cover the second half of the Seventieth Week—the great tribulation.

The church age will be characterized by spiritual deceptions, false Christs, wars, and rumors of wars (vv. 4–6; c.f. Luke 21:8–9; Mark 13:5–7). These are foreshadowings of the final week and the great tribulation in particular. Our indicator that these are expected for the entire church age is, "but the end is not yet" (v. 6).

What follows is the beginning of the Seventieth Week. Verses 7 and 8 speak of wars, famines, pestilences (disease), and earthquakes and call these the beginning of sorrows (c.f. Luke 21:10–11; Mark 13:8). This is the first half of the Seventieth Week and precedes the abomination of desolation (Dan. 9:27). Much of the military conflict that the man in linen described to Daniel in the vision of great warfare (Dan. 11:40–43) could be what will be occurring during the beginning of sorrows.

At this point, Luke gives us a passage that the other two gospel writers omit. He prefaces by saying, "But before all these" (Luke 21:12). What follows in Luke 21:12–24 are the persecutions of the early church (vv. 12–19) and then the destruction of Jerusalem by the Romans in 70 A.D. and the dispersion of the Jews until the fulfillment of the "times of the Gentiles" (vv. 20–24). This shows that Christ is exactly paralleling the prophecy of Daniel 9:26 and using the destruction of Jerusalem as a foreshadowing of the great tribulation. In a moment, we will see where Luke rejoins the discourse.

After Matthew covers the first half of the Seventieth Week, he continues with a brief overview of the second half of the Seventieth Week—the great tribulation (vv. 9–14; c.f. Mark 13:9–13). We have covered the prophecy of Christians being in the great tribulation and falling away because of the persecutions and spiritual deceptions already (vv. 9, 10, 13). Please notice that there is nothing in the text that would indicate that these verses are not for present-day Christians.

Further, we see that because of iniquity (lawlessness and wickedness), the love of many will grow cold (v. 12), another reason for believers to be on guard for their faith. Christ concludes with the statement that the gospel will be preached in all the world, and then the end will come. This is the Day of the Lord, and we now know another condition that will precede it, the worldwide preaching of the gospel.

What happens next is very important to understand. Christ doubles back to the midpoint of the Seventieth Week with a reference to the "abomination of desolation" (v. 15; c.f. Dan. 9:27) and continues with a much more detailed prophecy of this three-and-one-half-year period, including providing the name that we have been using all along—the great tribulation (c.f. Mark 13:14–20). Please note this is exactly how the prophecies of Daniel were presented, first in rough form, and then much more detail was added in subsequent prophecies. The more detailed description follows:

> [15]When ye therefore shall see the abomination of desolation, spoken of by Daniel the prophet, stand in the holy place, (whoso readeth, let him understand:) [16]Then let them which be in Judaea flee into the mountains: [17]Let him which is on the housetop not come down to take any thing out of his house: [18]Neither let him which is in the field return back to take his clothes. [19]And woe unto them that are with child, and to them that give suck in those days! [20]But pray ye that your flight be not in the winter, neither on the sabbath day: [21]For then shall be great tribulation, such as was not since the beginning of the world to this time, no, nor ever shall be. [22]And except those days should be shortened, there should no flesh be saved: but for the elect's sake those days shall be shortened. (Matt. 24:15–22)

Christ speaks of the abomination of desolation standing in the holy place, which we know from Daniel will happen at the midpoint of the Seventieth Week. He continues with a warning to believers to flee from Jerusalem because the times to come will be the worst ever on this earth. The horrific nature of the Antichrist's persecutions and wars will require Christ to return to prevent all humans from being extinguished. Notice the Lord is referring back to Daniel's prophecy and pointing us forward to Revelation, where we will receive even greater details about the Antichrist's persecutions and the abomination of desolation (Rev. 11:2; 12:6, 13–17; 13:5–8, 14–15; c.f. 2 Thess. 2:4). He continues by giving even more details with yet a second pass pertaining to the great tribulation (c.f. Mark 13:21–23):

> [23]Then if any man shall say unto you, Lo, here is Christ, or there; believe it not. [24]For there shall arise false Christs, and

false prophets, and shall shew great signs and wonders; insomuch that, if it were possible, they shall deceive the very elect. [25]Behold, I have told you before. [26]Wherefore if they shall say unto you, Behold, he is in the desert; go not forth: behold, he is in the secret chambers; believe it not. [27]For as the lightning cometh out of the east, and shineth even unto the west; so shall also the coming of the Son of man be. [28]For wheresoever the carcase is, there will the eagles be gathered together. (Matt. 24:23–28)

There will be many false alarms of Christ being here or there, but believers are told not to follow after them. Instead, we are told that his Second Coming will be completely visible and evident to all using two analogies (vv. 27–28). Before considering the analogies, we must first determine the correct point of comparison that Christ is intending. To do this, we use the surrounding text as well as other Bible teachings to inform our understanding.

The analogies of his Second Coming follow immediately after him saying not to be deceived into going to some desert or secret place to find him as false prophets will insist. The analogies teach a message that is quite contrary. It will not be secret, but rather it will be evident to all, just as a bolt of lightning can be seen from one end of the sky to the other or just as obvious as the location of a dead body is by the vultures ("eagles") circling around in the air.

The juxtaposition against the false alarms of a secret, unapparent coming informs our understanding of the analogies. This also agrees with what we learned in Daniel, that he will return in the "clouds of heaven" (Dan. 7:13) and that "every eye shall see him" (Rev. 1:7). These analogies are not teaching that his coming will be in the form of lightning or that there is some allegorical understanding that we should derive from the use of the word eagles. Simply, just as those events are visible and obvious to all, so will be his Second Coming.

Next, Christ moves on to teaching about the Day of the Lord, which will come "immediately after the tribulation of those days"—the great tribulation. Please recall that Luke presented a picture of the early church persecutions and destruction of the temple; this is the point at which he rejoins the narrative in Luke 21:25 (c.f. Mark 13:24–27):

> ²⁹Immediately after the tribulation of those days shall the sun be darkened, and the moon shall not give her light, and the stars shall fall from heaven, and the powers of the heavens shall be shaken: ³⁰And then shall appear the sign of the Son of man in heaven: and then shall all the tribes of the earth mourn, and they shall see the Son of man coming in the clouds of heaven with power and great glory. ³¹And he shall send his angels with a great sound of a trumpet, and they shall gather together his elect from the four winds, from one end of heaven to the other. (Matt. 24:29–31)

Since the Day of the Lord was covered in detail in a previous study, there is no reason to duplicate those teachings. However, it should be noted that this is what the Lord was referring to when he stated, "For the elect's sake those days shall be shortened" (v. 22). He will return before all humanity is wiped out. The elect are those who have prepared themselves for these times with a full understanding of what will be happening and have the truth of God's Word residing within them. They are those who will endure: "But he that shall endure unto the end, the same shall be saved" (v. 13). God can call these believers elect because he knows exactly who will believe in Christ, and of those, who will endure to the end. He knows those who will not be deceived (v. 24) or fall away in the face of hardships (v. 10) by his perfect "foreknowledge" (1 Pet. 1:2).

Significance of the Signs

> ³²Now learn a parable of the fig tree; When his branch is yet tender, and putteth forth leaves, ye know that summer is nigh: ³³So likewise ye, when ye shall see all these things, know that it is near, even at the doors. ³⁴Verily I say unto you, This generation shall not pass, till all these things be fulfilled. ³⁵Heaven and earth shall pass away, but my words shall not pass away. ³⁶But of that day and hour knoweth no man, no, not the angels of heaven, but my Father only. (Matt. 24:32–36)

There are four separate thoughts contained in this brief passage. The first and last speak to the significance of the signs that the Lord has just presented. The signs are meant to be an indicator to believers that the end is near since the exact time will be unknown. These points are so important that he devotes multiple analogies and parables to expand on them (vv. 37–51). The second and third thoughts are that the Jews will survive as a race until his return and that the events that he has just described will occur with absolute certainty.

The Lord conveys that the signs are meant to be an indicator to believers in the parable of the fig tree (v. 32) and follows with an interpretation of the parable (v. 33). Just as the tender branch and the budding leaves on the fig tree indicate that the summer is near, so do the signs that he has provided indicate that his Second Coming is near.

Second, he speaks of "this generation" that will not pass until "all these things be fulfilled." This can be interpreted in one of several ways since, in the Bible, the word generation has multiple meanings. In this context, however, I believe that the generation being referred to should be understood to mean the Jewish race.

In the Bible, the word "generation" (Greek *genea*)[1] can be used to describe (1) successive members of a genealogy (Matt. 1:1–17), (2) the duration of time occupied by each successive generation, i.e., 30–40 years, (3) all the people alive at a given point in time (Luke 1:48), or (4) a group or class of people possessing similar characteristics or pursuits. To determine the meaning in the text at hand, we must notice that the generation being spoken of will not pass until "all these things be fulfilled." Since all these things include the early church persecutions and the destruction of the temple (Luke 21:12–24), the entire church age (Matt. 24:4–6), and the future Seventieth Week, the only possible choice on the list is the last.

To confirm, we see that John the Baptist referred to the Pharisees and Sadducees as a "generation of vipers" (Matt. 3:7), and Jesus referred to the Pharisees in the same way (Matt. 12:34). They used the word to mean a "class" of people—unbelieving Jews. Further, the Lord Jesus had just finished excoriating the unbelieving Jews in Matthew 23, referring to them again as a "generation of vipers" (Matt. 23:33) and "this generation" (Matt. 23:36). I think we must conclude that the reference to "this generation" in the Olivet Discourse is this "class" of people, unbelieving Jews, and is telling us that the Jewish race will survive as a people until the return of Christ (c.f. Jer. 31:35–37).

---

1   Strong, *Concordance*, G1074.

Third, he speaks of the absolute certainty that the events will occur as described: "Heaven and earth shall pass away, but my words shall not pass away" (v. 35). The "words" referred to here are his prophecies, and what he is saying is that all the events *will* happen exactly as he says. The events that Christ describes must occur (Matt. 24:6; c.f. Rev. 1:1; 4:1; 22:6) before God's redemptive plan can be completed (Rev. 10:7).

And fourth, no one knows the "day and hour" of his return, only the Father (v. 36). Elsewhere, it is described as being like a "thief in the night" (1 Thess. 5:2; 2 Pet. 3:10; c.f. Rev. 16:15). Combined, these teach that the precise timing of his Second Coming will be unknown, and the "thief in the night" analogy creates an image of it being unexpected and unwelcome for those who are unprepared. For these reasons, believers are told to *watch* for the signs.

His Unexpected Return

> [37]But as the days of Noe were, so shall also the coming of the Son of man be. [38]For as in the days that were before the flood they were eating and drinking, marrying and giving in marriage, until the day that Noe entered into the ark, [39]And knew not until the flood came, and took them all away; so shall also the coming of the Son of man be. [40]Then shall two be in the field; the one shall be taken, and the other left. [41]Two women shall be grinding at the mill; the one shall be taken, and the other left. [42]Watch therefore: for ye know not what hour your Lord doth come. (Matt. 24:37–42)

The point of comparison of the analogy to the days of Noah is that they were completely unaware of the times they were in and only found out once it was too late. This is evident from the explanation that follows the analogy: "And knew not until the flood came, and took them all away." Thus, the flood was unexpected, they were unprepared, and it was a very unwelcome event!

Next, the Lord builds on this unexpected nature of his Second Coming with the analogy of the two in the field and two at the mill. Clearly, if they were aware that the Lord was coming that day, there would be no need for gathering in the field or grinding at the mill. Once again, this demonstrates the unexpected nature of his coming, followed by the warning to watch: "Watch therefore: for ye know not what hour your Lord doth come" (v. 42).

Because of the unexpected nature of the Lord's return, he gives us the signs that will immediately precede it so that we can be prepared and not caught by surprise. The following parables teach the necessity of this spiritual preparedness.

Watch and Be Wakeful

> [43]But know this, that if the goodman of the house had known in what watch the thief would come, he would have watched, and would not have suffered his house to be broken up. [44]Therefore be ye also ready: for in such an hour as ye think not the Son of man cometh. [45]Who then is a faithful and wise servant, whom his lord hath made ruler over his household, to give them meat in due season? [46]Blessed is that servant, whom his lord when he cometh shall find so doing. [47]Verily I say unto you, That he shall make him ruler over all his goods. [48]But and if that evil servant shall say in his heart, My lord delayeth his coming; [49]And shall begin to smite his fellowservants, and to eat and drink with the drunken; [50]The lord of that servant shall come in a day when he looketh not for him, and in an hour that he is not aware of, [51]And shall cut him asunder, and appoint him his portion with the hypocrites: there shall be weeping and gnashing of teeth. (Matt. 24:43–51)

These parables make it clear that the Lord expects the believer to be in a state of watchfulness and preparedness—spiritual wakefulness—at all times since the one who is not will be in for an unwelcome surprise when he returns (c.f. Mark 13:33–37). This message is quite contrary to the modern teaching of an "imminent expectation" of his Second Coming without any intervening signs to watch for.

Kingdom Parables

Three "kingdom parables" follow in Matthew 25. Each teaches a different lesson pertaining to the Lord's Second Coming. The parable of the virgins (Matt. 25:1–13) delineates between two types of believers, the wise and the foolish. The difference between them is their state of preparedness at his arrival. During the long time that the "bridegroom" has been away, the wise had sufficient oil, in this case representing faith, while the foolish didn't. It ends with this admonition: "Watch therefore, for ye know neither the day nor the hour wherein the Son of man cometh" (Matt. 25:13), making it clear that the Lord is giving us the signs that precede his Second Coming so that we are fully prepared at his arrival. In this case, the parable teaches the importance of remaining in the faith until Christ's return and not being among those who are "offended"—fall away.

The parable of the "talents" (Matt. 25:14–30) teaches how the Lord expects believers to bide their time while waiting for his return. The Lord is represented by a "man traveling into a far country," who has given his servants "talents" before his departure. In the parable, the talent is a large sum of money and represents the abilities and gifts given to each of us. Multiplying these talents should be thought of as bearing fruit for the Lord and making the most of the opportunities that we are entrusted with. Upon his return, it is the ones who have multiplied those talents, in his absence, that are rewarded. They are given responsibilities in the kingdom of God, "I will make thee ruler over many things," and eternal life, "Enter thou into the joy of thy lord" (Matt. 25:21, 23). The one who has done nothing with his "talent" is deemed "unprofitable" and thrown into hell: "And cast ye the unprofitable servant into outer darkness: there shall be weeping and gnashing of teeth" (Matt. 25:30).

This is a serious teaching since many now assert that a person has to do nothing more than believe to be saved. While it is absolutely true that by our faith alone we are saved and that the free gift of God is by his grace alone, not of our works (Eph. 2:8–9), there is still an obvious expectation the Lord has of his followers that is taught in this parable. After all, believers have been made for good works, which God has ordained for us (Eph. 2:10). And since the Lord cannot contradict himself, this multiplying of talents cannot be something he considers to be earning one's salvation. This is not an isolated concept limited to this parable alone. We are taught to be "doers of the word" and not just "hearers" (James 1:22). This parable teaches that we should be occupied with serving the Lord while we are waiting for his return.

The parable of the sheep and goats (Matt. 25:31–46) teaches that judgment will occur at his return. The good and the bad will be separated, much like what is taught in the parables of the fishing net (Matt. 13:47–50) and the wheat and the tares (Matt. 13:24–30; 37–43).

The first step in interpreting a passage in the Bible is to determine what kind of language it uses, literal or figurative, and if figurative, is it a parable or an allegory. This passage about the sheep and goats begins sounding like it may be a literal teaching: "When the Son of man shall come in his glory, and all the holy angels with him, then shall he sit upon the throne of his glory" (Matt. 25:31). However, it quickly transitions to language that we should interpret as being a parable, speaking of judging nations as a shepherd divides his sheep from the goats.

When interpreting a parable, it is important to know that there is one primary point that it is intended to convey.[2] In this case, it is the judgment and separation of believers from unbelievers. It is also important not to search for meaning in every detail of the parable since this treats it as if it were an allegory, where every detail usually does have a meaning.[3] Finally, any conclusions we make must be tested against clear Bible teachings and not allowed to determine doctrine.[4]

The reason for these statements is that some have used this parable to teach of a "judgment of nations" that Christ will engage in after his Second Coming. According to this teaching, all people will be lined up on the right or left, judged, and allowed to enter the kingdom or dispatched into hell. This understanding treats the parable as a literal teaching and results in a departure from what the Bible teaches in several ways. First, people are judged after they die: "It is appointed unto men once to die, but after this the judgment" (Heb. 9:27). Second, we have repeatedly seen that the judgment at the end of this world will be in destructive wrath upon Gentile nations and unbelievers, which will be expanded on in Revelation. And finally, there will be those of the nations that come against Jerusalem in the final battle of Armageddon who escape and return home (Isa. 66:19). They, and all the rest that are left alive from the nations, will come to Jerusalem every year to worship the Lord (Zech. 14:16). There are also clear references to "nations" (Zech. 14:19; Isa. 2:2–4; Dan. 7:14; Mic. 4:1–

---

2   Zuck, *Basic Bible Interpretation*, 215.
3   Zuck, *Basic Bible Interpretation*, 216.
4   Zuck, *Basic Bible Interpretation*, 217.

2; Ps. 22:27–28; 72:11; Mal. 3:12; Rev. 20:8; Zech. 8:20–23) and "people of the earth" (Zeph. 3:20) in the millennial kingdom. These contradict the teaching that all unbelievers will be judged and thrown into hell at the beginning of the millennial kingdom.

This, along with the previous teachings in Daniel and on the Day of the Lord, instructs us who will initially populate the millennial kingdom. The faithful remnant of Israel and Gentiles who survive the last day will enter this time in their natural bodies, and Old Testament saints and New Testament believers in Christ will enter in their glorified bodies.

Yet another example of being overly literal with this parable is that it has been used to teach that works-based salvation will be in place during the great tribulation. This is based on the statements that appear to teach that a person's willingness to help others will be determinative of whether they get eternal life or everlasting punishment (Matt. 25:34–45). Instead, it should be understood that willingness to help others is merely descriptive of true believers.

Statements such as these in a parable are ancillary elements and not intended to present an entirely new doctrine; they add "color" to the story instead. For example, the unprofitable servant in the parable that we just studied said, "Lord, I knew thee that thou art an hard man, reaping where thou hast not sown, and gathering where thou hast not strawed" (Matt. 25:24). This is clearly not intended to teach something new about the Lord's nature.

So, how is this parable to be interpreted in light of Scripture? There is a near-term, precursive fulfillment; and a more distant, final fulfillment. The precursive fulfillment will occur at Christ's Second Coming and is in the form of destructive wrath upon Gentile nations and unbelievers. The final fulfillment will occur at the great white throne judgment at the end of the millennium. This is when both church-age and millennium-age believers will enter into an eternal state with God, and all unbelievers will be sent into eternal punishment in the "lake of fire" (Matt. 25:46). These issues will be fully developed in the Revelation 19 and 20 teaching.

8

A Falling Away First

The Lord Jesus prayed these words before his crucifixion: "And now I am no more in the world, but these are in the world, and I come to thee. Holy Father, keep through thine own name those whom thou hast given me, that they may be one, as we are" (John 17:11). Please note that his prayer for the church was that we would all be "one"— united in truth. He considered this to be so important that he repeated the prayer three more times (John 17:21, 22, 23).

With the exception of Philemon, all of the epistles teach the necessity to adhere to the truth of God's Word. Some are directed at countering specific heresies, others at teaching doctrinal truths for the edification of the body of Christ. Some contain specific admonitions, such as these below, warning the believer to adhere to the truth as originally delivered to them:

> [3]Beloved, when I gave all diligence to write unto you of the common salvation, it was needful for me to write unto you, and exhort you that ye should earnestly contend for the faith which was once delivered unto the saints. (Jude 3)

> [15]Therefore, brethren, stand fast, and hold the traditions which ye have been taught, whether by word, or our epistle. (2 Thess. 2:15)

> [2]Now I praise you, brethren, that ye remember me in all things, and keep the ordinances, as I delivered them to you. (1 Cor. 11:2)

There are passages that admonish believers for their departure from the truth:

> [6]I marvel that ye are so soon removed from him that called you into the grace of Christ unto another gospel: [7]Which is not another; but there be some that trouble you, and would pervert the gospel of Christ. [8]But though we, or an angel from heaven, preach any other gospel unto you than that which we have preached unto you, let him be accursed. [9]As we said before, so say I now again, If any man preach any other gospel unto you than that ye have received, let him be accursed. (Gal. 1:6–9)

And Paul expresses great concern that believers may depart due to deception:

> [2]For I am jealous over you with godly jealousy: for I have espoused you to one husband, that I may present you as a chaste virgin to Christ. [3]But I fear, lest by any means, as the serpent beguiled Eve through his subtilty, so your minds should be corrupted from the simplicity that is in Christ. [4]For if he that cometh preacheth another Jesus, whom we have not preached, or if ye receive another spirit, which ye have not received, or another gospel, which ye have not accepted, ye might well bear with him. (2 Cor. 11:2–4)

Further, prophecies of apostasy are found:

> [1]But there were false prophets also among the people, even as there shall be false teachers among you, who privily shall bring in damnable heresies, even denying the Lord that bought them, and bring upon themselves swift destruction. [2]And many shall follow their pernicious ways; by reason of whom the way of truth shall be evil spoken of. [3]And through covetousness shall they with feigned words make merchandise of you: whose judgment now of a long time lingereth not, and their damnation slumbereth not. (2 Pet. 2:1–3)

With all of these warnings, the church has still managed to arrive at its current condition. A state that even the most casual observer would not mistake as being united—"one." Paul describes this force, which has been pulling the church away from the truth since its inception, as "the mystery of iniquity" (2 Thess. 2:7).

A Necessary Precondition—the Apostasy of the Church

> [1]Now we beseech you, brethren, by the coming of our Lord Jesus Christ, and by our gathering together unto him, [2]That ye be not soon shaken in mind, or be troubled, neither by spirit, nor by word, nor by letter as from us, as that the day of Christ is at hand. [3]Let no man deceive you by any means: for that day shall not come, except there come a falling away first, and that man of sin be revealed, the son of perdition; (2 Thess. 2:1–3)

The "falling away" (v. 3), Greek *apostasia*,[1] means a defection from the truth. This is not speaking of a general state of lawlessness or evil in the world but rather a departure from biblical truth by the church. The state of apostasy can exist only where previously there was the truth since, by definition, it is a departure from the truth.

This deteriorating condition of the church will continue to worsen until it has reached its peak. The Antichrist will not be "revealed" (v. 3) until the church has completely fallen away. This makes the apostasy of the church a necessary precondition for the rise of the Antichrist. And the rise of the Antichrist will be a necessary precondition for the return of the Lord. The Lord's return is referred to as "the coming of our Lord Jesus Christ" (v. 1), "the day of Christ" (v. 2), and "that day" (v. 3).

This brief passage teaches that we are not to expect an "any moment, imminent" ("at hand") return of the Lord since these precon-ditions must first be met (v. 2). And only after they have been met will the Lord return and "gather together" (rapture) believers to himself (v. 1). The Antichrist is referred to as the "man of sin" and the "son of perdition." These are descriptions of the man. Son of perdition means that he is destined to eternal damnation in the lake of fire. The text continues with additional descriptions of the Antichrist:

> [4]Who opposeth and exalteth himself above all that is called God, or that is worshipped; so that he as God sitteth in the temple of God, shewing himself that he is God.

---

1 Strong, *Concordance*, G646.

> ⁵Remember ye not, that, when I was yet with you, I told you
> these things? (2 Thess. 2:4–5)

Verse 4 adds to our knowledge gained from Daniel 8 and 11. The Antichrist will oppose and exalt himself above the God of heaven (Dan. 8:25; 11:36) and sit in the temple of God demanding worship (c.f. Rev. 13:4, 8, 15). This obvious blasphemy perpetrated by the Antichrist is what Paul refers to as being "revealed" (v. 3). It will occur at the midpoint of the Seventieth Week when the abomination of desolation is set up (Matt. 24:15) and he puts an end to daily temple services (Dan. 9:27). Up to that point, he will still appear as a savior, "and by peace shall destroy many" (Dan. 8:25), a hero riding on a "white horse" (Rev. 6:2).

The Restrainer

> ⁶And now ye know what withholdeth that he might be
> revealed in his time. ⁷For the mystery of iniquity doth
> already work: only he who now letteth will let, until he be
> taken out of the way. ⁸And then shall that Wicked be
> revealed, whom the Lord shall consume with the spirit of
> his mouth, and shall destroy with the brightness of his
> coming: (2 Thess. 2:6–8)

Paul had already spoken to the Thessalonians about these issues (v. 5). Here he is reminding them that something ("what withholdeth") is preventing the Antichrist from being revealed until "his time" (v. 6). Since the apostasy of the church is a necessary precondition for the rise of the Antichrist, logic dictates that a biblically sound church would be preventing it.

Next, he introduces the "mystery of iniquity," tells us that it is already at work at the time of the writing of this epistle, and that there is someone ("he") who is restraining it: "For the mystery of iniquity doth already work: only he who now letteth will let, until he be taken out of the way" (v. 7). The one who "letteth" (restrains) is the restrainer, and he will continue to hold back the advance of the mystery of iniquity until he is taken out of the way.

We know from v. 3 that the issue here is the falling away of the church. Later, Paul confirms this defection from the truth is the focus of his teaching when he describes the apostates: "They received not the love of the truth, that they might be saved" (v. 10) and, "That they all might be damned who believed not the truth" (v. 12). Further, he concludes this teaching by imploring believers to remain in the truth (v. 15). The reasonable inference from these points is that the mystery of iniquity is the force that is pulling the church away from the truth and that the restrainer is acting in a mitigating manner to limit this pull.

However, at a certain point, he will be taken out of the way so that the mystery of iniquity can progress to its fullest, resulting in the complete apostasy of the church. Once that has occurred, the Antichrist —"that Wicked"—will be revealed (v. 8). So, the way in which the restrainer is preventing the rise of the Antichrist is by holding back the apostasy of the church.

The effect of the mystery of iniquity on the church in Paul's day can be seen in passages like Galatians 1:6–9. They had already veered away from the truth. We will see more clear examples of the workings of the mystery of iniquity in the seven epistles of Revelation 2 and 3.

In the Bible, when we see the word "mystery," it means that God is revealing some truth to us that has previously remained hidden. In this case, the simplest way to describe the mystery of iniquity is the working of Satan within the church to corrupt and destroy it. The apostle John refers to this as the "spirit of antichrist" (1 John 4:3) and teaches that it was already at work when he was writing as well.

The importance of going into this level of detail is that it allows us to conclude that the church is an active participant in the rise of the Antichrist. We are also in a position to speculate who the restrainer may be since we have no further clues as to his identity. Notice the personal pronoun "he" (v. 7) referring to the restrainer.

Many have advanced the idea that he is the archangel Michael. What we know about Michael is that he is referred to as "your prince" (Dan. 10:21), the "great prince" who stands for the "children of thy people" (Dan. 12:1), and an "archangel" (Jude 9). This makes him a very high-ranking angel with authority over Israel and the Jews. This mystery of iniquity, however, is something that is acting on the church. Is it possible that Michael has authority over both Israel and the church? I guess so. But I think it's not the safest bet in this case. It may be another very high-ranking angel with authority over the church, but the Bible does not tell us of any such angel. So, the most reasonable conclusion is that it is the Holy Spirit who is holding back the advance of the mystery of iniquity, and consequently, the falling away of the church.

However, the identity of the restrainer is not an issue that we should get dogmatic about. The important points are (1) the church is heading away from the truth, (2) there is someone who is holding back the force that is responsible for this pull, (3) at a certain point he will step aside, (4) the mystery of iniquity will come to its fullest and the church will completely fall into apostasy, and (5) this falling away will be instrumental in the final rise of the Antichrist. It is only after all these things that the Lord will return, at which time he will destroy the Antichrist with the "brightness" (*epiphaneia*) of his "coming" (*parousia*) (v. 8).

Some teach that the restrainer is the Holy Spirit, and since he indwells believers, in order to stop his "restraining," it is necessary to remove the church from the earth before the Seventieth Week. Beware of compound logic like this. It is nothing more than an attempt to support a doctrine that otherwise has no biblical support. All the Holy Spirit has to do to stop his restraining is to step aside and let things go the way they have been going. He is in no way limited to acting only through believers. Instead, he can be directly limiting the extent to which Satan is allowed to influence the church. And when he relinquishes this role, the mystery of iniquity will be allowed to progress to its fullest.

A Strong Delusion

> [9]Even him, whose coming is after the working of Satan with all power and signs and lying wonders, [10]And with all deceivableness of unrighteousness in them that perish; because they received not the love of the truth, that they might be saved. [11]And for this cause God shall send them strong delusion, that they should believe a lie: [12]That they all might be damned who believed not the truth, but had pleasure in unrighteousness. (2 Thess. 2:9–12)

Verse 9 describes the Antichrist as satanically empowered and performing all forms of "signs and lying wonders" (c.f. Rev. 13:13–15; Matt. 24:24). The apostates are said to have "all deceivableness of

118

unrighteousness in them" (v. 10). The countless false doctrines that are circulating through Christianity are the "unrighteousness" that is said to be deceiving these people. This is exactly what the Lord Jesus warned about in the Olivet Discourse, that deceptions will be some of the greatest snares to believers.

Paul makes it quite clear that these professing believers have not received the truth but believe the lies to their own destruction (v. 10). In fact, they have such a desire to believe the lies ("pleasure in unrighteousness") that God sends a "strong delusion" (a lying or deluding spirit) upon them so that they *do* believe the lies (v. 11) and are turned over to the natural consequences of their desires: "That they all might be damned who believed not the truth, but had pleasure in unrighteousness" (v. 12).

These are incredibly strong statements that the Holy Spirit is making through the words of the apostle Paul. This is the same process that Paul describes in the epistle to the Romans: "For the wrath of God is revealed from heaven against all ungodliness and unrighteousness of men, who hold the truth in unrighteousness" (Rom. 1:18). He continues by describing unbelievers who want so much to disobey the will of God that "for this cause God gave them up unto vile affections" (Rom. 1:26). Further, because of their desire to disobey him, he sends a judgment upon them in the form of a "reprobate mind" (Rom. 1:28). It doesn't matter whether a person is a professing believer or in outright rebellion against God; if they want the lie badly enough, he will eventually turn them over to their desires.

Please note the two lies that are specifically addressed in the 2 Thessalonians passages. The first is the "at hand"—imminent—return of Christ, with no intervening signs to watch for (vv. 1–3). The second is "signs and lying wonders" (v. 9). "Imminence" is the corollary doctrine to pretribulationism. In fact, these two doctrines are simply circular in nature. Since these teachers assert a pretribulation rapture exists, then it follows that there cannot be any signs to watch for—making it imminent. Then they use the doctrine of imminence to validate their belief in pretribulationism. Once again, beware of compound logic that bases assertions on claims that are not valid in the first place.

The second kind of lie specifically mentioned is the use of "signs and wonders" by the Antichrist. For anyone who hasn't been watching, there has been an unbridled proliferation in the acceptance and practice of signs and wonders in modern Christianity. So much so that countless Christians are being encouraged to engage in practices such as unbiblical speaking in tongues, contemplative prayer (to receive personal revelation from God), unbiblical healing and deliverance, experientially oriented worship, and the list continues. In addition, in certain circles it is commonplace for people to be considered either a prophet or an apostle, or in some cases both.

This direction in which the church has been heading is playing right into the hands of Satan by creating the circumstances needed for the rise of the Antichrist. A large segment of professing believers will be primed to believe the satanic signs and wonders of the Antichrist. The Antichrist would have probably already been here but for the restraining efforts of the Holy Spirit delaying the apostasy, and consequently his arrival, until the fulness of the Gentiles has arrived (Rom. 11:25).

The Answer to Apostasy–the Truth

> [13]But we are bound to give thanks alway to God for you, brethren beloved of the Lord, because God hath from the beginning chosen you to salvation through sanctification of the Spirit and belief of the truth: [14]Whereunto he called you by our gospel, to the obtaining of the glory of our Lord Jesus Christ. [15]Therefore, brethren, stand fast, and hold the traditions which ye have been taught, whether by word, or our epistle. (2 Thess. 2:13–15)

Please notice the juxtaposition of the apostates in v. 12 against the true believers in v. 13. Key to this message is that our salvation is "through sanctification of the Spirit and belief of the truth." Paul's obvious intent by the exhortation to "stand fast, and hold the traditions which ye have been taught" (v. 15) is that those reading his words do not fall victim to the mystery of iniquity.

Concluding Thoughts

> [10]Now I beseech you, brethren, by the name of our Lord Jesus Christ, that ye all speak the same thing, and that there be no divisions among you; but that ye be perfectly joined

> together in the same mind and in the same judgment. [11]For
> it hath been declared unto me of you, my brethren, by them
> which are of the house of Chloe, that there are contentions
> among you. [12]Now this I say, that every one of you saith, I
> am of Paul; and I of Apollos; and I of Cephas; and I of
> Christ. [13]Is Christ divided? was Paul crucified for you? or
> were ye baptized in the name of Paul? (1 Cor. 1:10–13)

Paul admonished the church at Corinth for being divided and not one. The mystery of iniquity was at work in them as it is currently in the church today. The disunity in the church today is a readily apparent symptom of the apostasy that the mystery of iniquity has been fostering. This falling away of the church is going to happen just as certainly as Christ's Second Coming since it is a necessary precursor. But as believers, we can be prepared with the Word of God, thereby ensuring that we are not among those who want to believe the lies and have the strong delusion put upon us or among those who depart from the faith during the persecutions and tribulations.

Some may question whether God really would allow believers to go further into error by putting a strong delusion on them. To answer—he sent a "lying spirit" to the prophets of Ahab (1 Kings 22:19–23; 2 Chron. 18:18–22) and gave a "spirit of slumber" to the Jews (Rom. 11:8). Further, when Israel rebelled after God took them out of Egypt by making a golden calf and offering sacrifices to it (Ex. 32:1–6), God "gave them up to worship the host of heaven" (Acts 7:42). A clear pattern exists; those who want to go against the will of God do get a judgment put on them in this life.

As a reminder for those who may not have gotten the Revelation chart *The Time of the End*, please go to the publisher's website, www.watchfulservant.com, for a free download.

9

And I Will Not Blot Out His Name

Introduction (Rev. 1)

The apostle John was given the book of Revelation through a series of visions while in exile on the island of Patmos, under the reign of Emperor Domitian in approximately 95 A.D.[1] The book opens with an identification of it being the "Revelation of Jesus Christ," given to him by God, to show "his servants things which must shortly come to pass" (Rev. 1:1). Just as Christ was speaking to believers in the Olivet Discourse, he does so now and reaffirms that these prophecies *must* happen (Rev. 1:1; c.f. Rev. 4:1; 22:6; Matt. 24:6). This is followed by a blessing to all those who "read," "hear," and "keep" the words of this prophecy (Rev. 1:3).

The Lord Jesus appeared to John and identified himself as the "Alpha and Omega, the first and the last" (Rev. 1:11). He instructed John by saying, "Write the things which thou hast seen, and the things which are, and the things which shall be hereafter" (Rev. 1:19). John was to put them in a book and send it to seven specific churches in Asia Minor (Rev. 1:11). John provides a description of the Lord's appearance (Rev. 1:13–16) in which Christ is identified as the Son of Man. The Lord follows with yet an additional statement of his identity: "I am he that liveth, and was dead; and, behold, I am alive for evermore, Amen; and have the keys of hell and of death" (Rev. 1:18).

John describes the Lord as being "in the midst of the seven candlesticks" (Rev. 1:13) and that "he had in his right hand seven stars" (Rev. 1:16). The Lord provides the following explanation: "The mystery of

---

1   Walvoord, *Revelation*, 14–15.

123

the seven stars which thou sawest in my right hand, and the seven golden candlesticks. The seven stars are the angels of the seven churches: and the seven candlesticks which thou sawest are the seven churches" (Rev. 1:20).

The indicator that we have figurative language here, specifically a metaphor, is that the seven stars "are" the angels of the seven churches, and the seven candlesticks "are" the seven churches. Any time that something is said "to be" something that it literally is not, the Lord is letting us know that a metaphorical relationship must be inferred.[2] The seven "angels" should be understood to be the bishops or elders of the churches, and the way that a star would best represent them is that it is a beacon of God's light. In this case, they are in the hand of the Lord, implying his "holding" them with care and protection. The seven golden candlesticks (lamp stands) are a representation of the churches since a candlestick holds up a light for all to see, in this case God's light. This tells us how the Lord sees his church leaders and churches.

Epistles to the Churches (Rev. 2–3)

These seven epistles share a common format of having seven sections. Each is addressed to the "angel" of the church identified by its city, followed by an identification of Christ as the sender. The descriptions of Christ contain elements from the vision just given to John in Revelation 1. Then comes a commendation for what the church is doing well, followed by a rebuke for where the church has slipped. Next comes a call to repent and get back to the faith and truth, followed by an admonition for those that don't do this. The final section is a promise to those who "overcome." Not all of the letters contain all seven sections. Of the seven churches, two had remained faithful in all ways and have no rebuke, call to repent, or admonition. These are the churches at Smyrna and Philadelphia. The remaining five had all fallen in some way, and two of these, Sardis and Laodicea, have no commendation given to them. All believers should read these epistles carefully, and they should be studied in our churches. The mystery of iniquity was at work right from the beginning, as is evidenced in these epistles.

---

2   Zuck, *Basic Bible Interpretation*, 148-149.

The Promise to the Overcomer

This is the full promise to those who "overcome": "He that over-cometh, the same shall be clothed in white raiment; and I will not blot out his name out of the book of life, but I will confess his name before my Father, and before his angels" (Rev. 3:5). These are the words which the Lord Jesus spoke to the church at Sardis, and it is the same message that he gave to each of the seven churches in Revelation 2 and 3. When he spoke to the other six churches, he promised the over-comer either to be given eternal life or to be spared from eternal damnation. In this case, his statement contains both the promise of eternal life, "clothed in white raiment," and the guarantee of being spared from eternal damnation, "not blot out his name out of the book of life." In this promise to the church at Sardis, the statements are presented as equivalents, and one can see that the believer who does not overcome will have his name blotted out of the book of life and will not be clothed in white raiment.

This was the message to all seven churches, the necessity of which cannot be understated since five of the seven had already fallen in the eyes of the Lord. The message to the faithful—remain in the faith. The message to the fallen—get back in the faith and remain there. "To overcome" in these promises means to remain in the faith and the truth of God's Word. This is exactly what Christ meant when he stated, "But he that shall endure unto the end, the same shall be saved" (Matt. 24:13).

In Revelation, we will now see much more use of figurative language. In this case, the "white raiment" represents the righteousness of the saints, accounted to them through their belief in Christ (Rev. 19:8), and the "book of life" is God's book in which the names of all believers are recorded (Rev. 20:15).

To the church at Ephesus, Christ promised the overcomer "to eat of the tree of life, which is in the midst of the paradise of God" (Rev. 2:7), a reference to being given eternal life. To Smyrna, the over-comer "shall not be hurt of the second death" (Rev. 2:11). The "second death" is the eternal state of hell (Rev. 20:6, 14)—the "lake of fire." To Pergamos, the Lord promised "him that overcometh will I give to eat of the hidden manna, and will give him a white stone, and in the stone a new name written, which no man knoweth saving he that receiveth it" (Rev. 2:17), once again, figurative language speaking of eternal life. To Thyatira, the promises were to be given "power over the nations" (Rev. 2:26) and "the morning star" (Rev. 2:28), meaning to reign with Christ in the millennium as well as eternal life. To Philadelphia, the Lord promised to "write upon him the name of my God, and the name of the city of my God" (Rev. 3:12), meaning eternal life. And to Laodicea, the Lord will "grant to sit with me in my throne, even as I also overcame, and am set down with my Father in his throne" (Rev. 3:21), a reference to reigning with Christ.

The references to eternal punishment and reigning with Christ will be fulfilled in Revelation 20, and the references to eternal life will be fulfilled in Revelation 21 and 22. All of these statements are summarized at the end of Revelation by the following: "He that overcometh shall inherit all things; and I will be his God, and he shall be my son" (Rev. 21:7). It must also be noted that these are eschatological promises, describing the state in which a person will spend all eternity.

Just so that we know the importance of this teaching, on each occasion, it is either preceded or followed by, "He that hath an ear, let him hear what the Spirit saith unto the churches" (Rev. 3:22). This is meant as a teaching for these specific first century churches, all churches throughout the church age, and all believers, including those who find themselves in the great tribulation. It also confirms one of the essential teachings that we covered in our four general studies, the necessity for the believer to endure to the end. All of the other essentials of those studies will also be confirmed in these seven brief epistles.

The Five Fallen Churches

By the end of the first century, five of these seven churches had already fallen in some way. What is amazing is that two of them, Pergamos and Thyatira, were commended for their faith (Rev. 2:13, 19), yet they allowed "leaven" to enter in and now must get back to what they were originally taught.

The Transgressions

The church at Ephesus was strong in its rejection of evil and false apostles, but in the process, it had left its first love. The first love can only refer to Jesus, and if we read between the lines, they may well have redirected their love elsewhere, very possibly to fighting evil.

Pergamos, while never denying the faith of Christ, had slipped by allowing the "doctrine of Balaam" to enter. The account of Balaam can be found in Numbers 22–25. After Balaam was unable to curse Israel because of the Lord's protection over them, he gave council to the elders of Moab and Midian to entice them to worship their pagan idols: "And Israel abode in Shittim, and the people began to commit whoredom with the daughters of Moab. And they called the people unto the sacrifices of their gods: and the people did eat, and bowed down to their gods" (Num. 25:1–2). And, "Behold, these caused the children of Israel, through the counsel of Balaam, to commit trespass against the LORD in the matter of Peor, and there was a plague among the congregation of the LORD" (Num. 31:16).

Israel's transgression was "mingling" with the neighboring peoples and adopting their idol worship. This is a sin that Israel kept falling into time after time. The church at Pergamos had allowed this pagan worship to creep in: "To eat things sacrificed unto idols, and to commit fornication" (Rev. 2:14). They also had the "doctrine of the Nicolaitans." There is uncertainty as to what this is specifically. It may be a doctrine of abusing Christian liberty (c.f. Jude 4), or it may be the establishment of a "priest class" and "laity class" within the church. Either way, Pergamos was guilty of allowing idolatry, immorality, and heresy to enter, something that was not acceptable to the Lord.

Thyatira was commended for its works, service, faith, and patience but had also allowed in a false prophet and teacher, referred to as "Jezebel." She taught the people to "commit fornication, and to eat things sacrificed unto idols" (Rev. 2:20). This sounds much like the prophecy and warning of 2 Peter 2:1–22.

Sardis received no commendation. They had an outward appearance of being believers, "thou hast a name that thou livest," but in reality, were "dead" (Rev. 3:1). Laodicea received no commendation either. They were in a state of absolute indifference, referred to as being "neither cold nor hot" (Rev. 3:15). They relied on wealth, believing they had no need for the Lord.

Of these churches, only Thyatira and Sardis were said to have a small, faithful remnant within them. These were told, "I will put upon you none other burden. But that which ye have already hold fast till I come" (Rev. 2:24–25); and, "Thou hast a few names even in Sardis which have not defiled their garments; and they shall walk with me in white: for they are worthy" (Rev. 3:4). All of the rest had already fallen from grace by the working of the mystery of iniquity and were not prepared for the Lord's coming. This is what Christ meant by saying that the believer must overcome. It will be those who can resist all of these enticements, pulling them away from the faith and the truth, who will not have their names blotted out of the "book of life."

To summarize these transgressions, the churches had allowed the following to occur: (1) a redirecting of their first love to some other work, (2) mingling with the world by allowing in idolatry, immorality, and heresy, (3) seeking extra-biblical knowledge, in the form of false prophecy, and allowing false teachings, by not "testing the spirits" by the word of God, (4) just "going through the motions," giving the appearance of being alive, but actually being dead, and (5) trusting in riches and having no zeal for the Lord whatsoever. If any or all of these sound like they're describing today's church—that is because they are. These churches in Asia Minor were chosen by the Lord for a reason. They appear to be typical of the ways in which churches have been drawn away from the true faith. We will now see that all of these conditions are completely unacceptable to the Lord and had already resulted in these believers forfeiting their eternal life.

The Call to Repent and Admonition

Each of these five churches was given the call to repent and return to the original faith, followed by an admonition stating what would happen if they didn't. When all five are put together, we get a remarkable picture of how God deals with infidelity. And just as we saw the eschatological promises to those who overcome, here we see promises made to those who have fallen and don't get back on track with the Lord.

Ephesus was told to repent and return to doing the first works or the Lord will "remove thy candlestick out of his place" (Rev. 2:5). Repent means a change of mind, and to return to the first works means those that are consistent with a love of Jesus. To remove its candlestick means that the Lord will no longer consider it to be one of his churches. Pergamos was told, "Repent; or else I will come unto thee quickly, and will fight against them with the sword of my mouth" (Rev. 2:16). The sword of his mouth is a reference to the destructive judgment that the Lord will pour out on the Day of the Lord (Rev. 19:15, 21). To Thyatira, he said that since Jezebel was given the opportunity to repent, and had not, that he would render judgment upon her and her children in this life: "Behold, I will cast her into a bed, and them that commit adultery with her into great tribulation, except they repent of their deeds. And I will kill her children with death" (Rev. 2:22–23). The bed in v. 22 is a "sickbed" and constitutes a chastening of the Lord. Sardis was told, "Remember therefore how thou hast received and heard, and hold fast, and repent. If therefore thou shalt not watch, I will come on thee as a thief, and thou shalt not know what hour I will come upon thee" (Rev. 3:3). The message here is to return to the faith they were originally taught. Christ also speaks of an unexpected, unwelcome return, just as we saw his Second Coming described in the Olivet Discourse. And to Laodicea, the message to repent was in very figurative language: "I counsel thee to buy of me gold tried in the fire, that thou mayest be rich; and white raiment, that thou mayest be clothed, and that the shame of thy nakedness do not appear; and anoint thine eyes with eyesalve, that thou mayest see" (Rev. 3:18). If they don't repent, he will "spue" (vomit) them out of his mouth (Rev. 3:16).

These are very serious warnings. The Lord will no longer consider an offending church to be his, he will render physical judgment on these professing believers on the Day of the Lord, he will render chastening judgment during their lifetime, he will return unexpectedly, and he will completely reject (vomit) these people. This is how serious the Lord is about having a pure church waiting for him at his return and how important remaining in the faith *and* adhering to the truth is.

The Lord's desire to help us through this life is also evident from a brief passage at the end of the letter to the church of Laodicea: "As many as I love, I rebuke and chasten: be zealous therefore, and repent. Behold, I stand at the door, and knock: if any man hear my voice, and open the door, I will come in to him, and will sup with him, and he with me" (Rev. 3:19–20). This is the chastening—disciplinary correction (Heb. 12:6–7)—that the Lord promises all those he loves. The intent of which is to evoke repentance and to drive the individual back into his arms. The way that we "open the door" to the Lord is to repent and get back into biblical truth. When we do so, we will again be in communion with him: "I will come in to him, and will sup with him, and he with me."

Previously, we saw the prophecy that believers will depart from the faith (Matt. 24:10) and how this flies in the face of OSAS teaching. Here we have a confirmation that early Christians had already been led astray from the faith. OSAS teachers use the rationalization that if someone falls away from the faith, they must have never been truly saved. The elephant in the room with OSAS is that a believer has to have their name in the book of life before it can be blotted out, just as we studied that one must be in the faith before they can fall away. Thus, OSAS reasoning implies that God must have names in the book of life of people who aren't "truly saved."

The Bible teaches that believers can fall away for a variety of reasons, some of which we see in these five churches. I state this here again since these epistles confirm what was taught in a previous lesson. I am also convinced that this doctrine will lead many people, who consider themselves to be faithful Christians, to be drawn away from the faith. Just as it happened in the first century—so it will happen again in the future.

The Two Faithful Churches

The churches at Smyrna and Philadelphia were without fault before the Lord, and their epistles contain no rebuke, call to repent, or admonition. Instead, they contain an imperative to persevere, much like the statements to the faithful remnants at Thyatira and Sardis. To Smyrna, Christ said, "Be thou faithful unto death, and I will give thee a crown of life" (Rev. 2:10), and to Philadelphia, "Behold, I come quickly: hold that fast which thou hast, that no man take thy crown" (Rev. 3:11). The statement to Smyrna means to remain faithful through all persecutions and tribulations; and to Philadelphia, not to be deceived. In addition, these faithful churches were given the promises of tribulation for the purpose of testing (Smyrna) and preservation through tribulation (Philadelphia), exactly as taught in the Olivet Discourse (Matt. 24:9–10, 13).

The commendation to Smyrna reads, "I know thy works, and tribulation, and poverty, (but thou art rich) and I know the blasphemy of them which say they are Jews, and are not, but are the synagogue of

Satan" (Rev. 2:9). This is followed by a promise of tribulation for the purpose of testing: "Fear none of those things which thou shalt suffer: behold, the devil shall cast some of you into prison, that ye may be tried; and ye shall have tribulation ten days: be thou faithful unto death, and I will give thee a crown of life" (Rev. 2:10). The crown of life is an eschatological promise of eternal life. It must be understood that the promises of tribulation and eternal life for those who remain in the faith are not only for those at Smyrna but to all church-age believers: "He that hath an ear, let him hear what the Spirit saith unto the churches" (Rev. 2:11).

The commendation to Philadelphia reads, "I know thy works: behold, I have set before thee an open door, and no man can shut it: for thou hast a little strength, and hast kept my word, and hast not denied my name" (Rev. 3:8). This is followed by a promise of living, judging, and reigning with him: "Behold, I will make them of the synagogue of Satan, which say they are Jews, and are not, but do lie; behold, I will make them to come and worship before thy feet, and to know that I have loved thee" (Rev. 3:9). And finally, a promise of preservation through the great tribulation for their fidelity to him: "Because thou hast kept the word of my patience, I also will keep thee from the hour of temptation, which shall come upon all the world, to try them that dwell upon the earth" (Rev. 3:10).

To determine what Revelation 3:10 is teaching, we must examine it in two pieces. The first is the "hour of temptation." Temptation means trial and testing. Hour can be used to mean a literal hour or short period of time. It could also mean a "season" or "time," as in a "time of testing," i.e., the great tribulation. I think it is perfectly reasonable to infer the latter meaning.

Next, we must determine the meaning of "keep thee from." "Keep" (Greek *tēreō*)[3] means to watch or to guard. It is used in these verses to mean "guard while in the presence of danger":[4]

> [11]And now I am no more in the world, but these are in the world, and I come to thee. Holy Father, keep through thine own name those whom thou hast given me, that they may be one, as we are. [12]While I was with them in the world, I

---

3   Strong, *Concordance*, G5083.
4   Gundry, *Church and Tribulation*, 58.

> kept them in thy name: those that thou gavest me I have kept, and none of them is lost, but the son of perdition; that the scripture might be fulfilled. (John 17:11–12)

Further, in Revelation 3:10, *tēreō* is used in conjunction with the preposition *ek* in the phrase "keep thee from." There is only one other time these two words are used together like this: "I pray not that thou shouldest take them out of the world, but that thou shouldest keep them from the evil" (John 17:15). In this verse, *tēreō ek* are used in "keep them from" the evil, clearly speaking of protection while in the presence of danger, not the removal from that danger.

Notice the Lord's prayer that the Father would not "take them out" of the world. In this portion of the verse, "take them out" is *airō*[5] *ek*, which means "to lift up or away from." This is exactly what one would expect if describing a rapture of the church from the earth, and in this verse it is juxtaposed against the prayer for preservation.

It seems that if what the Lord meant in Revelation 3:10 was to take the church out of the world before the great tribulation that John would have used *airō ek* instead of *tēreō ek*. For these reasons, I believe that the correct interpretation of "keep thee from the hour of temptation" (Rev. 3:10) is that the Lord will preserve believers through the great tribulation.

Any time there is a passage such as this that can have multiple interpretations or may be unclear, it is necessary to reconcile our understanding with other clear Bible teachings. In this case, the understanding of Revelation 3:10 presented here is in conformity with the teaching of the church being raptured on the Day of the Lord after the dead are raised. It is also in agreement with the earlier study that taught the preservation of those who remain in the faith. The portion of the Day of the Lord that the believer will not be present for is the final vial of God's wrath and the wrath of the Lamb since we will be raptured immediately before this, at Christ's appearing, and will be returning with him at that point (Rev. 19:14).

---

5   Strong, *Concordance*, G142.

10

The Seal Judgments

Next, we transition into the prophetic chapters of Revelation. This is when we will be using everything that we have learned thus far about prophetic symbolism and figurative language to interpret the teachings. Further, we will continue to receive clues that the entire book of Revelation is providing far greater detail to Daniel's time of the end—the Seventieth Week—and to the prophecies of Christ in the Olivet Discourse.

These prophecies have been delivered in multiple visions, which should be considered to be separate prophecies whose placement in the Seventieth Week must be determined. This means that they do not simply progress consecutively, in sequential order, but rather layer one on top of the other for concurrent fulfillment. This is how the prophecies of Daniel were presented and how the Lord covered the great tribulation, using multiple layers of prophecy, in the Olivet Discourse. This was also the universally understood style of presentation in John's day.[1] Additionally, the separate visions will be shown to highlight the activities of different participants during the Seventieth Week, each having a different role during this time of judgment and chastening.

These prophecies consist of three series of seven judgments each: seals, trumpets, and vials. Each of these is interrupted between the sixth and seventh judgment with a parenthetical section. There are also four interludes. The first, Revelation 12, teaches about Satan, Israel, and the church. The second, Revelation 13, teaches about the Antichrist and the false prophet. The third, Revelation 14, shows a

---

1   Gundry, *Church and Tribulation*, 74–77.

spiritual firstfruits and harvest at the end of the age. And the fourth, Revelation 17–18, teaches about the harlot Babylon (religious Rome), future governmental Rome (ten kings), the Antichrist, and the Antichrist system. After these judgments and interludes, Revelation 19 shows the Day of the Lord and the battle of Armageddon in great detail. Revelation 20 is a picture of the first resurrection and rapture of living believers and the establishment of the kingdom of God on earth —the millennial kingdom. And Revelation 21–22 show the eternal state with God in a new heaven and earth. But before all these things were revealed to John, he was brought up to heaven in the spirit and shown a beautiful picture of worship and the book containing Daniel's vision of great warfare, which Daniel was instructed to "shut up" (close) and "seal" (Dan. 12:4, 9).

John Brought up to Heaven (Rev. 4)

> [1]After this I looked, and, behold, a door was opened in heaven: and the first voice which I heard was as it were of a trumpet talking with me; which said, Come up hither, and I will shew thee things which must be hereafter. [2]And immediately I was in the spirit: and, behold, a throne was set in heaven, and one sat on the throne. (Rev. 4:1–2)

John will now be told the things that must occur in the future. He was brought up to heaven in the spirit to be in the presence of God, who appeared as beautiful precious stones surrounded by a rainbow:

> [3]And he that sat was to look upon like a jasper and a sardine stone: and there was a rainbow round about the throne, in sight like unto an emerald. [4]And round about the throne were four and twenty seats: and upon the seats I saw four and twenty elders sitting, clothed in white raiment; and they had on their heads crowns of gold. (Rev. 4:3–4)

John saw God surrounded by twenty-four elders, clothed in white raiment, having gold crowns on their heads. We now begin to see the use of symbolic numbers; the number twelve represents God's perfect government on earth. This was the number of Jacob's sons, patriarchs of the twelve tribes of Israel. It was also the number of apostles Jesus chose to spread the gospel. Here, the twenty-four elders may represent both Old Testament and New Testament saints reigning with God in heaven (c.f. Rev. 5:9, 10). The white raiment shows that they have been redeemed through the blood of Christ, and their golden crowns represent rulership with God and eternal life. John continues with further descriptions as follows:

> 5And out of the throne proceeded lightnings and thunderings and voices: and there were seven lamps of fire burning before the throne, which are the seven Spirits of God. (Rev. 4:5)

The number three can often represent the Trinity.[2] Here we see lightning, thundering, and voices proceeding from the throne of God. Seven often means God's perfection and completeness.[3] Here it is used to depict the Holy Spirit (c.f. Zech. 4:10; Isa. 11:2). Notice the use of metaphor once again in the statement that the "seven lamps of fire" are "the seven Spirits of God." As we studied earlier, this is intending to create an implicit relationship between the Holy Sprit and the lamps. In this case, it means that the Holy Spirit provides God's illumination to the world and the fire can be a reference to God's judgment. Understanding metaphor will become increasingly important, especially when we get to the two prophets of Revelation 11. John also describes four beasts surrounding God's throne:

> 6And before the throne there was a sea of glass like unto crystal: and in the midst of the throne, and round about the throne, were four beasts full of eyes before and behind. 7And the first beast was like a lion, and the second beast like a calf, and the third beast had a face as a man, and the fourth beast was like a flying eagle. 8And the four beasts had each of them six wings about him; and they were full of eyes within: and they rest not day and night, saying, Holy, holy, holy, Lord God Almighty, which was, and is, and is to come. (Rev. 4:6–8)

These creatures, described here as beasts, bear a striking resemblance to the seraphims (Isa. 6:2–13) and the cherubims (Ezek. 1:5-28; 10:1–22). The most reasonable interpretation is that they are very high-ranking angels who are in God's presence to serve him. Revelation 4

---

2   Bullinger, *Number in Scripture*, 75.
3   Bullinger, *Number in Scripture*, 107.

concludes with a passage showing worship in heaven and the statement that God is the creator of all things and that all things have been created for his pleasure:

> [9]And when those beasts give glory and honour and thanks to him that sat on the throne, who liveth for ever and ever, [10]The four and twenty elders fall down before him that sat on the throne, and worship him that liveth for ever and ever, and cast their crowns before the throne, saying, [11]Thou art worthy, O Lord, to receive glory and honour and power: for thou hast created all things, and for thy pleasure they are and were created. (Rev. 4:9–11)

God Holds Daniel's Sealed Vision (Rev. 5)

What follows is quite amazing. God holds a book in his right hand that contains writing inside and is sealed on the outside with seven seals. No one is worthy to open the book except for the Lord Jesus:

> [1]And I saw in the right hand of him that sat on the throne a book written within and on the backside, sealed with seven seals. [2]And I saw a strong angel proclaiming with a loud voice, Who is worthy to open the book, and to loose the seals thereof? [3]And no man in heaven, nor in earth, neither under the earth, was able to open the book, neither to look thereon. [4]And I wept much, because no man was found worthy to open and to read the book, neither to look thereon. [5]And one of the elders saith unto me, Weep not: behold, the Lion of the tribe of Juda, the Root of David, hath prevailed to open the book, and to loose the seven seals thereof. (Rev. 5:1–5)

Since "book" can also be translated as a scroll, many commentators have noted the similarity to a title deed in ancient times. They conclude that the proper interpretation should be that it represents a deed to the earth. In the absence of any other possibilities, I would fully agree with this. However, Daniel was given two visions that he was told to "shut up" (close, conceal). The second of which, he was told to "shut up" (close) and "seal" because it was for the time of the end: "But thou, O Daniel, shut up the words, and seal the book, even to the time of the end: many shall run to and fro, and knowledge shall be increased"

(Dan. 12:4). This was the vision of great warfare (Dan. 10–12), for which we were given the interpretation pertaining to the Seventieth Week in Daniel 11:35–12:3.

The interpretation spoke of the battles and wars, which will be occurring during the Seventieth Week, and focused on the activities of the Antichrist and the other nations at that time. There are striking parallels between this and what we will see when the seals are removed from this book in Revelation 6. Further, now is the time for these prophecies to be known, as spoken to John by an angel: "Seal not the sayings of the prophecy of this book: for the time is at hand" (Rev. 22:10). For these reasons, I believe that it is proper to understand this book, which is now in the hand of God, to be the vision given to Daniel. And when each of the seals is removed, John is given a portion of Daniel's vision to record for us. At this point in the vision, the Lord Jesus appears to John as a Lamb:

> [6]And I beheld, and, lo, in the midst of the throne and of the four beasts, and in the midst of the elders, stood a Lamb as it had been slain, having seven horns and seven eyes, which are the seven Spirits of God sent forth into all the earth. [7]And he came and took the book out of the right hand of him that sat upon the throne. (Rev. 5:6–7)

After the Lord takes the book, a beautiful scene of worship in heaven follows:

> [8]And when he had taken the book, the four beasts and four and twenty elders fell down before the Lamb, having every one of them harps, and golden vials full of odours, which are the prayers of saints. [9]And they sung a new song, saying, Thou art worthy to take the book, and to open the seals thereof: for thou wast slain, and hast redeemed us to God by thy blood out of every kindred, and tongue, and people, and nation; [10]And hast made us unto our God kings and priests: and we shall reign on the earth. (Rev. 5:8–10)

We see that there are those who have been redeemed by the blood of Jesus in heaven and that they will live and reign with him in the millennial kingdom (vv. 9, 10). Also, we see the symbolic use of the number four in the statement that he has "redeemed us" from "every kindred, and tongue, and people, and nation" (v. 9). The number four symbolically represents events that are from all directions of the compass, as we have previously seen. It also speaks of the entire world or worldwide events.[4] In the case above, those who have been redeemed come from the entire world.

The scene in heaven continues with an innumerable host of angels joining the elders and beasts, confirming that the Lord is worthy to receive "power, and riches, and wisdom, and strength, and honour, and glory, and blessing" (v. 12):

> [11]And I beheld, and I heard the voice of many angels round about the throne and the beasts and the elders: and the number of them was ten thousand times ten thousand, and thousands of thousands; [12]Saying with a loud voice, Worthy is the Lamb that was slain to receive power, and riches, and wisdom, and strength, and honour, and glory, and blessing. (Rev. 5:11–12)

Once again, we see the sevenfold symbolism for God's perfection and completeness. The use of these symbolic numbers is so prevalent in Revelation that it is necessary to become acquainted with them before we move on to the prophecies. Following this, all creation joins in the praise and pronounces a fourfold blessing upon God:

> [13]And every creature which is in heaven, and on the earth, and under the earth, and such as are in the sea, and all that are in them, heard I saying, Blessing, and honour, and glory, and power, be unto him that sitteth upon the throne, and unto the Lamb for ever and ever. [14]And the four beasts said, Amen. And the four and twenty elders fell down and worshipped him that liveth for ever and ever. (Rev. 5:13–14)

The First Four Seals–the Antichrist, World Powers

With each seal that the Lord Jesus opens on this book, John is given a portion of Daniel's vision. There are a total of seven seals, representing the perfect completion of God's indignation upon mankind. The first four in the series are depicted as riders on horses. I believe that it is quite reasonable to interpret this as representing judgments

---

4   Bullinger, *Number in Scripture*, 84–86.

rendered by men and man's kingdoms. The number four points to the worldwide scope of the judgments. This is where we will begin to see the activities of different participants in the Seventieth Week depicted in separate visions. We know that God uses ungodly men and kingdoms to render judgments from earlier studies. This passage of prophecy reads as follows:

> [1]And I saw when the Lamb opened one of the seals, and I heard, as it were the noise of thunder, one of the four beasts saying, Come and see. [2]And I saw, and behold a white horse: and he that sat on him had a bow; and a crown was given unto him: and he went forth conquering, and to conquer. [3]And when he had opened the second seal, I heard the second beast say, Come and see. [4]And there went out another horse that was red: and power was given to him that sat thereon to take peace from the earth, and that they should kill one another: and there was given unto him a great sword. [5]And when he had opened the third seal, I heard the third beast say, Come and see. And I beheld, and lo a black horse; and he that sat on him had a pair of balances in his hand. [6]And I heard a voice in the midst of the four beasts say, A measure of wheat for a penny, and three measures of barley for a penny; and see thou hurt not the oil and the wine. [7]And when he had opened the fourth seal, I heard the voice of the fourth beast say, Come and see. [8]And I looked, and behold a pale horse: and his name that sat on him was Death, and Hell followed with him. And power was given unto them over the fourth part of the earth, to kill with sword, and with hunger, and with death, and with the beasts of the earth. (Rev. 6:1–8)

Upon opening of the first seal, John saw a rider on a white horse who was sent out to conquer (vv. 1–2). This rider was given a crown, meaning that he was put in this position by God to serve God's purposes. He rode a white horse, indicating that he will appear as a savior. And he held a bow but no arrows. Combined, these depict the Antichrist appearing on the scene, who was said to destroy "by peace" (Dan. 8:25) and will be accepted as a saving hero by Israel (Dan. 9:27; John 5:43) and the world (Rev. 13:8).

With the second seal, John saw a red horse, indicating war, blood-shed, and death (vv. 3–4). This rider was "given" power, meaning authority, to "take peace from the earth" (v. 4). God's indignation with mankind is being rendered through these wars. These terrible events will result in a true church, with the "chaff" being burned off—the purging spoken of in an earlier study.

With the third seal, John saw a black horse (vv. 5–6), indicating famine (c.f. Lam. 5:10). A pair of balances may well represent scarcity of food, and a day's wages ("a penny") will only be able to purchase enough for one person's daily needs ("a measure"). This statement is juxtaposed against "hurt not the oil and the wine." Oil and wine are items that the rich indulge in. Stated like this, it may well mean that the poor will starve, but the rich will continue in their indulgent ways.

With the fourth seal, John saw a pale horse whose rider's name was "Death" (vv. 7–8). He was given authority to kill one-quarter of the earth's population with persecutions, famine, and "beasts of the earth." This latter reference, when combined with the pale green color (Greek *chlōros*)[5] of the horse, may well mean what the Lord spoke of as "pestilences" (Matt. 24:7)—fatal diseases.

In these four seals, we see the arrival of the Antichrist and the wars, famines, bloodshed, and diseases that follow. This is the same picture that the Lord presented: "For nation shall rise against nation, and kingdom against kingdom: and there shall be famines, and pestilences, and earthquakes, in divers places" (Matt. 24:7). He referred to these as "the beginning of sorrows" (Matt. 24:8)—the first half of the Seven-tieth Week. I believe it is reasonable to place these events in that period, preceding the abomination of desolation.

The Fifth Seal–the Church in the Great Tribulation

Immediately following the description of the beginning of sorrows in the Olivet Discourse, the Lord spoke of the great tribulation as follows: "Then shall they deliver you up to be afflicted, and shall kill you: and ye shall be hated of all nations for my name's sake" (Matt. 24:9). This is precisely what we see next upon the opening of the fifth seal:

---

5   Strong, *Concordance*, G5515.

⁹And when he had opened the fifth seal, I saw under the altar the souls of them that were slain for the word of God, and for the testimony which they held: ¹⁰And they cried with a loud voice, saying, How long, O Lord, holy and true, dost thou not judge and avenge our blood on them that dwell on the earth? ¹¹And white robes were given unto every one of them; and it was said unto them, that they should rest yet for a little season, until their fellowservants also and their brethren, that should be killed as they were, should be fulfilled. (Rev. 6:9–11)

We know these souls will be Christian martyrs, killed during the great tribulation for their testimony of Jesus Christ (v. 9). They are seen in heaven, under the altar, because upon death, believers are immediately in the presence of the Lord (Phil. 1:23; 2 Cor. 5:8). Also, they have been given their white robes, meaning they are dressed in the righteousness of Christ because they believe in him. When they asked when their deaths would be avenged, they were informed that there are still more to be martyred.

This is exactly what the Lord meant when he said, "But he that shall endure unto the end, the same shall be saved" (Matt. 24:13). These are the believers who will remain in the faith and truth until the end and are now seen in the presence of the Lord. The fulfillment of his promise of preservation is seen in these believers. We can also place these events in the great tribulation since the Lord prophesied Christian persecutions and martyrdom occurring after the beginning of sorrows when the abomination of desolation occurs (Matt. 24:9–22; c.f. Rev. 12:17).

So, where will the rest of the church be at this time? Still on earth—in the great tribulation. Their eventual disposition will be either martyrdom (v. 11), death under some other circumstances, or remaining alive until the Lord's Second Coming. I believe it is reasonable to place the timing of this seal early in the great tribulation after the Antichrist has been revealed.

Also, these believers under the altar are "souls"—not yet glorified. Dispensationalists would have you believe that the church has already been raptured by this point and that believers have already been given their glorified bodies. Here we see God's Word plainly refuting these assertions.

The Sixth Seal–the Day of the Lord Announced

The opening of the sixth seal brings us to a very important point in the Seventieth Week, the announcement of the Day of the Lord:

> [12]And I beheld when he had opened the sixth seal, and, lo, there was a great earthquake; and the sun became black as sackcloth of hair, and the moon became as blood; [13]And the stars of heaven fell unto the earth, even as a fig tree casteth her untimely figs, when she is shaken of a mighty wind. [14]And the heaven departed as a scroll when it is rolled together; and every mountain and island were moved out of their places. [15]And the kings of the earth, and the great men, and the rich men, and the chief captains, and the mighty men, and every bondman, and every free man, hid themselves in the dens and in the rocks of the mountains; [16]And said to the mountains and rocks, Fall on us, and hide us from the face of him that sitteth on the throne, and from the wrath of the Lamb: [17]For the great day of his wrath is come; and who shall be able to stand? (Rev. 6:12–17)

All of the signs that are to immediately precede the Lord's Second Coming are seen in this passage. The sun will be darkened and the moon turned to blood (v. 12; c.f. Joel 2:31; Isa. 13:10; Matt. 24:29), there will be celestial and seismic disturbances (vv. 13–14; c.f. Isa. 13:13; 34:4; Luke 21:25), and men's hearts will fail from fear (vv. 15–16; c.f. Isa. 2:19–21; Luke 21:26). In v. 16, we see that those fleeing want to hide from the face of God ("him that sitteth on the throne") and from the wrath of Jesus ("the Lamb"). The opening of this seal signifies the beginning of the last day of this world, at which time Christ will return in glory (Matt. 24:30; Rev. 19:11–21) to claim what is rightfully his (Col. 1:16). All of the events of the Day of the Lord will now be happening between this signal of its beginning and the seventh seal, the signal of its end. And as we saw in Daniel, these events will be presented to us in separate prophecies, which layer one upon the other to create a complete picture of the events on that day.

God's Preservation of His People

Revelation 7 presents a parenthetical section of prophecy between the sixth and seventh seals. As noted, each of the three series of seven judgments (seals, trumpets, vials) contains a section like this between the sixth and seventh judgment. Interpretation of these sections can present a considerable challenge. I have observed that commentators often read these and then follow by adding details that aren't in the text to advance a predetermined doctrine. I have taken this into consideration and done my absolute best not to engage in this sort of interpretation. It must also be stated that the events in these sections should be understood not to necessarily occur between the sixth and seventh judgments where they are placed in the text.

With prayer and a desire to be obedient to God's Word, I have concluded that the proper approach to understanding these parentheses is to first step back and determine the big picture that God is presenting to us. After making that determination, the details in the text and the entirety of God's Word should be used to confirm that understanding and the proper placement within the Seventieth Week. That being said, I see Revelation 7 as a picture of God's preservation of his people, the faithful remnant of Israel and the church. The first half of the chapter pertains to Israel, and the second, to the church.

Faithful Israel Sealed for Preservation

[1]And after these things I saw four angels standing on the four corners of the earth, holding the four winds of the earth, that the wind should not blow on the earth, nor on the sea, nor on any tree. [2]And I saw another angel ascending from the east, having the seal of the living God: and he cried with a loud voice to the four angels, to whom it was given to hurt the earth and the sea, [3]Saying, Hurt not the earth, neither the sea, nor the trees, till we have sealed the servants of our God in their foreheads. [4]And I heard the number of them which were sealed: and there were sealed an hundred and forty and four thousand of all the tribes of the children of Israel. (Rev. 7:1–4)

This section begins with John describing four angels standing on the four "corners" of the earth, holding back the "four winds" from blowing on the earth, the sea, and the trees (v. 1). This is highly figurative language, but we know that four relates to the entirety of the earth and that winds can refer to great turmoil that will soon ensue. In v. 2, another angel informs us that this wind (turmoil) is referring to the first four angels "hurting" (rendering destructive judgment) the earth, sea, and trees and that they are appointed by God ("given") to do so. They are told to refrain from their destructive activities until the "servants" of God can be sealed in their foreheads (v. 3). In v. 4, we are told these servants number 144,000 and that they are Jews from all the tribes of Israel.

The first point to take from this passage is that there will be four angels rendering judgments during the great tribulation and that those judgments will be directed at the earth, sea, and trees. This is critical to a proper understanding of the first four trumpet judgments, which we will be studying in Revelation 8. Second, these judgments must not proceed until a group of 144,000 Jewish "servants" have been sealed.

Many have noted the word "servant" and concluded that these are Jewish believers in Christ who will be preaching the gospel during the great tribulation. This assertion can be refuted as follows: (1) The use of the word servant does not automatically make these Jews believers in Christ. Both Moses (Josh. 12:6; 2 Kings 18:12; Mal. 4:4) and Joshua (Josh. 5:14; Judg. 2:8) are referred to as servants of the Lord. (2) Sealing them for protection is an indicator that they are not believers since there would be no need to seal believers in Christ, who are "sealed" by the Holy Spirit from the moment that they believe (Eph. 1:13). (3) Jews will not be saved until the end of the great tribulation when Christ returns in glory and pours out the Holy Spirit on them. Until then, they are still unbelievers. (4) There is no Bible passage that can be referenced to confirm that these Jews will be preaching the gospel.

It is my contention that this group of Jews is the faithful remnant of Israel that God will call (Joel 2:32; Rom. 11:15, 26), bring through the great tribulation, and save on the last day. As we studied earlier, God does promise his faithful Jews that he will preserve them through the chastening fire. We will see in the study that follows that this is exactly what this seal provides for them, protection from judgments that will come (Rev. 9:4). This is the group of Jews that God calls his "servants" who "sought" him (Isa. 65:8–10). He will separate faithful Israel from the unfaithful during the great tribulation (Isa. 65:12–15). These are the Jews with whom God will make a new covenant (Jer. 31:31).

The only reference point that we are given to determine the timing of this event within the Seventieth Week is that it will occur prior to the judgments of the four angels. In revelation 8, we will learn that the first four trumpet judgments appear to be what these angels will be responsible for since they cause great harm to the earth, sea, and trees. It is reasonable to conclude that those will occur during the great tribulation, and for this reason, I believe that it is a fair guess that the sealing of these Jews will occur around the time of the abomination of desolation. The remainder of Revelation 7 that pertains to the sealing of this faithful remnant (vv. 5–8) identifies the number from each tribe that will be sealed as 12,000.

The Preserved Church in Heaven

After being shown the faithful remnant of Israel being sealed for protection, John saw a vast multitude in heaven, clothed in white robes, giving praise to God and Jesus along with the angels, four beasts, and the elders:

> [9]After this I beheld, and, lo, a great multitude, which no man could number, of all nations, and kindreds, and people, and tongues, stood before the throne, and before the Lamb, clothed with white robes, and palms in their hands; [10]And cried with a loud voice, saying, Salvation to our God which sitteth upon the throne, and unto the Lamb. [11]And all the angels stood round about the throne, and about the elders and the four beasts, and fell before the throne on their faces, and worshipped God, [12]Saying, Amen: Blessing, and glory, and wisdom, and thanksgiving, and honour, and power, and might, be unto our God for ever and ever. Amen. (Rev. 7:9–12)

At this point, we know that these are believers in Christ because of the white robes they are wearing and that they are from the entire world by the fourfold reference "of all nations, and kindreds, and people, and tongues." In v. 12, we see a sevenfold blessing to God and Jesus, "Blessing, and glory, and wisdom, and thanksgiving, and honour, and power, and might, be unto our God for ever and ever. Amen." Next, one of the elders asks John a question:

> [13]And one of the elders answered, saying unto me, What are these which are arrayed in white robes? and whence came they? [14]And I said unto him, Sir, thou knowest. And he said to me, These are they which came out of great tribulation, and have washed their robes, and made them white in the blood of the Lamb. [15]Therefore are they before the throne of God, and serve him day and night in his temple: and he that sitteth on the throne shall dwell among them. [16]They shall hunger no more, neither thirst any more; neither shall the sun light on them, nor any heat. [17]For the Lamb which is in the midst of the throne shall feed them, and shall lead them unto living fountains of waters: and God shall wipe away all tears from their eyes. (Rev. 7:13–17)

Verse 14 tells us exactly who these believers are—the tribulation church. It is confirmed for us that they are believers in Christ because they have "washed their robes, and made them white in the blood of the Lamb." The next bit of information is that they came "out of" great tribulation. The Greek preposition for "out of" is *ek*[6] and means "out from within."[7] This means that these believers were in the great tribulation before they were taken out of it.

There is also an amazing timing reference in v. 15, which places this event after the Day of the Lord. It is the statement that they "serve him day and night in his temple." Looking forward to Revelation 15, we see that "no man was able to enter into the temple, till the seven plagues of the seven angels were fulfilled" (Rev. 15:8). This is speaking of the temple in heaven and tells us that no person will be allowed to enter until after the last of the seven vial judgments has been poured out. This makes it impossible for the tribulation church, shown to be in heaven in this vision, to be serving God in his temple at any time earlier than the end of the Seventieth Week.

Verses 16–17 show the fulfillment of God's promises to believers. They endured, he preserved them through the tribulation, and his promise of preservation is now seen as having been fulfilled. Earlier,

---

6   Strong, *Concordance*, G1537.
7   Gundry, *Church and Tribulation*, 55.

after the fifth seal was opened, we saw great tribulation martyrs under the throne in heaven. Now we see the entire tribulation church, those that were martyred and those that remained until the end, having received the blessings of God for their enduring faith.

This is the purified church that Christ died for (Eph. 5:27). We now see the intended effect of the great tribulation on the church. It has been purged, cleansed, and refined. There will be no nominal believers in this group.

The Seventh Seal–the Day of the Lord Completed

The culmination of the seven seal judgments is presented at the beginning of Revelation 8:

> ¹And when he had opened the seventh seal, there was silence in heaven about the space of half an hour. ²And I saw the seven angels which stood before God; and to them were given seven trumpets. ³And another angel came and stood at the altar, having a golden censer; and there was given unto him much incense, that he should offer it with the prayers of all saints upon the golden altar which was before the throne. ⁴And the smoke of the incense, which came with the prayers of the saints, ascended up before God out of the angel's hand. ⁵And the angel took the censer, and filled it with fire of the altar, and cast it into the earth: and there were voices, and thunderings, and lightnings, and an earthquake. (Rev. 8:1–5)

There are four distinct events happening in this brief passage. First, the opening of the seventh seal is followed by thirty minutes of silence in heaven (v. 1). Second, we are introduced to seven angels standing before God, to whom seven trumpets are given (v. 2). These will be the angels who sound the trumpets in the judgments that follow this passage. Third, another angel is introduced, holding a golden censer, who offers incense and the prayers of all the saints to God (vv. 4–5). Finally, a fivefold judgment signifying the end of this world is given (v. 5).

It is easy to understand four of the five elements of this judgment: voices, thundering, lightning, and an earthquake. But what is meant by the angel taking the censer, filling it with fire from the altar, and throwing it down upon the earth (v. 5)? Fire is often a symbol of God's judgment. I contend this is the visual representation given to John that is later described as the great hail at the end of the trumpet and vial judgments.

Let's look at the events that mark the end of this world at the last trumpet and vial. The trumpets end with, "And the temple of God was opened in heaven, and there was seen in his temple the ark of his testament: and there were lightnings, and voices, and thunderings, and an earthquake, and great hail" (Rev. 11:19). The first four are a repeat of what we saw at the end of the seals, and the fifth is the great hail. The vials end as follows:

> [18]And there were voices, and thunders, and lightnings; and there was a great earthquake, such as was not since men were upon the earth, so mighty an earthquake, and so great. [19]And the great city was divided into three parts, and the cities of the nations fell: and great Babylon came in remembrance before God, to give unto her the cup of the wine of the fierceness of his wrath. [20]And every island fled away, and the mountains were not found. [21]And there fell upon men a great hail out of heaven, every stone about the weight of a talent: and men blasphemed God because of the plague of the hail; for the plague thereof was exceeding great. (Rev. 16:18–21)

Verse 18 gives us the four events that we know from the seventh seal: voices, thundering, lightning, and a great earthquake. Verses 19–20 provide much more detail about the earthquake. Finally, v. 21 tells us the fifth event, the great hail, and provides much more detail about that event. Please note the weight of these hailstones is a "talent." Depending on the metal, a talent can weigh anywhere from 100 to 200 pounds. Assuming these are 100 pounds, it must be inferred that these are no ordinary hailstones but are of supernatural origin—the angel in this case. This is exactly how God provided prophecy for us in Daniel, first in rough form, with imagery and in visions, then with each subsequent prophecy, he provided greater detail and moved away from the imagery to the literal interpretations.

In the earlier study of the Day of the Lord, we took a brief look at how Daniel presented different events that occur on the last day in separate prophecies. We also took a brief look ahead at the final seal, trumpet, and vial judgments and observed that each presents a picture of different events on that day. When we understand that there are multiple prophecies with concurrent fulfillment and a common endpoint, each layering more detail upon the other, then what initially appears to be quite a mystery—the angel who casts fire from the altar down to the earth—now fits together like the final piece of the puzzle. I believe that this angel and his actions are one of many little clues that the Lord gives us throughout Revelation to help us put together this puzzle more accurately.

Also, the number five may indicate God's provision, fullness, and grace.[8] In this case, it signifies the completion (fullness) of God's indignation upon the unbelieving world and grace for believers. This is the point at which he will have avenged the deaths of his martyrs (Rev. 6:10) and completed his redemptive plan for this world (Rev. 11:15–19). He will have poured out his wrath on the nations and those who remain of the harlot religious system (Rev. 16:17–21) and destroyed the Antichrist and his armies at the battle of Armageddon (Rev. 19:15–21). He will have also given his believers the eternal life that he has promised and will begin his reign on earth (Rev. 20:4–6).

In summary, the sixth seal announces the beginning of the Day of the Lord and the seventh marks its culmination. There are two earthquakes involved here. The first occurs at the sixth seal and is among the signs that precede the Lord's Second Coming (Rev. 6:12). It will result in every mountain and island being moved out of their places (Rev. 6:14). The second occurs at the seventh seal and is among the signs that signal the end of this world (Rev. 8:5). This second earthquake is far more devastating, and we are told that there has never been one of this magnitude since man was on earth (Rev. 16:18). The consequences of this earthquake include every mountain and island being completely destroyed: "And every island fled away, and the mountains were not found" (Rev. 16:20).

After this analysis, the logical question is what actually happens at the seventh seal? It appears that all we are told of is a period of silence in heaven, followed by prayers offered to God, concluding with the fivefold judgment at the end. It is important to note that the silence

---

8   Bullinger, *Number in Scripture*, 92.

149

observed at the seventh seal is in heaven. Meanwhile, the scene on earth will be anything but silent. As we continue through Revelation, we will be given all of the events that fill this thirty-minute void in subsequent prophecies.

11

The Trumpet Judgments

We will now begin to study the trumpet judgments. The seven judgments are presented in three groupings. The first consists of four judgments, the second of two, and finally the last consists of one judgment. The first group of four will destroy parts of the earth, seas, trees, and more. The parenthetical section on God's preservation (Rev. 7) taught us to be looking for destructive judgments rendered by angels. These judgments were to specifically target the earth, seas, and trees (Rev. 7:2–3). We have additional evidence that angels will be involved in great tribulation judgments. At the seventh seal, there was the visual image of judgment (angel throwing the fire down on the earth), and subsequent prophecies show the literal effect (the great hail). For these reasons and others that will soon be presented, I believe that the judgments of the four angels (Rev. 7:2–3), which we were told to expect, are what we will now have revealed to us in the first four trumpets that follow.

The second group of two judgments will be performed by demons released from the pit and the Euphrates River. The final judgment of the seven will be the return of the Lord Jesus to complete the "mystery of God" and reclaim the earth for himself. The prophecies alternate between visual imagery and literal descriptions, just as we saw with the great hail.

The First Four Trumpets–Judgments by Angels

The sounding of trumpets was used for a variety of reasons in Israel (Num. 10), not the least of which was to "blow an alarm" in advance of going to war with an enemy: "And if ye go to war in your land against the enemy that oppresseth you, then ye shall blow an alarm with the trumpets; and ye shall be remembered before the LORD your God, and ye shall be saved from your enemies" (Num. 10:9). The enemy during the great tribulation will be Satan. These four judgments are as follows:

> [6]And the seven angels which had the seven trumpets prepared themselves to sound. [7]The first angel sounded, and there followed hail and fire mingled with blood, and they were cast upon the earth: and the third part of trees was burnt up, and all green grass was burnt up. [8]And the second angel sounded, and as it were a great mountain burning with fire was cast into the sea: and the third part of the sea became blood; [9]And the third part of the creatures which were in the sea, and had life, died; and the third part of the ships were destroyed. [10]And the third angel sounded, and there fell a great star from heaven, burning as it were a lamp, and it fell upon the third part of the rivers, and upon the fountains of waters; [11]And the name of the star is called Wormwood: and the third part of the waters became wormwood; and many men died of the waters, because they were made bitter. [12]And the fourth angel sounded, and the third part of the sun was smitten, and the third part of the moon, and the third part of the stars; so as the third part of them was darkened, and the day shone not for a third part of it, and the night likewise. [13]And I beheld, and heard an angel flying through the midst of heaven, saying with a loud voice, Woe, woe, woe, to the inhabiters of the earth by reason of the other voices of the trumpet of the three angels, which are yet to sound! (Rev. 8:6–13)

After the seven angels prepared to sound (v. 6), the first sounded his trumpet and John saw hail and fire mingled with blood cast down on the earth (v. 7). This is the vision, and what followed are the literal effects on the earth. One-third of the trees and all of the grass was burned up. This is very much like the plague of hail and fire that was poured out on Egypt before Israel was freed from slavery (Ex. 9:22–26). This judgment in Egypt was performed by God and was very specifically targeted. Those of Egypt that brought their cattle in from the field were spared (the men and their cattle) as well as all the children of Israel in Goshen (Ex. 9:19–21, 26).

After the second angel sounded, John saw a burning mountain thrown into the sea (v. 8). The result was one-third of the sea turning to blood, one-third of all the ocean life being killed, and one-third of all ships being destroyed (vv. 8–9). How this will actually manifest when it occurs is open to speculation; however, it may well be a giant asteroid hitting the earth. This also bears resemblance to the rivers of Egypt being turned to blood (Ex. 7:17–21).

When the third angel sounded, John saw a great burning star fall from heaven (v. 10). This resulted in one-third of the rivers and springs being poisoned (vv. 10–11). Once again, exactly how this will manifest is open to speculation. However, it is definitely some sort of supernatural attack since the effects are limited to poisoning only fresh waters.

The fourth sounded, and one-third of the light from the sun, moon, and stars ceased to shine (v. 12). This is speaking of something directly affecting the sun since it will not shine for a third of the day. Once again, this points to supernatural intervention and corroborates the assertion that these are the judgments of the angels in Revelation 7:2–3.

Just as before, there are four judgments in the first part of this series, pointing to worldwide events. They bear striking similarity to the plagues of Egypt, which were supernaturally caused by God. The damage that results fits the description of the judgments of the four angels (Rev. 7:2–3), harming the earth, sea, and trees. Also, they are beyond the scope of what could be considered natural or man-made cataclysms. For these reasons, I believe that we have just been shown the actions of another participant in the judgments of the great tribulation—the four angels—and that God has set apart his faithful remnant, in advance, for preservation with a seal (Rev. 7:3). Just as Israel was protected in Exodus (Ex. 8:22; 9:4, 11, 26; 10:23), so will those with the seal be protected from these judgments. The seal on the forehead can well be thought of like the blood on the door posts and lintel (Ex. 12:23) that resulted in Israel being spared the deaths of their firstborn when God instituted the Passover.

The final verse of Revelation 8 names the next three trumpets "woes." After the actions of these angels, God plans to set loose demons that have been bound in the pit and the Euphrates River upon unbelieving humanity during the great tribulation.

The First Two Woes–Judgments by Demons

[1]And the fifth angel sounded, and I saw a star fall from heaven unto the earth: and to him was given the key of the bottomless pit. [2]And he opened the bottomless pit; and there arose a smoke out of the pit, as the smoke of a great furnace; and the sun and the air were darkened by reason of the smoke of the pit. [3]And there came out of the smoke locusts upon the earth: and unto them was given power, as the scorpions of the earth have power. [4]And it was commanded them that they should not hurt the grass of the earth, neither any green thing, neither any tree; but only those men which have not the seal of God in their foreheads. (Rev. 9:1–4)

Revelation 9 opens with the fifth angel sounding his trumpet. We begin with an interesting comparison. In v. 1, John saw a star fall from heaven, to whom the key to the bottomless pit was given. The pronoun "he," in this case, is contrasted to the pronoun "it," which we saw used in reference to the great star that fell from heaven after the third trumpet (Rev. 8:10). This star here, after the fifth trumpet, should be understood to be referring to a being of some sort, and since the key "was given," an angel is the most logical conclusion. Use of the word "fall" implies that it is Satan or one of his fallen angels. This can be compared to when an angel of God is given the key to the bottomless pit and is said to have "come down" from heaven (Rev. 20:1). The most reasonable conclusion is that this star represents Satan and that the timing of this event is at the midpoint of the Seventieth Week when he is expelled from heaven by the archangel Michael and his angels (Rev. 12:7–9).

The bottomless pit, to which he was given the key, is the Greek *abussos*.[1] This is a place in hell that holds the souls of men and demons —fallen angels. In the Old Testament it is called "the pit" (Isa. 24:18; Ezek. 26:20; 31:14–18; 32:18–30). In the New Testament, it is referred to as the "deep" (Luke 8:31; Rom. 10:7) and the "bottomless pit"

---

1 Strong, *Concordance*, G12.

(Rev. 9:1, 2, 11; 11:7; 17:8; 20:1, 3). This is the first mention of this place in Revelation but not the last. As we progress in these studies, it will be shown that the Antichrist will rise from this place (Rev. 11:7; 17:8; c.f. Isa. 24:18) and that Satan will be bound there during the millennial kingdom (Rev. 20:1–3). It is important to note that Satan is not in this pit at any time before he is bound and thrown in at the Second Coming.

The one holding the key now opened the pit and smoke came out, as from a "great furnace" (v. 2), confirming our understanding of what this pit is—hell. Next, John saw "locusts" emerge from the smoke, which were given authority to hurt all people who do not have the seal of God in their forehead (vv. 3–4). Their torment will be like that of a scorpion. Notice what they are not allowed to harm—the earth, grass, or trees. These were for the angels of God to damage. Here, the sealed faithful remnant is specifically identified for protection (v. 4). This confirms our understanding of God's purpose in sealing these Jews before the start of the trumpet judgments—preservation through the great tribulation. Based on where the locusts came from, the smoke of the great fire, the limited nature of their mission, and the one who is their "king" (Rev. 9:11), it must be concluded that these are demons being unleashed on unbelievers. Next, we see a description of the torment they will execute:

> 5And to them it was given that they should not kill them, but that they should be tormented five months: and their torment was as the torment of a scorpion, when he striketh a man. 6And in those days shall men seek death, and shall not find it; and shall desire to die, and death shall flee from them. (Rev. 9:5–6)

They will not be permitted to kill anyone, just cause torment like a scorpion sting for the duration of five months. God is in control of this, as evidenced by the phrase "to them it was given." These demons are being used by God to pour out his indignation on unbelieving humanity. What follows is further evidence that these locusts symbolically represent demons:

> 7And the shapes of the locusts were like unto horses prepared unto battle; and on their heads were as it were

155

crowns like gold, and their faces were as the faces of men.
[8]And they had hair as the hair of women, and their teeth
were as the teeth of lions. [9]And they had breastplates, as it
were breastplates of iron; and the sound of their wings was
as the sound of chariots of many horses running to battle.
[10]And they had tails like unto scorpions, and there were
stings in their tails: and their power was to hurt men five
months. (Rev. 9:7–10)

Verses 7–10 detail exactly what John saw. The descriptions make it evident that these locusts are not ordinary insects of some sort. Just as beasts were used as symbols of kingdoms, these insects are symbols of demons. We should understand that what we are being given here are figurative depictions of their attributes. Being like "horses unto battle" may be speaking of strength in battle, and "faces of men" may be referring to intelligence. These are all subject to interpretation and we should not get dogmatic over these points. However, it is important to understand that it is highly unlikely there will be visible demons flying around, appearing like these, when the time comes.

When we see animals or insects being described in ways that are simply not possible in the natural world, we know that God is using symbolic imagery to convey information to us. In the prophecies of Joel 2, the same process was used. God blended prophecies of the destruction caused by locusts in Joel's day with the locust demon-army that will come in advance of the Day of the Lord. The same kinds of supernatural attributes are seen in Joel's locust horde:

[4]The appearance of them is as the appearance of horses;
and as horsemen, so shall they run. [5]Like the noise of
chariots on the tops of mountains shall they leap, like the
noise of a flame of fire that devoureth the stubble, as a
strong people set in battle array. [6]Before their face the
people shall be much pained: all faces shall gather blackness.
[7]They shall run like mighty men; they shall climb the wall
like men of war; and they shall march every one on his ways,
and they shall not break their ranks: [8]Neither shall one
thrust another; they shall walk every one in his path: and
when they fall upon the sword, they shall not be wounded.
[9]They shall run to and fro in the city; they shall run upon

the wall, they shall climb up upon the houses; they shall enter in at the windows like a thief. (Joel 2:4–9)

Immediately after this description, Joel transitions to the Day of the Lord. He continues by showing the signs which will precede the Second Coming and describes the Jews being saved on that last day (Joel 2:10–32). John continues with the following:

> [11]And they had a king over them, which is the angel of the bottomless pit, whose name in the Hebrew tongue is Abaddon, but in the Greek tongue hath his name Apollyon. [12]One woe is past; and, behold, there come two woes more hereafter. (Rev. 9:11–12)

These demons have a leader, the angel of the bottomless pit, who is named Abaddon (destruction) and Apollyon (destroyer). More than likely, these are referring to Satan. More importantly, we have just been introduced to yet another participant in the judgments of the great tribulation—demons. The next woe will only serve to confirm this assertion.

> [13]And the sixth angel sounded, and I heard a voice from the four horns of the golden altar which is before God, [14]Saying to the sixth angel which had the trumpet, Loose the four angels which are bound in the great river Euphrates. [15]And the four angels were loosed, which were prepared for an hour, and a day, and a month, and a year, for to slay the third part of men. [16]And the number of the army of the horsemen were two hundred thousand thousand: and I heard the number of them. (Rev. 9:13–6)

After the sounding of the sixth trumpet, John heard a voice from the altar telling the angel that just sounded to let loose the four angels that have been bound in the Euphrates River. This is the only place in the Bible that we read of these angels. The only similarity to the four angels of God that wrought destruction upon the earth, seas, and trees in the first four trumpets is the number. Again, four refers to worldwide judgment. But these are demons since no angel of God is ever referred to as being bound. They will be released on unbelieving humanity for the purpose of killing one-third of mankind, and the army of demons that they will lead numbers 200 million. This is not an army of men, nor should it be confused with the armies from the east, which will come to the battle of Armageddon under the sixth vial and will be men (Rev. 16:12–16). The description that follows confirms this:

> [17]And thus I saw the horses in the vision, and them that sat on them, having breastplates of fire, and of jacinth, and brimstone: and the heads of the horses were as the heads of lions; and out of their mouths issued fire and smoke and brimstone. [18]By these three was the third part of men killed, by the fire, and by the smoke, and by the brimstone, which issued out of their mouths. [19]For their power is in their mouth, and in their tails: for their tails were like unto serpents, and had heads, and with them they do hurt. (Rev. 9:17–19)

This army of demons was seen by John as riders on horseback. Once again, the supernatural descriptions speak of demonic entities, which have been given power by God to kill people. John describes them killing with fire, smoke, and brimstone from their mouths, and they will be able to hurt with their tails. These are the visual images that John was given. How this will manifest in reality is open to speculation.

We know from the fifth trumpet that faithful Jews will not be harmed by these demons. It should be understood that believers in Christ will not be either. In previous studies we covered numerous passages of God's promise to preserve believers, and earlier in Revelation it was shown that a reasonable interpretation of Revelation 3:10 was a promise of preservation through the great tribulation. These judgments show us what the "hour of temptation" (Rev. 3:10) will look like, and the following passage shows exactly at whom they will be directed—unbelievers:

> [20]And the rest of the men which were not killed by these plagues yet repented not of the works of their hands, that they should not worship devils, and idols of gold, and silver, and brass, and stone, and of wood: which neither can see, nor hear, nor walk: [21]Neither repented they of their murders, nor of their sorceries, nor of their fornication, nor of their thefts. (Rev. 9:20–21)

This is the first of three times in Revelation that we will see unbelievers unwilling to repent, even after being tortured and watching others like themselves die. Prophecies like this make it quite clear why God has to put an end to this world in the way that he intends to. This level of evil will not come to an end on its own. He told his people to hide and wait until the indignation passed since he will punish those who do evil: "Come, my people, enter thou into thy chambers, and shut thy doors about thee: hide thyself as it were for a little moment, until the indignation be overpast. For, behold, the LORD cometh out of his place to punish the inhabitants of the earth for their iniquity: the earth also shall disclose her blood, and shall no more cover her slain" (Isa. 26:20–21).

Even though believers won't be subject to these supernatural judgments, they will be persecuted and killed at the hands of the Antichrist. That was shown after the fifth seal by the souls under the altar in heaven and in previous studies where God promised his church persecutions.

The Great Tribulation Witnesses

As with the seal judgments, a parenthetical section (Rev. 10:1–11:14) is given to us between the sixth and seventh trumpets. This section will be evaluated in the same manner as before, first from a distance to determine God's big picture, then in detail. The primary focus of this section is to present the activities of two witnesses, empowered by God, who will prophesy to the world and render judgments on those who oppose them during the great tribulation. The ministry of these witnesses is detailed in Revelation 11, and in order to be able to understand Revelation 10, we must first lay some groundwork.

Old Testament prophecy states that Elijah will come before the Day of the Lord: "Behold, I will send you Elijah the prophet before the coming of the great and dreadful day of the LORD" (Mal. 4:5). This is why Christ's disciples asked him why the scribes said that Elijah must come first (Matt. 17:10). To which he answered, "Elias truly shall first come, and restore all things. But I say unto you, That Elias is come already" (Matt. 17:11–12).

The Lord is not contradicting himself here. The prophecy of Malachi has a dual fulfillment. The first was when John the Baptist came in the "spirit and power" of Elijah (Luke 1:17), exactly what the Lord meant when he said that "Elias is come already" (Matt. 17:12; c.f. Matt 11:14). The second arrival of Elijah will precede the Lord's Second Coming and is what the Lord was referring to when he said, "Elias truly shall first come, and restore all things" (Matt. 17:11).

For this reason, there is general agreement among commentators that one of the two witnesses in Revelation 11 will be Elijah. The identity of the second is not nearly as evident, so much speculation exists. Some say it will be Moses since he was with Elijah at the transfiguration. Others say Enoch since he was taken to heaven by God. I contend that the answer to the question is found in Revelation 10, immediately preceding the discussion of the two witnesses.

The Commissioning of John

> ¹And I saw another mighty angel come down from heaven, clothed with a cloud: and a rainbow was upon his head, and his face was as it were the sun, and his feet as pillars of fire: ²And he had in his hand a little book open: and he set his right foot upon the sea, and his left foot on the earth, ³And cried with a loud voice, as when a lion roareth: and when he had cried, seven thunders uttered their voices. ⁴And when the seven thunders had uttered their voices, I was about to write: and I heard a voice from heaven saying unto me, Seal up those things which the seven thunders uttered, and write them not. (Rev. 10:1–4)

This vision begins with John seeing another angel from heaven, who stands with one foot on the sea and one on the earth, holding a little book in his hand open. Standing on the sea and earth may well signify ownership. The little book, I contend, is the first of Daniel's "shut up" (closed) visions (Dan. 8), the vision of the evening and the morning. Daniel was instructed to conceal this vision since it was going to be for the future—a time for which John was now writing.

After this, the angel cried in a loud voice, like a lion, and what followed were the voices of "seven thunders" (v. 3). This is important —John was just about to write what these seven thunders said but was told not to by a voice from heaven. Daniel was given a vision, allowed to write it but then told to shut it up. John heard these seven voices and was told not to write them but to "seal" them. Daniel's vision was written so it could be passed on to someone else. What could it mean when John was told not to write something that he heard? The only possibility I can think of is that *he* will be the one to deliver what these seven thunders said to the world. The passage continues as follows:

> ⁵And the angel which I saw stand upon the sea and upon the earth lifted up his hand to heaven, ⁶And sware by him that liveth for ever and ever, who created heaven, and the things that therein are, and the earth, and the things that therein are, and the sea, and the things which are therein, that there should be time no longer: ⁷But in the days of the voice of the seventh angel, when he shall begin to sound, the mystery of God should be finished, as he hath declared to his servants the prophets. (Rev. 10:5–7)

The angel then stood with his hand to heaven and swore by God "that there should be time no longer" (v. 6). This means that the end of the world has arrived. He confirms that the end will occur at the seventh trumpet since the "mystery of God" will be finished at that time (v. 7). The mystery of God is the completion of his redemptive plan for this world: Jews will be redeemed, believers in Christ will be raised from the dead, the dead in Christ and living believers will be given their glorified bodies, and Christ's reign on earth will begin. This is another one of the endpoints of the Seventieth Week that we covered in the Day of the Lord study. This final trumpet will be sounded at the end of this parenthetical section in Revelation 11. The passage continues as follows:

> ⁸And the voice which I heard from heaven spake unto me again, and said, Go and take the little book which is open in the hand of the angel which standeth upon the sea and upon the earth. ⁹And I went unto the angel, and said unto him, Give me the little book. And he said unto me, Take it, and eat it up; and it shall make thy belly bitter, but it shall be in thy mouth sweet as honey. ¹⁰And I took the little book out of the angel's hand, and ate it up; and it was in my mouth sweet as honey: and as soon as I had eaten it, my

> belly was bitter. [11]And he said unto me, Thou must prophesy again before many peoples, and nations, and tongues, and kings. (Rev. 10:8–11)

John was instructed to eat the little book; it was sweet as honey in his mouth but bitter in his belly. This means that John was now given Daniel's vision of the Day of the Lord (c.f. Ezek. 2:8–3:3). His reaction seems to indicate this: sweet—Jews saved, Christians glorified; bitter—destructive wrath poured out on unbelievers. He now has the vision and will be able to write it for us. It may well be what we see in Revelation 19.

But what about the seven thunders? John was told that he must prophesy again before the entire world: "Many peoples, and nations, and tongues, and kings" (v. 11). I believe that this is the clue we needed to determine who the second prophet will be—John. He is the only one who can deliver what the seven thunders said. What these seven thunders may be is open to speculation. However, I think a very reasonable conclusion is that there will be seven more judgments during the great tribulation. We will now see that these two witnesses —John and Elijah—will be empowered by God to render judgments of their own. The passage continues in Revelation 11:

The Two Witnesses

> [1]And there was given me a reed like unto a rod: and the angel stood, saying, Rise, and measure the temple of God, and the altar, and them that worship therein. [2]But the court which is without the temple leave out, and measure it not; for it is given unto the Gentiles: and the holy city shall they tread under foot forty and two months. (Rev. 11:1–2)

John was given a measuring rod and told to measure the temple of God, the altar, and those who worship there. This is added evidence that there will be a temple in Jerusalem before the great tribulation for the Antichrist to desecrate (Dan. 9:27). Measuring appears to be signifying ownership by God.[2] This is further confirmed by the angel telling John not to measure the outer court of the temple since it, and Jerusalem ("the holy city"), will be under Gentile control for forty-two months. This forty-two months will be the great tribulation, the final

---

2   Walvoord, *Revelation*, 178.

three-and-one-half-year period, during which the Antichrist will be permitted to rule the world.

> ³And I will give power unto my two witnesses, and they shall prophesy a thousand two hundred and threescore days, clothed in sackcloth. ⁴These are the two olive trees, and the two candlesticks standing before the God of the earth. (Rev. 11:3–4)

Next, John introduces us to two witnesses who will prophesy during the great tribulation, here specified as 1,260 days. There are references in this chapter that indicate these two witnesses will be men. The first is found in the metaphorical statement of them being the "two olive trees" and "two candlesticks" standing before God (v. 4). This bears striking similarity to how God referred to Joshua and Zerubbabel (Zech. 4:2–6; 11–14) as two olive trees and two olive branches, providing oil for a golden candlestick—Israel.

Since the Holy Spirit is figuratively referred to as oil, the "two olive trees" appear to be speaking of these two great tribulation witnesses as being empowered by God to fulfill their mission as vessels through which the Holy Spirit will flow. The candlestick is a reference to them being God's light to the world. They will also be supernaturally empowered to destroy their enemies and render judgments on them and the world.

> ⁵And if any man will hurt them, fire proceedeth out of their mouth, and devoureth their enemies: and if any man will hurt them, he must in this manner be killed. ⁶These have power to shut heaven, that it rain not in the days of their prophecy: and have power over waters to turn them to blood, and to smite the earth with all plagues, as often as they will. (Rev. 11:5–6)

They will be allowed to finish their testimony, and only after they have fulfilled their mission will they be killed.

> ⁷And when they shall have finished their testimony, the beast that ascendeth out of the bottomless pit shall make war against them, and shall overcome them, and kill them. (Rev. 11:7)

This is now the first reference we see in Revelation to a beast that rises from the bottomless pit. We previously saw that demons will be let loose from the pit and allowed to render specific judgments on unbelieving humanity. As we continue, it will become evident that this beast from the pit is none other than the Antichrist (c.f. Rev. 17:8, 11).

> [8]And their dead bodies shall lie in the street of the great city, which spiritually is called Sodom and Egypt, where also our Lord was crucified. [9]And they of the people and kindreds and tongues and nations shall see their dead bodies three days and an half, and shall not suffer their dead bodies to be put in graves. [10]And they that dwell upon the earth shall rejoice over them, and make merry, and shall send gifts one to another; because these two prophets tormented them that dwelt on the earth. (Rev. 11:8–10)

After these prophets are killed by the Antichrist, their bodies will be left on the street in Jerusalem, referred to here as Sodom and Egypt. These are references to the moral filth of Sodom and spiritual idolatry and occult practices of Egypt. Their bodies will be seen by the entire world, and once again, we see the fourfold reference used by God to convey that.

Two additional pieces of information have been provided to confirm that these witnesses will be men. First, they will be killed by the Antichrist (v. 7); and second, their dead bodies will lie in the street (v. 8). Many commentators have treated these witnesses as being symbolic of something other than two men. The similarity of the metaphorical references given to these witnesses to those of Joshua and Zerubbabel (v. 4), the types of judgments they will execute (vv. 5–6), the description of their deaths, and the prophecy that follows (v. 12), showing them being in the resurrection, are why I believe they will be literal men.

These prophets will be active during the great tribulation so their deaths will occur only three-and-one-half days before the Second Coming. Notice what the world does—all the people rejoice and send gifts to each other. The deaths of these prophets will be a welcome event to these unbelievers since they have been rendering judgments on the people of the earth and preaching the Word. More than likely they have also been responsible for seven more judgments—the seven thunders—the details of which we do not know. I believe their deaths may well be the "peace and safety" that Paul is referring to in the third verse of this passage speaking of the Day of the Lord:

> [1]But of the times and the seasons, brethren, ye have no need that I write unto you. [2]For yourselves know perfectly that the day of the Lord so cometh as a thief in the night. [3]For when they shall say, Peace and safety; then sudden destruction cometh upon them, as travail upon a woman with child; and they shall not escape. (1Thess. 5:1–3)

The world thinks they have put an end to their torment but the Second Coming—the third woe—is about to happen:

> [11]And after three days and an half the Spirit of life from God entered into them, and they stood upon their feet; and great fear fell upon them which saw them. [12]And they heard a great voice from heaven saying unto them, Come up hither. And they ascended up to heaven in a cloud; and their enemies beheld them. (Rev. 11:11–12)

Verses 11 and 12 show exactly what happens when the Lord appears in the clouds. The dead rise first and the living are gathered together with them. Just as in Daniel, where we were never given all of the events of the Day of the Lord in any one prophecy, the same applies here. We are told about these two prophets being raised from the dead because they are the primary focus of this parenthetical section; however, it is at this time that all the dead will rise as well. So, they are part of the resurrection of the dead, which is the first event to happen on the Day of the Lord after Christ appears in the clouds. Immediately after this, we are given additional events that occur on the Day of the Lord:

> [13]And the same hour was there a great earthquake, and the tenth part of the city fell, and in the earthquake were slain of men seven thousand: and the remnant were affrighted, and gave glory to the God of heaven. [14]The second woe is past; and, behold, the third woe cometh quickly. (Rev. 11:13–14)

The earthquake here must be the one that announces the Day of the Lord—the sixth seal. This is because we are told that the third woe still remains, and that is where we see the fivefold judgment of the end, which includes the final great earthquake. The city referenced is Jerusalem. Seven thousand will die in this earthquake. There is also evidence that the Lord pours out the Holy Spirit on faithful Israel in the statement, "The remnant were affrighted, and gave glory to the God of heaven." They have now seen the one they pierced on this last day and will mourn for him (Zech. 12:10). Additional events and details of this day will be seen in subsequent prophecies.

The Third Woe–the World Now Belongs to Christ

God closes out this chapter by presenting the final trumpet judgment, showing the worship in heaven, and providing confirmation that the seventh trumpet brings us to yet another endpoint for this world:

> 15And the seventh angel sounded; and there were great voices in heaven, saying, The kingdoms of this world are become the kingdoms of our Lord, and of his Christ; and he shall reign for ever and ever. 16And the four and twenty elders, which sat before God on their seats, fell upon their faces, and worshipped God, 17Saying, We give thee thanks, O Lord God Almighty, which art, and wast, and art to come; because thou hast taken to thee thy great power, and hast reigned. 18And the nations were angry, and thy wrath is come, and the time of the dead, that they should be judged, and that thou shouldest give reward unto thy servants the prophets, and to the saints, and them that fear thy name, small and great; and shouldest destroy them which destroy the earth. 19And the temple of God was opened in heaven, and there was seen in his temple the ark of his testament: and there were lightnings, and voices, and thunderings, and an earthquake, and great hail. (Rev. 11:15–19)

Please note the seventh seal provided only a very rough framework for the prophecies of the end of this world. All of the details of the redemption, wrath, and destruction are provided later in Revelation. In this passage, the emphasis is on God's redemptive plan—the mystery of God—being completed (Rev. 10:7). The voices in heaven confirm that the entire world has now become the Lord's (v. 15). Worship in heaven follows because the Lord has taken what is rightfully his. They confirm that his wrath has been poured out and that it is now the time to judge the living and the dead (v. 18, c.f. 2 Tim. 4:1; 2 Cor. 5:10; Rom. 14:10). The passage closes with the fivefold judgment of the end: voices, thundering, lightning, an earthquake, and a great hail. Just as in Daniel, God has added another layer of detail to the framework established in the seal judgments. This time, giving specific prophecies of three additional participants in the great tribulation—angels, demons, and witnesses—and ending with the Day of the Lord.

Concluding Thoughts

Earlier, it was stated that the faithful remnant of the Jews as well as the believing church will be protected from these supernatural judgments rendered by angels and demons. The Jews will be protected by virtue of the seal given to them by God and true believers by being indwelled by the Holy Spirit. If this is the case, what possible reason could God have for allowing the church to be present on earth during the great tribulation? To answer this question it is first necessary to understand that the church presently is comprised of three distinctly identifiable groups: (1) False professors—individuals who claim faith in Christ but knowingly are not believers. John describes such individuals as being of the antichrist spirit (1 John 2:18–19). Their purpose is to disrupt the church and lead people away from the truth. (2) Professing believers—individuals who profess Christ but are not in biblical truth. These are believers in "another Jesus," "another Spirit," or "another gospel" (2 Cor. 11:3–4). The Lord Jesus describes these professing believers as those who have chosen the "wide gate" (Matt. 7:13–23). (3) True believers—individuals who believe in the Christ of the Bible and hold to the truth.

Individuals in the first two groups should not expect any protection through these supernatural judgments. The reason for the false professors being unprotected is obvious; however, the professing believers deserve a closer examination. In the Sermon on the Mount, Jesus teaches that believers must enter through the "strait" (narrow) gate. To understand this teaching, the passage must be considered in its entirety (Matt. 7:13–23). The Lord instructs us to seek the strait gate and says that there will be few who find it (Matt. 7:13–14). He follows by teaching to beware of false prophets and how they can be identified by their fruits (Matt. 7:15–20). He concludes by making it clear that those who have chosen the wide gate are professing believers since they will address him as "Lord" and claim to have performed many signs and wonders in his name (Matt. 7:21–23). His response to these individuals will be that he never knew them (Matt. 7:23) and that they will not inherit the kingdom of heaven (Matt. 7:21). The fact that these people call him Lord, but Christ states that he never knew them can mean only one thing; they are professing believers who have never been in the truth and consequently never indwelled by the Holy Spirit.

Further, he describes the gate they have entered as being the wide one. This, combined with the prophecy of apostasy in the church (2 Thess. 2:3–12), means that many professing Christians will fall into this category. They will be subject to the supernatural judgments studied earlier as well as those that we will study in Revelation 16—the wrath of God. There is a reason for them to be in the great tribulation—to be brought to the true faith through the terrible conditions that will ensue. The unfortunate reality is that many will be part of the chaff that gets burned off.

The third group identified earlier, true believers, will be the ones who have God's promises of preservation and protection through the great tribulation. However, there are two ways individuals in this group can go. The first is to "endure" until the end (Matt. 24:13). These will be the ones who "overcome" (Rev. 2–3), and the promise of eternal life will be theirs. But since the Lord prophesied that there will be those who fall away during the great tribulation (Matt. 24:10), we know that not all will endure until the end. These, who do not overcome, will have their names blotted out of the book of life (Rev. 3:5). The important thing to note is that God speaks of blotting names from the book where only true believers will be listed. To be blotted out of this book means that the individual must have been a true believer at some point. This teaches that God does not consider a Christian's enduring to the end to be a certainty. It also means that the Lord Jesus will return to the spotless church that he died for (Rev. 19:6–9; c.f. Eph. 5:27).

12

The Interludes

Israel, Satan, the Church (Rev. 12)

The next section of Revelation, chapters 12–14, consists of three interludes. They are followed by another series of seven judgments, presented as vials being poured out on the earth—the wrath of God. A fourth interlude follows this in Revelation 17–18. These interludes provide additional information about different participants in the Seventieth Week and are presented through highly symbolic imagery. Revelation 12 opens as follows:

> [1]And there appeared a great wonder in heaven; a woman clothed with the sun, and the moon under her feet, and upon her head a crown of twelve stars: [2]And she being with child cried, travailing in birth, and pained to be delivered. [3]And there appeared another wonder in heaven; and behold a great red dragon, having seven heads and ten horns, and seven crowns upon his heads. [4]And his tail drew the third part of the stars of heaven, and did cast them to the earth: and the dragon stood before the woman which was ready to be delivered, for to devour her child as soon as it was born. [5]And she brought forth a man child, who was to rule all nations with a rod of iron: and her child was caught up unto God, and to his throne. (Rev. 12:1–5)

The woman presented in v. 1 is Israel. She is pictured in glory, clothed in the sun, her feet on the moon. The crown of twelve stars refers to the twelve tribes of Israel (c.f. Gen. 37:9–11). Israel is referred to as the wife of God (Isa. 54:5–6), and in general, a woman is used in Revelation to symbolically refer to a religious system. Later, a harlot will be used to refer to religious Rome and a chaste bride to refer to the church. The woman is depicted as giving birth (v. 2), and her child is Christ (Isa. 66:7).

Verse 3 introduces Satan as a great red dragon (c.f. Rev. 12:9). He is shown to rebel against God and draw away one-third of the angels with him (v. 4). Afterwards, he seeks to destroy Christ as soon as he is born (v. 4). Christ is born of the virgin Mary and brought up to heaven after his crucifixion (v. 5).

The imagery used to depict Satan includes seven heads and ten horns. The seven heads may well represent the consecutive satanic kingdoms that have reigned throughout history (c.f. Rev. 17:10). The ten horns represent future Rome, with its ten concurrently ruling leaders (c.f. Dan. 2:44; 7:24).

The Antichrist will also be shown as having seven heads and ten horns, indicating his connection to Satan. In the case of Satan, the crowns are on the seven heads, showing his influence throughout all time. In the case of the Antichrist, the crowns are on the ten horns (Rev. 13:1), showing his connection to future Rome. The important message is that the Antichrist has a profound association with Satan and will be satanically empowered (Rev. 13:4), but the two are distinctly separate entities. Considerable prophetic foreshortening occurs between verses 5 and 6:

> [6]And the woman fled into the wilderness, where she hath a place prepared of God, that they should feed her there a thousand two hundred and threescore days. [7]And there was war in heaven: Michael and his angels fought against the dragon; and the dragon fought and his angels, [8]And prevailed not; neither was their place found any more in heaven. [9]And the great dragon was cast out, that old serpent, called the Devil, and Satan, which deceiveth the whole world: he was cast out into the earth, and his angels were cast out with him. (Rev. 12:6–9)

Verse 6 shows Israel fleeing the persecutions of the Antichrist. This will occur at the abomination of desolation when the Antichrist breaks his covenant with Israel and desecrates the temple. The language speaks of God providing refuge ("she hath a place prepared of God") for Israel in Gentile nations ("the wilderness") for 1,260 days, the duration of the great tribulation.

Verses 7–9 show a war in heaven between Satan and his demons and the archangel Michael and his angels. Michael is victorious and Satan and his demons are thrown out of heaven (c.f. Isa. 14:12–15; Ezek. 28:12–16). Until this point, Satan has been able to enter into God's presence in heaven (Job 1:6–12; 2:1–7). During the great tribulation, he will no longer have this access and will increase his efforts to destroy the Jews and Christians since he knows his time is limited. The prophetic foreshortening between verses 5 and 6 brings us up to the abomination of desolation, thus it is reasonable to assume that the war in heaven will occur at that time. This passage continues with the following:

> [10]And I heard a loud voice saying in heaven, Now is come salvation, and strength, and the kingdom of our God, and the power of his Christ: for the accuser of our brethren is cast down, which accused them before our God day and night. [11]And they overcame him by the blood of the Lamb, and by the word of their testimony; and they loved not their lives unto the death. [12]Therefore rejoice, ye heavens, and ye that dwell in them. Woe to the inhabiters of the earth and of the sea! for the devil is come down unto you, having great wrath, because he knoweth that he hath but a short time. [13]And when the dragon saw that he was cast unto the earth, he persecuted the woman which brought forth the man child. [14]And to the woman were given two wings of a great eagle, that she might fly into the wilderness, into her place, where she is nourished for a time, and times, and half a time, from the face of the serpent. [15]And the serpent cast out of his mouth water as a flood after the woman, that he might cause her to be carried away of the flood. [16]And the earth helped the woman, and the earth opened her mouth, and swallowed up the flood which the dragon cast out of his mouth. [17]And the dragon was wroth with the woman, and went to make war with the remnant of her seed, which keep the commandments of God, and have the testimony of Jesus Christ. (Rev. 12:10–17)

Satan will no longer be able to slander Jews or Christians in heaven (v. 10), and v. 11 shows how believers will overcome him, by belief in Christ ("the blood of the Lamb") and their testimony. This is a picture of what Jesus told believers in the Olivet Discourse—endure until the end. Satan will persecute Israel (v. 13), but the Jews will be helped by God, "given two wings of a great eagle, that she might fly into the wilderness" (v. 14). This is figurative language speaking of God's provision for the faithful remnant. Jews will be able to flee from Israel to a safe place of protection, "the wilderness," for the duration of the great tribulation, "time, and times, and half a time" (v. 14).

The figurative language of v. 15, "the serpent cast out of his mouth water as a flood," speaks of the intensity of the persecutions. But there will be those nations that help the Jews, referred to as "the earth" (v. 16). In addition to persecuting Israel, Satan will also persecute Christians, "the remnant of her seed" (v. 17). Christ is Israel's seed, and his followers will be that remnant. This is confirmed by the state-ment that they "keep the commandments of God, and have the testi-mony of Jesus Christ" (v. 17).

The important thing to take from this is that the intensity of perse-cutions of Jews and Christians will increase dramatically during the great tribulation and that God will provide for his people through this time (vv. 14, 16; c.f. Rev. 3:10). Also, this passage teaches of both Jews and Christians in the great tribulation. Israel and the Jews get very little mention in the book of Revelation. The first mention was at the sealing of the faithful remnant (Rev. 7:1–8), and there was a brief allusion to the moment of their salvation (Rev. 11:13); this is the only other mention. Jerusalem is mentioned, and the events surrounding the battle of Armageddon will be studied later, but this is the extent of what we are taught about the Jewish people during the Seventieth Week.

The Unholy Trinity (Rev. 13)
The First Beast-the Antichrist and His Kingdom

Revelation 13 begins with a new vision. We will now be told much more about Daniel's fourth beast (Dan. 7:7). Just as in Daniel, this beast represents future Rome, the Antichrist, and the Antichrist kingdom. Which of these is being spoken of must be determined based on the context of the passage. There was a very limited description of this beast's appearance in Daniel 7; we now see much greater detail:

> ¹And I stood upon the sand of the sea, and saw a beast rise up out of the sea, having seven heads and ten horns, and upon his horns ten crowns, and upon his heads the name of blasphemy. ²And the beast which I saw was like unto a leopard, and his feet were as the feet of a bear, and his mouth as the mouth of a lion: and the dragon gave him his power, and his seat, and great authority. (Rev. 13:1–2)

The Kingdom-One-World Government

Verse 1 informs us of a beast with ten horns rising from the sea, just as we saw in Daniel 7. The reference to the sea means that the Antichrist and his kingdom will rise out of the Gentile nations. This kingdom will rise to power as the ten-leader, future Rome (c.f. Dan. 2:41–43; 7:7), and by the midpoint of the Seventieth Week, the kingdom will become entirely the Antichrist's (c.f. Dan. 7:24–25; Rev. 17:12–13).

In Daniel 7, the fourth beast represented Rome and its global political, governmental, economic, and religious rule (Dan. 7:23). By the end of Revelation 13, we will see each of these elements of future Rome usurped by the Antichrist and rolled into his Antichrist kingdom. Revelation 17 will provide much more detail about the reuniting of political/governmental Rome with its religious component prior to the establishment of the Antichrist kingdom.

The ten horns with crowns symbolically speak of political leaders who have been given authority. All ten together on this one beast points to a single global governing entity comprised of ten concurrently ruling leaders (c.f. Dan. 2:40–44; 7:7–8, 23–25). The global extent of this rule is confirmed in v. 7: "Power was given him over all kindreds, and tongues, and nations." This governing power will first be exercised by future Rome and then by the Antichrist. We will get the details of how this power transfers from future Rome to the Antichrist in Revelation 17.

This beast has seven heads, just as described in the vision of Satan (Rev. 12:3). This shows a profound connection to Satan (c.f. vv. 2, 4). We will be told the symbolic meaning of these heads in Revelation 17. This beast is described with attributes of the first three beasts of

Daniel 7: a leopard, a bear, and a lion (v. 2). This may mean that all of the satanic evil of those three previous kingdoms will be present in this final kingdom. We are also told that the beast will be satanically empowered (v. 4); "the dragon" will give him his power, seat, and authority (v. 2).

The Antichrist

> [3]And I saw one of his heads as it were wounded to death; and his deadly wound was healed: and all the world wondered after the beast. [4]And they worshipped the dragon which gave power unto the beast: and they worshipped the beast, saying, Who is like unto the beast? who is able to make war with him? [5]And there was given unto him a mouth speaking great things and blasphemies; and power was given unto him to continue forty and two months. [6]And he opened his mouth in blasphemy against God, to blaspheme his name, and his tabernacle, and them that dwell in heaven. (Rev. 13:3–6)

In Revelation 11, we got a little hint of the identity of the Antichrist when we were told that the beast would ascend out of "the bottomless pit" (Rev. 11:7). Now in Revelation 13, we receive three messages much like the one in v. 3 (Rev. 13:3, 12, 14), each providing more specific detail. Verse 3 states that one of the seven heads of the beast received an apparently deadly wound which was healed. Verse 12 states that the wound was deadly and that the one being referred to is the Antichrist since the context speaks of the false prophet causing all unbelievers to worship this man. Verse 14 confirms that it is the Antichrist being spoken of and that he does live after this head wound. After this "healing," the whole world will be amazed and follow this man (v. 3).

Revelation 17 provides even more information about this event. There is confirmation again that the beast will rise out of the pit (Rev. 17:8), and there are three other mentions that are very interesting. They essentially say that the beast existed at some prior time, now doesn't exist, but will exist again in the future. This is captured in the statement "the beast that was, and is not, and yet is" (Rev. 17:8). They read as follows:

> [8]The beast that thou sawest was, and is not; and shall ascend out of the bottomless pit, and go into perdition: and they that dwell on the earth shall wonder, whose names were not written in the book of life from the foundation of the world, when they behold the beast that was, and is not, and yet is. (Rev. 17:8)

> [11]And the beast that was, and is not, even he is the eighth, and is of the seven, and goeth into perdition (Rev. 17:11).

Notice the people of the world will actually see ("behold") this beast from the pit (Rev. 17:8). I believe that when combined with the teaching of the deadly head wound, which is healed, what is being described is a satanic resurrection. When the Holy Spirit relinquishes his restraining role and the mystery of iniquity is allowed to progress to its fullest, Satan will be allowed to perform this resurrection. This beast from the pit will then indwell the Antichrist. This "resurrection event" will be one of the primary reasons why the entire world will follow and worship this man. The apostasy of the church will be complete at this point.

It appears that Satan may be allowed to raise the soul of the most evil man in history to fill the role of the Antichrist during the great tribulation. The timing of this resurrection and indwelling of the Antichrist by this beast can most reasonably be assumed to occur at the midpoint of the Seventieth Week. This is when the Antichrist will be "revealed" (2 Thess. 2:3), break his covenant with Israel (Dan. 9:27), and set up the abomination of desolation (Dan. 9:27; 12:11; Matt. 24:15). The Antichrist's eventual end will be to "go into perdition"— the lake of fire (Rev. 17:8 c.f. Rev. 19:20). Because of the similarity of the Lord's description of his own incarnation and death (Rev. 1:18) to the description of this beast's (Rev.17:8, 11), I believe that it is not a demon rising from the pit, but rather the soul of a man.

Returning to Revelation 13, vv. 4–6 provide further details of the Antichrist which are in complete agreement with what we learned in Daniel, with one notable addition—that the whole unbelieving world will worship the Antichrist and Satan (v. 4). We are told that Satan ("the dragon") will be empowering the Antichrist (c.f. Dan. 8:24–25) and that he will be seemingly invincible in war (c.f. Dan. 11:36–45). Also, he will speak incredible blasphemies against God (c.f. Dan. 7:7–

11, 23–25) and will be allowed to continue for forty-two months (c.f. Dan. 7:25; 12:7). We also learn the identity of the "god of forces" (Dan. 11:38–39) that he will worship—Satan—and that this will be whom he will "acknowledge and increase with glory" (Dan. 11:39). The remainder of this passage continues as follows:

> [7]And it was given unto him to make war with the saints, and to overcome them: and power was given him over all kindreds, and tongues, and nations. [8]And all that dwell upon the earth shall worship him, whose names are not written in the book of life of the Lamb slain from the foundation of the world. [9]If any man have an ear, let him hear. [10]He that leadeth into captivity shall go into captivity: he that killeth with the sword must be killed with the sword. Here is the patience and the faith of the saints. (Rev. 13:7–10)

Throughout the New Testament, believers in Christ are referred to as saints. When spoken of collectively (v. 7), this means the church. As we studied previously, the church will be undergoing a refining/ purging during the great tribulation, just as Israel will be. The Antichrist's rule will be worldwide (v. 7), and he will be allowed to perform his God-ordained role for forty-two months—the great tribulation.

Verse 8 again teaches that the Antichrist will be worshipped by all those who do not have their names written in the book of life. This speaks of worldwide worship of the beast by all unbelievers and fallen Christians. Looking ahead in Revelation 13 (vv. 12, 15), we see that what is being spoken of here is the prophecy of a one-world religion— Antichrist worship. Currently, there is a tremendous push within Christianity for ecumenism, the unification of all professing believers. This unity, however, can only be achieved by further compromise of biblical doctrine. What is seen here is the endpoint of this kind of thinking— the one-world religion—with the Antichrist seated as God in the temple (c.f. 2 Thess. 2:4).

The "captivity" spoken of (v. 10) is succumbing to Antichrist worship and taking the mark of the beast (Rev. 13:16), which will be discussed shortly. Notice the one being warned is the one who leads people into this captivity. I think it is reasonable to infer that this warning can be applied to pastors and churches that teach doctrines that will cause people to fall into this captivity. These leaders will be held responsible, just as the lawless unbelievers and the Antichrist ("he that killeth with the sword") will be. Falling into this captivity is juxtaposed against remaining faithful throughout these trials, which is described as the "patience and the faith of the saints." This is exactly what believers are told to do in every epistle in Revelation 2 and 3, stay faithful through the horrible and challenging circumstances until the Lord's return.

The Second Beast–the False Prophet

There was a little clue in Daniel 7 that I called special attention to. In the angel's interpretation, the four beasts that Daniel saw were first described as coming up from the sea (Dan. 7:3) and then later said to arise from the earth (Dan. 7:17). It is important to understand that God uses later prophecies to add detail and clarity to earlier ones. This was the case in Daniel 2 and 7. In Daniel 2, the final kingdom that was crushed by the stone was only presented to us as ten toes, representing the final ten-king, future Rome. Later in Daniel 7, we learned about a little horn that will arise from among these ten kings. We used this information to update our understanding of the prophecy. Here we encounter the same type of prophetic update. Just as we were introduced to the Antichrist in Daniel 7 (the little horn), we now are introduced to yet one more principal—the false prophet—the beast that John saw coming up out of the earth:

> [11]And I beheld another beast coming up out of the earth; and he had two horns like a lamb, and he spake as a dragon. [12]And he exerciseth all the power of the first beast before him, and causeth the earth and them which dwell therein to worship the first beast, whose deadly wound was healed. [13]And he doeth great wonders, so that he maketh fire come down from heaven on the earth in the sight of men, (Rev. 13:11–13)

The seemingly unresolved issue of Daniel 7, the beasts originating from two different places, now makes sense. The Antichrist will not be working alone in his chastening role on humanity; he will have an accomplice. In v. 11, this second beast is described as arising from the earth, having two horns like a lamb, and speaking like a dragon. This symbolic imagery points to a wolf in sheep's clothing (c.f. Matt. 7:15). The horns of a lamb speak of the appearance of godliness because of the lamb reference, but speaking like a dragon means the words are from Satan. The "earth" that he will arise from may well mean the "world system," which is always at odds with Christianity (c.f. 1 John 2:15–17; 3:1; John 15:19; James 4:4). Put together, this points to someone who is a representative of the world system, speaking satanic lies but appearing Christ-like. This understanding of the symbolic meaning of "the earth" is further confirmed in v. 12 where he is said to cause "the earth and them which dwell therein to worship the first beast."

In Revelation 13, we are not given a name for this beast. But later (Rev. 16:13; 19:20; 20:10), he is given a name that corresponds to this interpretation—the false prophet. Also, the descriptions in these later references makes it evident that he is a man, just like the Antichrist. Further, just like the beast that rises from the sea (Rev. 13:1) represents the man (Antichrist) and his Antichrist kingdom, this beast can be understood to symbolize the man (false prophet) and the system that he represents—the world system disguised by a thin veneer of godliness. This man will be the ecclesiastical head of the Antichrist's religious system since he will be the one to get unbelievers to worship the beast (v. 12).

One-World Religion

In v. 12, we are told that this false prophet will cause everyone to worship the beast and that he will perform amazing signs and wonders (v. 13). The false prophet's signs and wonders will be how the deceptions are advanced:

> 14And deceiveth them that dwell on the earth by the means of those miracles which he had power to do in the sight of the beast; saying to them that dwell on the earth, that they should make an image to the beast, which had the wound by a sword, and did live. 15And he had power to give life unto the image of the beast, that the image of the beast should both speak, and cause that as many as would not worship the image of the beast should be killed. (Rev. 13:14–15)

Through his deceptions (v. 14), the false prophet will convince the masses to make a statue of the Antichrist ("image"), and he will have the power to make this statue speak and kill those who will not worship it (v. 15). This is virtually the same thing that Nebuchadnezzar did (Dan. 3), with the exception that under the Antichrist, there will be incredible, satanically empowered signs and wonders occurring. These deceptions will be how the Antichrist consolidates all worship to himself and Satan (vv. 4, 8, 12). The result will be a one-world religious system with mandatory worship; rebellion will be punishable by death. It is quite reasonable to infer that this statue is what the Lord was speaking of when he warned of the abomination of desolation that will "stand" in the "holy place" (Matt. 24:15). Based on that, it can be inferred that this will occur at the midpoint of the Seventieth Week.

One-World Economic System

¹⁶And he causeth all, both small and great, rich and poor, free and bond, to receive a mark in their right hand, or in their foreheads: ¹⁷And that no man might buy or sell, save he that had the mark, or the name of the beast, or the number of his name. ¹⁸Here is wisdom. Let him that hath understanding count the number of the beast: for it is the number of a man; and his number is Six hundred threescore and six. (Rev. 13:16–18)

Participation in the Antichrist economic system will require a mark, commonly referred to as the mark of the beast. This mark will be in an individual's right hand or forehead (v. 16), and it will take one of three forms: "a mark" (some kind of a stamp or image), "the name of the beast," or "the number of his name" (v. 17). With this mark, the Antichrist will also have a one-world economic system under his control. This is the final piece of the puzzle to fully understand the Antichrist kingdom. His kingdom will have worldwide political and governmental control (vv. 1, 7), worldwide religious control (v. 15), and worldwide economic control (v. 17). There will be no other system on this earth, and the unholy trinity—Satan, the Antichrist, and the false prophet—will be allowed to execute God's indignation on the people of this planet. In v. 18, we are told the number of the beast, 666, and more importantly, that it is the number of a man. This means that there will be a man who will fill this role in the future.

Concluding Thoughts

Several issues that stem from the study of the two beasts require some speculation. For that reason, I have placed them in this concluding section. First, the symbolism pertaining to the second beast presents some interesting interpretive challenges. From earlier studies in Daniel, we know that God uses the beast symbol to represent a world empire. However, the remainder of the description of this beast (horns like a lamb, speaking like a dragon, rising from the earth) and the name given to him (false prophet) could well be applied to the apostate church (2 Thess. 2: 3, 7, 9–12). From earlier studies, we know that the apostate church plays a major role in the rise of the Antichrist, and yet there is no place in Revelation where it is mentioned—except for maybe here as the second beast.[1] The only potential problem with this conclusion is that the beast symbolism doesn't fit unless God has chosen not to use a woman to symbolically represent this religious system—apostate Christianity—but a beast instead. If that is the case, then the false prophet, having the outward appearance of a man of God but speaking and performing satanic words and miracles, may well be a representative of the fallen church. It may be that God considers the apostate church to be nothing more than the world system with a thin veneer of godliness, which is how the false prophet was described earlier.

Also, deception is said to be the primary tool used by Satan (Rev. 12:9; 20:3) and the false prophet (Rev. 13:14; 19:20), and the miracles of the false prophet are the means of advancing this deception (Rev. 13:14). Keep in mind that Satan has been working on this for the entire church age. By the time the Antichrist arrives on the scene, the church will no longer have the discernment to separate truth from fiction. There will be some lie of Satan that almost everyone on earth will believe, resulting in them worshiping a man as if he were Christ on earth (c.f. 2 Thess. 2:4). To understand this more fully we must first understand what the Antichrist really is.

---

1   The identity of the harlot (Rev. 17) will be shown to be yet another false religious system and not the apostate church.

The term antichrist (Greek *antichristos*)[2] means "against Christ" or "instead of Christ." In the case of the Antichrist, he will fill both roles, being both opposed to (Rev. 13:5, 6) and a substitute for Christ (Rev. 13:4, 8, 12, 15). The Bible uses this term in both a narrow sense (1 John 2:18), referring to the final Antichrist and a broad sense (1 John 2:22; 2 John 7), referring to all antichrists throughout the church age.

There is yet another term used for those who claim to be Christ— false Christs (Greek *pseudochristos*).[3] These are the individuals that the Lord Jesus spoke of in the Olivet Discourse saying, "For there shall arise false Christs, and false prophets, and shall shew great signs and wonders; insomuch that, if it were possible, they shall deceive the very elect" (Matt. 24:24; c.f. Mark 13:22). This was said by the Lord when he was describing the conditions that will exist during the great tribulation. The elect will be those with the discernment to know that these miracles are of the devil.

Next, we must understand why Christ performed miracles during his earthly ministry. It was to confirm his identity as the Messiah. He expelled demons from people (Matt. 12:24–29) to demonstrate that he was greater than Satan and raised the dead to confirm his identity (John 11:4, 15) and signify that he was sent by God (John 11:42). It seems that Satan will employ the same kind of strategy by having the false prophet perform all sorts of amazing miracles to fool people into believing that the Antichrist is actually Christ.

There will also be others who will be performing miracles to support their claims that they are Christ—the false Christs of the Olivet Discourse. When put together, the false resurrection of the Antichrist, his claim of being Christ, and others making similar claims and showing signs and wonders, I think it is possible that Satan's final lie will be that man can be God. This was the original lie in the garden of Eden (Gen. 3:5) and may well be the deception that Satan will use to entice people to worship the Antichrist and take the mark of the beast.

In addition to deception, coercion will be a prominent feature of the Antichrist kingdom as well. Those without the mark of the beast will

---

2   Strong, *Concordance*, G500.
3   Strong, *Concordance*, G5580.

be shut out of the economic system, and those who will not worship his image will be killed. Later, we will learn that taking the mark will constitute an unforgivable sin and will be associated with worshipping the man (Rev. 14:9–11). This latter point, however, makes me think that deception will still be the primary tool (c.f. Rev. 19:20) and that the mark may be some sort of symbol of believing the Antichrist's "gospel message."

It may be that the mark is the sign that people will have to take in order to attain god-like status and have eternal life under this satanic lie. The true Jesus gives us eternal life by our believing in him, while Satan will deceive people into taking a mark that indicates his owner-ship of them. This sort of thing will only be possible in a world in which the vast majority is ignorant of biblical truth. This is why the mystery of iniquity is such an important part of Satan's plan and why it was stated earlier that the apostate church will play an active role in the rise of the Antichrist.

Another consequence of this system is that it will be very easy to identify true believers in Christ and set them up as the enemy. We know that the Antichrist will be blaspheming God (Rev. 13:6) and persecuting believers. It wouldn't be too difficult for him to convince everyone that Christians are to blame for all the world's problems. And since he will portray himself as Christ, it is plausible that he will also portray the true God of heaven as the devil.

Firstfruits–Angels–Harvest (Rev. 14)

Revelation 14 opens with a new vision. We are introduced to yet another group of 144,000. The reason for identifying them as another group is that the only similarity to the 144,000 of Revelation 7 is the number, and the primary difference is that these are Christians. The imagery in this chapter is highly symbolic, and before continuing, a brief explanation of Jewish agricultural feasts (holy convocations) is necessary.

God instituted three agricultural feasts for Israel: the Feast of First-fruits (Lev. 23:9–14), the Feast of Harvest (Ex. 23:16, 34:22; Lev. 23:15–22; Num. 28:26), and the Feast of Ingathering (Ex. 23:16, 34:22; Lev. 23:33–44). The Feast of Firstfruits was to be observed on the second day of the Feast of Unleavened Bread. It was held in the early spring and was to be a time of gratitude for God's provision. Before they ate of the harvest, the Jews were to bring a sheaf (2 quarts) of their grain harvest to the priest to be offered to God (Lev. 23:14). This feast was fulfilled at Christ's resurrection (1 Cor. 15:20–23) and provides assurance to believers of their resurrection at Christ's Second Coming.

The Feast of Harvest coincides with the Feast of Weeks (Pentecost), and the Jews were again to bring a grain offering, this time of the first-fruits of the wheat harvest (Ex. 34:22). This was the day on which Christ established his church. Some 3,000 Jews came to Christianity (Acts 2:41) after the Holy Spirit descended on the disciples and Peter preached the gospel.

The Feast of Ingathering coincides with the Feast of Tabernacles (Lev. 23:33–44) and occurs at the end of the harvest season. Once again, the Jews were instructed to make offerings to God.

I believe that what we see in Revelation 14 is the spiritual representation of these latter two agricultural feasts. The chapter opens with the Feast of Harvest and closes with the Feast of Ingathering. They are separated by messages given by three angels, a statement of how true believers will persevere in the faith during the great tribulation, and a blessing pronounced on believers who die in Christ.

Christian Firstfruits

> [1]And I looked, and, lo, a Lamb stood on the mount Sion, and with him an hundred forty and four thousand, having his Father's name written in their foreheads. [2]And I heard a voice from heaven, as the voice of many waters, and as the voice of a great thunder: and I heard the voice of harpers harping with their harps: [3]And they sung as it were a new song before the throne, and before the four beasts, and the elders: and no man could learn that song but the hundred and forty and four thousand, which were redeemed from the earth. [4]These are they which were not defiled with women; for they are virgins. These are they which follow the Lamb whithersoever he goeth. These were redeemed from among men, being the firstfruits unto God and to the Lamb. [5]And in their mouth was found no guile: for they are without fault before the throne of God. (Rev. 14:1–5)

John describes a company of 144,000 standing with Jesus on Mount Zion (v. 1). This is a spiritual Zion since the scene is taking place before the throne in heaven (v. 3). These 144,000 were redeemed from the earth (vv. 3, 4), being the souls of Christians since redemption can only be in Jesus Christ. This is confirmed since they were faultless before God (v. 5). The only way that is possible is by belief in Christ. Verse 4 tells us that they lived exemplary Christian lives ("not defiled with women") and followed Jesus ("the Lamb") at all times. Not defiled with women points to these being men. One final point, they have the Father's name written in their foreheads, speaking of them belonging to God. Each of these points identifies them as being a different group from those in Revelation 7:1–8.

The earlier group was comprised of Jews, they were sealed for preservation with a seal of God, not his name, and they were presum-ably both men and women. The 144,000 Jews will be alive on earth throughout the Seventieth Week, protected through the great tribula-tion, and enter into the millennial kingdom in their natural bodies. The 144,000 of Revelation 14 have lived and died as Christians, are now with the Lord in heaven as souls, and will be offered as a firstfruits of the entire church age in anticipation of the final harvest. The most reasonable placement of this event within the Seventieth Week would be at its beginning.

Since this group in Revelation 14 is described as exemplary Chris-tians and have been given a special position before God, to be able to sing a song that no one else could learn (v. 3), I believe that God has chosen the most devoted Christians of the entire church age to be in this group. And just as the Jews were to offer the best of their harvest at the Feast of Firstfruits and the Feast of Harvest, so will God do by offering these Christians as a firstfruits to himself and Jesus: "Being the firstfruits unto God and to the Lamb" (v. 4). The agricultural feasts of Israel were not only a picture of gratitude, they were also a picture of faith that the eventual harvest would be abundant. This seems to be exactly what this firstfruits offering is pointing to, the abundant harvest at the end of the great tribulation, which is shown symbolically at the end of Revelation 14.

Paul spoke of the Feast of Firstfruits being fulfilled at Christ's resurrection (1 Cor. 15:20). It may be said that the Feast of Harvest

(Pentecost/firstfruits of the wheat harvest) was initially fulfilled by the establishment of the church, and finally, at this firstfruits offering of souls. The salvation plan that is pictured in the Jewish agricultural feasts will be completed at the end of the Seventieth Week. The seed was planted at Pentecost, the firstfruits of the church age offered at the beginning of the Seventieth Week, and the harvest at the end—Christ's Second Coming.

Messages of Angels

> ⁶And I saw another angel fly in the midst of heaven, having the everlasting gospel to preach unto them that dwell on the earth, and to every nation, and kindred, and tongue, and people, ⁷Saying with a loud voice, Fear God, and give glory to him; for the hour of his judgment is come: and worship him that made heaven, and earth, and the sea, and the fountains of waters. ⁸And there followed another angel, saying, Babylon is fallen, is fallen, that great city, because she made all nations drink of the wine of the wrath of her fornication. ⁹And the third angel followed them, saying with a loud voice, If any man worship the beast and his image, and receive his mark in his forehead, or in his hand, ¹⁰The same shall drink of the wine of the wrath of God, which is poured out without mixture into the cup of his indignation; and he shall be tormented with fire and brimstone in the presence of the holy angels, and in the presence of the Lamb: ¹¹And the smoke of their torment ascendeth up for ever and ever: and they have no rest day nor night, who worship the beast and his image, and whosoever receiveth the mark of his name. (Rev. 14:6–11)

The vision continues with three angels delivering specific messages to all of the world (vv. 6–11). The first preaches the gospel to all the world, the second announces the fall of Babylon, and the third announces the consequence of taking the mark of the beast and worshipping the beast—eternal damnation. Considering the highly symbolic presentation of this vision, beginning with the firstfruits imagery and ending with the harvest imagery, I think it would be incorrect to consider these messages to be any less symbolic. Consequently, I do not expect an actual angel to be the one who preaches the gospel to the entire world (c.f. Matt. 24:14) or announces the other messages either. How these messages will be delivered to all of humanity is open to speculation. However, one thing is certain; God will make sure that everyone gets the news and, therefore, will be without excuse at Christ's Second Coming. I do think it is quite reasonable to assume that these messages will get out to everyone through the preaching of the two witnesses and other believers during the great tribulation (Rev. 12:11).

The first message is the gospel of salvation through Jesus Christ alone, combined with an exhortation to fear and worship the true God of heaven, creator of everything. Again, we see the use of the fourfold reference to the people of the world (v. 6) and to all of creation as well (v. 7), signifying that all will hear the gospel message and that God is the creator of the universe. There will most certainly be some other gospel preached by the Antichrist and his church leader, the false prophet. Their gospel, and signs confirming it, will be convincing enough for many to follow them instead of the true God. The exhortation to worship the true God contains the warning that the hour of his judgment is at hand.

The second angel makes a twofold reference to the fall of Babylon (v. 8). The name Babylon is used in a symbolic, spiritual sense, much like the names Sodom and Egypt were used to refer to Jerusalem (Rev. 11:8). It speaks of all rebellion against God and all false and idolatrous worship. We are given a little hint that the name Babylon will be used to convey multiple meanings by it being called "that great city" and also referred to with the feminine personal pronoun "she." Her activities have justified God's wrath upon all nations; what she is guilty of is fornication. The fornication is spiritual, and the mysteries of these statements, along with an explanation of the twofold reference to her fall will be fully explained in Revelation 17 and 18. What we will learn later is that Babylon is referring to an idolatrous world religious system as well as a worldwide spiritual state which encompasses all false worship and material idolatry.

The third angel presents a very ominous message to those who take the mark of the beast and worship him (vv. 9–11)—there will be no avoiding the wrath of God. And if anyone thinks that this wrath will be limited to physical punishment on earth, it is clearly stated that it will be eternal torment in the lake of fire (vv. 10–11). The most devastating part of this message is that there seems to be no way to escape this outcome once an individual has taken the mark, making this an unforgivable sin. This speaks of the horrendous blasphemies that one will be agreeing to by taking the mark of the beast and accepting the Antichrist's "gospel" message. Even participation in the idolatrous Babylon religious system can be forgiven (Rev. 18:4), but not this.

Blessings for Believers

> [12]Here is the patience of the saints: here are they that keep the commandments of God, and the faith of Jesus. [13]And I heard a voice from heaven saying unto me, Write, Blessed are the dead which die in the Lord from henceforth: Yea, saith the Spirit, that they may rest from their labours; and their works do follow them. (Rev. 14:12–13)

Each of the previous two interludes contains a message of how believers will make it through the great tribulation—by their enduring faith. In Revelation 12, believers were said to overcome by their faith and testimony, and hold to these, even at the cost of their lives (Rev. 12:11). In Revelation 13, the enduring faith of believers was juxtaposed against the activities of false prophets and the lawless (Rev. 13:10). In Revelation 14, believers are identified as those who "keep the commandments of God, and the faith of Jesus." Once again, their enduring faith is referred to as "patience," and a blessing has now been pronounced upon those who die for their faith. These are all references to Christians in the great tribulation and teach of the circumstances that believers will face in the not-too-distant future. The success of the mystery of iniquity is evidenced by the fact that virtually no churches are preparing their congregants for these coming times.

The Harvest

> [14]And I looked, and behold a white cloud, and upon the cloud one sat like unto the Son of man, having on his head a golden crown, and in his hand a sharp sickle. [15]And another angel came out of the temple, crying with a loud voice to him that sat on the cloud, Thrust in thy sickle, and reap: for the time is come for thee to reap; for the harvest

> of the earth is ripe. [16]And he that sat on the cloud thrust in his sickle on the earth; and the earth was reaped. [17]And another angel came out of the temple which is in heaven, he also having a sharp sickle. [18]And another angel came out from the altar, which had power over fire; and cried with a loud cry to him that had the sharp sickle, saying, Thrust in thy sharp sickle, and gather the clusters of the vine of the earth; for her grapes are fully ripe. [19]And the angel thrust in his sickle into the earth, and gathered the vine of the earth, and cast it into the great winepress of the wrath of God. [20]And the winepress was trodden without the city, and blood came out of the winepress, even unto the horse bridles, by the space of a thousand and six hundred furlongs. (Rev. 14:14–20)

The final part of this vision was presented to John through harvest imagery. This is a symbolic representation of what will be occurring at Christ's Second Coming. On earth, this will be the conclusion of God's redemptive plan that was pictured in the three Jewish agricultural feasts. This will be the "harvest" at the end of the season (church age) and the fulfillment of the Feast of Ingathering.

The imagery presented here closely follows, in both form and substance, the parables of Christ. This is the same message as that presented in the parables of the wheat and tares (Matt. 13:24–30), the fishing net (Matt. 13:47–50), and the sheep and goats (Matt. 25:31–46). That message is that the good (those in Christ) will be separated from the bad (unbelievers).

As presented earlier, this separation of believers from unbelievers will occur in two stages. The first, at the end of this world, is when believers will be given their immortal bodies and unbelievers will experience the final vial of God's wrath (Rev. 16) and the wrath of the Lamb—the Day of the Lord. The second, at the end of the millennial kingdom, is when unbelievers will experience the second death—be thrown into the lake of fire (Rev. 20:15).

There are two important messages contained in this vision. First, there are two reapers. The first of whom is Christ ("the Son of Man"), shown coming in the clouds (vv. 14–16; c.f. Dan. 7:13; Acts 1:11), and the second is an angel (vv. 17–20). Christ is shown to reap those that are his, and the angel to reap the unbelievers. The second message is that there is no separation in time between the harvest of these two groups. The consistent message is that believers and unbelievers will be together on earth until the Day of the Lord, at which time they will be separated (c.f. Matt. 13:30).

This vision uses winepress imagery (vv. 19–20) to represent God's destructive wrath. I believe that because of its highly symbolic nature, we are not being given a literal teaching of the amount of bloodshed (v. 20) but rather are being told that his wrath will be overwhelming.

13

The Wrath of God

Revelation 15 opens with another vision. In v. 1, we are introduced to seven angels who have the seven final judgments, described as the "wrath of God." We must distinguish between these judgments and the Day of the Lord, the "wrath of the Lamb" (Rev. 6:16). During the great tribulation, both Jesus and the Father will be rendering judgments, which are identified as being distinctly separate. Christ's wrath will all be poured out on the last day after the resurrection of the dead and rapture of living believers (Rev. 19). God's wrath will be poured out over some period of time during the great tribulation. The precise starting point for God's wrath is not specified; however, the endpoint —the seventh vial—is on the Day of the Lord and coincides with the seventh seal and seventh trumpet.

Preparations in Heaven

> [1]And I saw another sign in heaven, great and marvellous, seven angels having the seven last plagues; for in them is filled up the wrath of God. [2]And I saw as it were a sea of glass mingled with fire: and them that had gotten the victory over the beast, and over his image, and over his mark, and over the number of his name, stand on the sea of glass, having the harps of God. [3]And they sing the song of Moses the servant of God, and the song of the Lamb, saying, Great and marvellous are thy works, Lord God Almighty; just and true are thy ways, thou King of saints. [4]Who shall not fear thee, O Lord, and glorify thy name? for thou only art holy: for all nations shall come and worship before thee;

for thy judgments are made manifest. ⁵And after that I looked, and, behold, the temple of the tabernacle of the testimony in heaven was opened: ⁶And the seven angels came out of the temple, having the seven plagues, clothed in pure and white linen, and having their breasts girded with golden girdles. ⁷And one of the four beasts gave unto the seven angels seven golden vials full of the wrath of God, who liveth for ever and ever. ⁸And the temple was filled with smoke from the glory of God, and from his power; and no man was able to enter into the temple, till the seven plagues of the seven angels were fulfilled. (Rev. 15:1–8)

After being introduced to the seven angels, we are told of believers in heaven who have gotten victory over the beast (v. 2). Here we see those who kept "the commandments of God, and the faith of Jesus" (Rev. 14:12). There is a beautiful scene of singing and praise (v. 3), and these believers pronounce that all nations (everyone on earth) will worship before the Lord Jesus and that his judgments will be "made manifest"—evident to all (v. 4). These believers died "in the Lord" and have now been given the rest that was promised to them (Rev. 14:13).

Following this, John saw the final preparations in heaven for the pouring out of God's wrath on unbelievers (vv. 5–8). The temple in heaven was opened, and each of the seven angels was given a vial filled with one of God's judgments—"the wrath of God" (v. 7). We are also given the timing reference for the earliest possible time that a man can enter into the temple (v. 8; c.f. Rev. 7:15), after the seventh vial judgment—the end of the great tribulation.

The Vial Judgments

¹And I heard a great voice out of the temple saying to the seven angels, Go your ways, and pour out the vials of the wrath of God upon the earth. ²And the first went, and poured out his vial upon the earth; and there fell a noisome and grievous sore upon the men which had the mark of the beast, and upon them which worshipped his image. ³And the second angel poured out his vial upon the sea; and it became as the blood of a dead man: and every living soul died in the sea. ⁴And the third angel poured out his vial

upon the rivers and fountains of waters; and they became blood. (Rev. 16:1–4)

God's wrath consists of seven judgments, which are symbolically depicted as being contained in vials that are poured out on the earth by angels. The first vial will result in a sore developing on those who have taken the mark of the beast and worship his image. This is much like the sixth judgment that God put on Egypt during the days of Moses (Ex. 9:8–11). This sore will selectively target unbelievers (v. 2), just as the judgment in Egypt targeted only Egyptians (Ex. 9:11). This also gives us a timing reference for when these judgments will begin— during the great tribulation. This is because it will be a judgment on those who have taken the mark of the beast and worship his image, events which will only be possible after the abomination of desolation.

The second and third vials will cause the oceans and fresh waters to be turned to blood (vv. 3–4). These are different judgments from the second and third trumpets (Rev. 8:8–11) since those only affected one-third of the oceans and fresh waters. These will affect them all and must therefore occur at some time after the second and third trumpets. This is very much like the first of God's judgments performed in Egypt by the hand of Moses (Ex. 7:19–25).

> [5]And I heard the angel of the waters say, Thou art righteous, O Lord, which art, and wast, and shalt be, because thou hast judged thus. [6]For they have shed the blood of saints and prophets, and thou hast given them blood to drink; for they are worthy. [7]And I heard another out of the altar say, Even so, Lord God Almighty, true and righteous are thy judgments. (Rev. 16:5–7)

Verses 5–7 show two angels proclaiming God's judgments to be righteous. Under the fifth seal (Rev. 6:11), martyred saints in heaven were told to wait until this time for their deaths to be avenged.

> [8]And the fourth angel poured out his vial upon the sun; and power was given unto him to scorch men with fire. [9]And men were scorched with great heat, and blasphemed the name of God, which hath power over these plagues: and they repented not to give him glory. [10]And the fifth angel poured out his vial upon the seat of the beast; and his

> kingdom was full of darkness; and they gnawed their
> tongues for pain, [11]And blasphemed the God of heaven
> because of their pains and their sores, and repented not of
> their deeds. (Rev. 16:8–11)

The fourth and fifth vials will result in a period of scorching heat from the sun, followed by a period of darkness that will come over the Antichrist's seat of government (vv. 8–11). God previously used darkness during the time of Moses as the ninth judgment on Egypt (Ex. 10:21–23). That judgment did not affect the Jews (Ex. 10:23), and I see no reason to believe that God will not provide the same kind of protection to his people (believers and the faithful remnant of Israel) during these great tribulation judgments. Also, under these judgments, we see that followers of the Antichrist will be blaspheming God and unwilling to repent (vv. 9, 11), just as they were under the judgments rendered by demons (Rev. 9:20–21).

> [12]And the sixth angel poured out his vial upon the great
> river Euphrates; and the water thereof was dried up, that the
> way of the kings of the east might be prepared. [13]And I saw
> three unclean spirits like frogs come out of the mouth of
> the dragon, and out of the mouth of the beast, and out of
> the mouth of the false prophet. [14]For they are the spirits of
> devils, working miracles, which go forth unto the kings of
> the earth and of the whole world, to gather them to the
> battle of that great day of God Almighty. (Rev. 16:12–14)

The sixth vial prepares the way for the nations of the east (China, North Korea, India) to mount a ground offensive against Jerusalem (v. 12; c.f. Zech. 12:2–3; 8–10; 14:1–4) by drying up the Euphrates River. John also saw three demon spirits, which appeared like frogs, come out of the mouths of Satan, the Antichrist, and the false prophet (v. 13). These spirits will work some sorts of signs and wonders ("miracles") and cause all the nations of the world to come against Israel and Jerusalem (v. 14; c.f. Joel. 3:2; Zech. 14:2). God used frogs in the second judgment on Egypt (Ex. 8:5), and here we see them being used to gather the armies of the world to Israel.

> [15]Behold, I come as a thief. Blessed is he that watcheth, and
> keepeth his garments, lest he walk naked, and they see his

shame. [16]And he gathered them together into a place called in the Hebrew tongue Armageddon. [17]And the seventh angel poured out his vial into the air; and there came a great voice out of the temple of heaven, from the throne, saying, It is done. (Rev. 16:15–17)

Just as in the seal and trumpet judgments, there is a parenthesis between the sixth and seventh vials. This one is very short and directed at believers. It can be summarized by the statement "watch and be wakeful." The Lord restates that his coming will be unexpected—"like a thief" (c.f. 1 Thess. 5:2; 2 Pet. 3:10)—and pronounces a blessing on those who watch for the signs that will precede his return (c.f. Matt. 24:32–33; 42–43) and remain in a state of spiritual preparedness (c.f. Matt. 24:44). This is what the figurative language of v. 15 means.

Verse 16 returns to the three demon spirits and informs us that they will gather all the armies of the world to Mount Megiddo ("Armageddon," Hebrew: Har-Megiddon) for the final battle of "that great day of God Almighty" (v. 14)—the Day of the Lord. This is where the phrase "battle of Armageddon" comes from. These armies will be destroyed by the Lord at his Second Coming (Rev. 19:11–21). The seventh angel poured out his vial and John heard the voice of God announce, "It is done" (v. 17).

> [18]And there were voices, and thunders, and lightnings; and there was a great earthquake, such as was not since men were upon the earth, so mighty an earthquake, and so great. [19]And the great city was divided into three parts, and the cities of the nations fell: and great Babylon came in remembrance before God, to give unto her the cup of the wine of the fierceness of his wrath. [20]And every island fled away, and the mountains were not found. [21]And there fell upon men a great hail out of heaven, every stone about the weight of a talent: and men blasphemed God because of the plague of the hail; for the plague thereof was exceeding great. (Rev. 16:18–21)

The plagues of Egypt were God's judgments upon the gods of Egypt (Ex. 12:12). In these vials, we see very similar judgments being poured out on the unbelievers and blasphemers of the great tribulation. The final vial (vv. 18–21) is the culmination of these judgments and will unleash an unparalleled barrage of destruction upon mankind and the world. This vial will release thunder, lightning, voices, an earthquake, and a great hail. This is the same fivefold event shown at the end of the seal and trumpet judgments.

This final judgment of God will destroy all the cities of the world (v. 19), and the earthquake will be so intense that all the mountains fall and islands disappear (v. 20). The hailstones are described as weighing 100 pounds ("a talent"), and men will still be blaspheming God (v. 21). The great city (v. 19) is Jerusalem, and the earthquake will divide it into three parts (c.f. Zech. 14:4). This is when the Lord Jesus will step foot on the Mount of Olives and save his people from the armies arrayed against Jerusalem (c.f. Zech. 14:3–4).

We also see the second reference to Babylon in Revelation. The important message to take from this passage is that she came into "remembrance" to God (v. 19). The mystery of "Babylon the Great" will be revealed in the next chapter of Revelation. We will find out that this religious system will be destroyed by the ten rulers of political Rome at the midpoint of the Seventieth Week. From that time forward, all political, governmental, economic, and religious control will be under the Antichrist. At the end of the great tribulation, when the seventh vial is poured out, God will "remember" the abominations of Babylon and purge all remaining remnants of this system from the earth.

Concluding Thoughts

The great tribulation will be a worldwide judgment of God upon humanity, and Israel will play a central role in all of the events. In Revelation, we learn that the little horn role of Daniel 7 will be filled by two men, the Antichrist and the false prophet. By virtue of the satanically empowered signs and wonders, they will deceive the vast majority into believing that the Antichrist is God on earth.

To oppose their lies and coercive measures, God will raise two prophets, who will profess the gospel of Jesus Christ and work God-empowered miracles to confirm their message as well as render judgments on those who oppose them. This will be yet another battle that will be raging during the great tribulation, in addition to all of the other judgments.

The events that are described in God's prophecies will most certainly take place. However, some of the motivations that will be the driving forces behind these events are not clearly stated. For instance, the Antichrist will make his final seat of power in Jerusalem, but by the end of the great tribulation, he will have all the armies of the world united in an effort to destroy the city and her people.

We know that he will be successful in demonizing the two prophets since all the world will celebrate their deaths (Rev. 11:7–10). I suspect that the three demon spirits that John saw leaving from the mouths of Satan, the Antichrist, and the false prophet may well deceive people into thinking that Jerusalem and the Jews must be destroyed for the torments to stop or that the Antichrist's "gospel" promises (whatever they may be) can't be realized until these people and city are wiped off the face of the earth.

Either way, we know that Satan is behind these deceptions and that his goal is to persecute and destroy Christians and Jews since he knows his time is limited after being thrown out of heaven (Rev. 12:15–17). We also know that it is Jesus Christ whom the Antichrist and the other nations of the great tribulation are ultimately at war with (Rev. 17:14; 19:19). In the end, the deceptions will work, all the world will get united behind the idea of destroying the Jews and Israel, and God will use this final indignation on his people, the Jews, to save them and turn them to the Lord.

14

Babylon the Great

Revelation 17 and 18 present us with one of the most interesting interpretive challenges in the Bible. John describes a new vision in which he saw a woman riding a beast. The beast is ten-horned, future Rome, introduced to us in Daniel 7 and further described in Revelation 13. In Revelation 13, we understood the beast to represent future Rome, the Antichrist, as well as the Antichrist kingdom—the global political, governmental, economic, and religious system. The beast of Revelation 17 is the same beast, with the exception of having its religious component presented separately from the other components of the empire. This religious component is given the name "Babylon the Great," which is a symbolic name intended to teach us the spiritual character of this aspect of Rome. This image of a woman on the beast shows that political/governmental Rome will rise in the form of the ten-king empire prophesied in Daniel and reunite with its religious arm —the woman. All aspects of Rome will once again be present on earth as a worldwide empire.

Further, Babylon the Great is presented to us as both a woman (vv. 3–5) and a city (v. 18). The woman is a symbolic image, and the city presents both a literal and a figurative meaning. This is done because there is more to Babylon the Great than can be presented in just the woman symbol. To convey his full message, God uses figurative references to a city as well. The important thing to keep in mind is that the references to a woman and a city in Revelation 17 and 18 are all speaking of this one part of Rome—Babylon the Great.

The Woman

> [1]And there came one of the seven angels which had the seven vials, and talked with me, saying unto me, Come hither; I will shew unto thee the judgment of the great whore that sitteth upon many waters: [2]With whom the kings of the earth have committed fornication, and the inhabitants of the earth have been made drunk with the wine of her fornication. [3]So he carried me away in the spirit into the wilderness: and I saw a woman sit upon a scarlet coloured beast, full of names of blasphemy, having seven heads and ten horns. [4]And the woman was arrayed in purple and scarlet colour, and decked with gold and precious stones and pearls, having a golden cup in her hand full of abominations and filthiness of her fornication: [5]And upon her forehead was a name written, MYSTERY, BABYLON THE GREAT, THE MOTHER OF HARLOTS AND ABOMINATIONS OF THE EARTH. [6]And I saw the woman drunken with the blood of the saints, and with the blood of the martyrs of Jesus: and when I saw her, I wondered with great admiration. [7]And the angel said unto me, Wherefore didst thou marvel? I will tell thee the mystery of the woman, and of the beast that carrieth her, which hath the seven heads and ten horns. (Rev. 17:1–7)

One of the seven angels informed John that he will tell him the judgment of the "great whore" who sits upon "many waters" (v. 1). The "whore" reference is the same kind of language that God used to describe Israel when they would chase after other gods (Deut. 31:16; Judg. 2:17; Num. 25:1–3; 2 Chron. 21:13), and it refers to spiritual whoredom. What Israel did to earn this condemnation was to "mingle" with the surrounding nations and adopt their idolatrous worship practices. Further, God spoke of Israel as an unfaithful wife (Ezek. 16), and the book of Hosea portrays this through the allegory of Hosea's marriage. The significance of this is that Israel had a professed relationship with God but played the harlot with all of the neighboring pagan deities. To apply these analogies to the whore on the beast, one would say that she professes Christianity while engaging in spiritual harlotry.

Her harlotry is described as fornication (v. 2). Again, this is to be understood in the spiritual sense. The picture it conveys is unfaithfulness to God. Israel's whoredoms spoke of her engaging in the abominations of neighboring nations, pagan practices, and idol worship. This harlot's fornications should be understood to mean the same sorts of abominations. Her fornication is figuratively depicted as wine, with which she has intoxicated the citizenry of the world (v. 2). The reference to the whore sitting on "many waters" (v. 1) points to her influence over many nations. Later, it will be explained as meaning all the peoples of the world (v. 15). This means that people all over the world have believed her lies and engaged in her blasphemous worship.

Her harlotry is not limited to the spiritual, however. The "fornication" with kings (political leaders) speaks of yet another form of religious impurity, mingling religion with politics and exerting dominion and control over governments of the world. Later, we will see that she reigns over the "kings of the earth" (v. 18).

After this brief interpretation, the angel showed John a vision of the woman (v. 3). At this point we are given symbolic imagery to add to what we have been told in the first two verses. The symbol of a woman points to a religious system, just as we saw previously used in Revelation 12 to refer to Israel. Verses 4–5 continue to describe the woman, both visually and with a title on her forehead. Her idolatry is twofold. She is shown in costly apparel and precious stones, pointing to material idolatry, and the golden cup in her hand is full of the "abominations and filthiness of her fornication," pointing to spiritual idolatry (v. 4).

Her title is Babylon the Great, and it is preceded by "Mystery" (v. 5). When we see "mystery" in the Bible, it indicates that God is revealing something that has previously been hidden. Further, the name Babylon must be understood in the spiritual sense, just as when Jerusalem was referred to spiritually as Sodom and Egypt (Rev. 11:8). Babylon was known for its rebellion against God (Gen. 11:1–9) and is considered to be the birthplace of all idolatrous worship under Nimrod. The Babylon reference and woman symbol point to a rebellious, idolatrous religious system. Combined with the rest of the title, "Mother of Harlots and Abominations of the Earth," indicates that she is the first ("mother") of many other harlots.

Following this, we are told of some of her exploits. She is drunk with the blood of saints and martyrs (v. 6). This points to her perse-cuting and killing true believers in Christ. Later, in v. 9, we are told that she is seated (located) on seven "mountains." Historically, Rome has been known as the city on seven hills.[1] Further, commentators generally agree that Peter used the spiritual name "Babylon" as a refer-ence to Rome when he closed his first epistle (1 Pet. 5:13).[2] All of the attributes presented thus far, including persecuting and killing true believers in Christ,[3] ruling over the governments of the world,[4] and committing spiritual harlotry,[5] when combined, point to this woman on the beast being the Roman Catholic Church.[6]

There is a noteworthy relationship between the harlot and the beast that she is riding as well. She is seen as seated on the beast (v. 3), which presents the image of her directing and guiding the beast. She is also said to be carried by the beast (v. 7), which presents the image of her being supported by the beast. There is a mutually beneficial rela-tionship expressed in this, where each advances and furthers the agenda of the other, with the ultimate endpoint being the rise of the Antichrist to world domination. God will allow this relationship to continue until it is no longer needed.

The Beast

[8]The beast that thou sawest was, and is not; and shall ascend out of the bottomless pit, and go into perdition: and they that dwell on the earth shall wonder, whose names were not written in the book of life from the foundation of the world, when they behold the beast that was, and is not, and yet is. [9]And here is the mind which hath wisdom. The seven heads are seven mountains, on which the woman sitteth. [10]And there are seven kings: five are fallen, and one is, and the other is not yet come; and when he cometh, he must

---

1   Hislop, *Two Babylons*, 3, Introduction.
2   Longman, *Expositor's Bible Commentary*, vol. 13, p. 356; Wenham, *New Bible Commentary*, 1370.
3   Hunt, *Woman Rides the Beast*, 243–262.
4   Hunt, *Woman Rides the Beast*, 229–241.
5   McCarthy, *Gospel According to Rome*.
6   Hunt, *Woman Rides the Beast*, 67–85.

continue a short space. [11]And the beast that was, and is not, even he is the eighth, and is of the seven, and goeth into perdition. (Rev. 17:8–11)

Just as in Daniel, this prophecy consists of a vision (vv. 3–6), followed by the interpretation by an angel (vv. 7–18). The description of the beast began in v. 3 and resumes in v. 8. In v. 3, the color of the beast was added to the description that we were given in Revelation 13. Scarlet (v. 3) is red and presents the image of bloodshed. We have determined that the beast can refer to future Rome, the Antichrist, or the Antichrist kingdom. It is up to us to determine which is being discussed based on the context presented. As discussed in the earlier study on the Antichrist, v. 8 is referring to the "resurrection event" of the Antichrist, which will occur at the midpoint of the Seventieth Week. In this case, the "beast" is referring to the man—the Antichrist.

The seven heads have a dual meaning (v. 9). The first, which we have already considered, is that the "seven mountains" are a reference to the seven hills of Rome, meaning that the harlot is seated (located) in Rome. The second meaning is that there are "seven kings," the number of kingdoms that the beast represents. The angel informed John that five are in the past for him, one currently rules, and one is yet to come (v. 10). After that seventh kingdom, there will be an eighth, who will be the Antichrist—the beast (v. 11). This indicates that the kingdoms follow one another, and since we will later see that the ten concurrent leaders of future Rome are represented by the horns, the most plausible explanation for the "seven kings" is seven consecutive kingdoms. Remember that king and kingdom are used interchangeably (Dan. 7:17, 23).

Daniel's prophecies told us of four of these consecutive kingdoms: Babylon, Medo-Persia, Greece, and Rome. At the time of John's writing of Revelation, the ruling empire was Rome. This makes Rome the sixth kingdom since the angel specified that the ruling kingdom at that time was the sixth (v. 10). Since there were two kingdoms that oppressed Israel before Daniel's prophecies, it is reasonable to conclude that they were left out of the list for Daniel but are included here. Those two were Egypt and Assyria. This means that the first six of John's kingdoms are Egypt, Assyria, Babylon, Medo-Persia, Greece, and Rome.

We must also remember that future, ten-king Rome was considered to be part of Daniel's fourth kingdom. So, the sixth kingdom in John's list includes both historic Rome and future Rome. We also know that the eighth is the Antichrist from the pit (v. 11). All that remains to determine is the identity of the seventh kingdom. Of this kingdom, the angel said, "And the other is not yet come; and when he cometh, he must continue a short space" (v. 10). This identifies the seventh kingdom as being short-lived and places it between future, ten-king Rome and the Antichrist. There is only one possibility for this kingdom, and it is spelled out in the next passage of prophecy:

> 12And the ten horns which thou sawest are ten kings, which have received no kingdom as yet; but receive power as kings one hour with the beast. 13These have one mind, and shall give their power and strength unto the beast. 14These shall make war with the Lamb, and the Lamb shall overcome them: for he is Lord of lords, and King of kings: and they that are with him are called, and chosen, and faithful. (Rev. 17:12–14)

Here we see future, ten-king Rome (v. 12), and the angel told John that they have not yet received their kingdom as of the time of his writing. Neither have they received it yet, but we know they will rise as a world power at some time in the future and reunite with religious Rome. This will be the future manifestation of Daniel's fourth and John's sixth kingdom. Remember from Daniel that the Antichrist will arise after these ten kings come to power (Dan. 7:20, 24). Thus, the seventh kingdom will be these ten, plus the Antichrist: "But receive power as kings one hour with the beast" (v. 12). This coalition of the ten plus the Antichrist will reign as the seventh kingdom for a "short space" (v. 10), "one hour" (v. 12). After this, the ten will collectively agree to give their power exclusively to the Antichrist (v. 13), who will then be the eighth of John's kingdoms (v. 11).

The important message here is that the seventh kingdom cannot arise until after the sixth comes to power. And since the sixth has not yet arisen, there is no way that the seventh has already come and gone. At the time of the writing of this book, the next event on the prophetic timeline, concerning these kingdoms, is the rise of future, ten-king Rome. Following that, the Antichrist will arise as an eleventh among them, they will rule the world for a short time in that configuration, and then power will be transferred exclusively to the Antichrist. At that point, his forty-two month reign on earth will begin (Dan. 7:25; 9:27; 12:7; Rev. 13:5).

Verse 14 contains two promises for believers. The first is that this global empire of evil will be at war with Christ. Implicit in this is the promise of persecution of Christians (c.f. Matt. 24:9; Rev. 12:17). The second is that there is only one Lord—Jesus Christ—and when he returns with his "called," "chosen," and "faithful" (glorified believers), he will be victorious.

The Woman Is That Great City

> ¹⁵And he saith unto me, The waters which thou sawest, where the whore sitteth, are peoples, and multitudes, and nations, and tongues. ¹⁶And the ten horns which thou sawest upon the beast, these shall hate the whore, and shall make her desolate and naked, and shall eat her flesh, and burn her with fire. ¹⁷For God hath put in their hearts to fulfil his will, and to agree, and give their kingdom unto the beast, until the words of God shall be fulfilled. ¹⁸And the woman which thou sawest is that great city, which reigneth over the kings of the earth. (Rev. 17:15–18)

Verse 15 provides additional details about the harlot. Previously (v. 9), we saw she was seated (figuratively speaking of her location) on seven "mountains" (Rome). Here, we also see that the "many waters" that she was described as being seated on (v. 1) is a reference to all the peoples of the world. This is speaking of the global influence of her harlotry, causing countless people of the world to be "drunk with the wine of her fornication" (v. 2). Referring back to v. 4, the harlot is shown holding a cup filled with the abominations of her fornication (spiritual idolatry) and is adorned in costly attire and jewelry (material idolatry). Her idolatry is twofold—spiritual and material—and her influence over the world encompasses both of these types of idolatry. The "drunkenness" that she has spread throughout the world consists of false worship and rebellion against God as well as an obsession with material possessions.

At verse 16, it becomes evident why, in this prophecy, God has chosen to separate the formal religious component of Rome from the rest of the empire. The ten political rulers will hate the harlot and fulfill God's will by destroying her (v. 17). That is what is meant by the figurative language "make her desolate and naked, and shall eat her flesh, and burn her with fire" (v. 16). This tells us that political/governmental Rome will destroy its religious arm—Roman Catholicism—and afterwards, hand the entire empire over to the Antichrist. He will be allowed to reign "until the words of God shall be fulfilled" (v. 17), until the "indignation be accomplished" (Dan. 11:36). Remember, the Antichrist will serve as God's chastening tool on humanity for the duration of God's indignation. When God's indignation has been fulfilled, the chastening tool will have served his purpose, and God will put an end to him and the great tribulation.

The timing of this "desolation" of the harlot can most reasonably be assumed to occur at the midpoint of the Seventieth Week—the abomination of desolation, the revelation of the Antichrist (2 Thess. 2:3). At that point, the formal religion of Roman Catholicism will no longer exist and Rome will be destroyed, "burn her with fire" (v. 16). In the lament for the harlot that follows (Rev. 18:9–24), we will see that the worldwide material idolatry that she has fostered will come to an end as well. It will be replaced by the mark of the beast—the Antichrist's economic system. During the great tribulation, there will only be one religion in the world, Antichrist worship, and all the other aspects of future Rome—namely, political, governmental, and economic will be under the Antichrist's control as well.

This harlot is also identified as "that great city" which rules over all the kings of the earth (v. 18). Rome and her popes have exerted dominion over world political powers for centuries; however, there are yet additional interpretations of this description of the harlot as a city. Any time we see something in the Bible that is said "to be" something that it literally is not, we have an indicator that God is presenting a figurative reference. That was the case with the seven stars and seven candlesticks in Revelation 1 and the two olive trees and two candlesticks in Revelation 11. Both were metaphorical descriptions of the subjects of those passages. The same applies here, and I believe it is proper to understand the "great city" of v. 18 as more than just the city of Rome. Up to this point, the name Babylon the Great has been used in the narrow sense, focused on Rome and the Church of Rome. The descriptions and lament that follow indicate that we should also consider a broader understanding of this term to include all false and idolatrous worship as well as all material idolatry.

God uses multiple types of figurative language throughout the Bible. A metonym is one of those figures of speech in which a word is used to mean something that it is associated with.[7] In the case of a city name being used as a metonym, it can refer to either the people of that city or the spiritual state of that city. Jesus used the names of the cities Chorazin and Bethsaida as a way of referring to the people of those cities: "Woe unto thee, Chorazin! woe unto thee, Bethsaida! for if the mighty works, which were done in you, had been done in Tyre and Sidon, they would have repented long ago in sackcloth and ashes" (Matt. 11:21). And previously, we saw the names Sodom and Egypt used to refer to the spiritual states associated with them (Rev. 11:8).

Symbolically, the woman, Babylon the harlot, speaks of the organized religious system. However, Babylon the city, speaks on multiple levels. The literal is a reference to Rome, the city. The figurative (metonym), on the first level, speaks of the people throughout the world who are engaged in false and idolatrous worship. On the second level, it speaks of the nature of the sin and idolatry—the worldwide spiritual state. We will see that the spiritual state of Babylon extends to all ungodly worship and religious idolatry, as well as material idolatry (Rev. 18:1–3). These figurative references to a "city" describe a people and a worldwide spiritual condition, which extends beyond the narrow focus on the Church of Rome presented throughout Revelation 17. From this point forward, the descriptions of Babylon blend together and alternate between the narrow focus (Rome) and the broad (all ungodliness and materialism).

When the ten political leaders of future Rome destroy the harlot and the literal city (Rome), the organized religious system will come to an end. However, the two figurative cities will still exist, the people and the spiritual state. With these distinctions, we can now understand the two destructions of Babylon that are spoken of. The first is the destruction of the "harlot"—the organized religious system. It will occur at

---

7   Zuck, *Basic Bible Interpretation*, 150.

the midpoint of the Seventieth Week and will be performed by the ten kings of future Rome (Rev. 17:16–17). The second is the destruction of the figurative cities—all remaining ungodly worship and idolatry and the people who engage in them. It will occur at the seventh vial, at the end of the great tribulation, and will be performed by God (Rev. 16:19). This is because the spiritual state of Babylon and the idolatry will still exist in the hearts of people (c.f. Ezek. 14:1–4) even after the destruction of Rome. Those who do not part with the idolatry of Babylon the Great will have God's judgment poured out on them in the form of a hundred-pound hailstone. As we proceed, it will now be necessary to determine which of the manifestations of Babylon the Great is being referred to in the lament that follows. But first, John tells us more about the two figurative cities.

> [1]And after these things I saw another angel come down from heaven, having great power; and the earth was lightened with his glory. [2]And he cried mightily with a strong voice, saying, Babylon the great is fallen, is fallen, and is become the habitation of devils, and the hold of every foul spirit, and a cage of every unclean and hateful bird. [3]For all nations have drunk of the wine of the wrath of her fornication, and the kings of the earth have committed fornication with her, and the merchants of the earth are waxed rich through the abundance of her delicacies. (Rev. 18:1–3)

John now saw another angel from heaven, whose glory lightened the entire earth (v. 1). In v. 2, we again see the twofold reference to the fall of Babylon the Great (c.f. Rev. 14:8; Isa. 21:9). Considerable debate surrounds the significance of this twofold reference, and there is no reason to become dogmatic over the meaning. There are two equally plausible interpretations of this statement. The first is simply a reference to the two demises of Babylon, the first at the midpoint of the Seventieth Week and the second at the seventh vial. The second interpretation looks at the placement of this twofold announcement and notes that it is preceded by the description of the physical destruction of Rome and Roman Catholicism (Rev. 17:16) and followed by a description of the all-encompassing extent of her spiritual fall. I think it is quite reasonable to infer that these are the two falls being spoken of, the physical destruction and the spiritual fall. This would make the angel's statement read as follows: "Babylon the Great is fallen (destroyed by the ten kings), is fallen (into absolute idolatry and rebellion against God)."

We are told that Rome's spiritual fall is absolute: "And is become the habitation of devils, and the hold of every foul spirit, and a cage of every unclean and hateful bird" (v. 2). This is figurative language which means that every possible kind of hideous and abominable practice and worship has found its way into Rome. How can this possibly be? considering that Rome professes herself to be the only true Christian church. The simple answer is religious syncretism. This is the process of amalgamating or fusing different systems of belief or religion into one. This is precisely what the Roman Catholic Church has been doing in its worldwide missionary efforts throughout history.[8] The process has been one of assimilating local pagan worship into its practices by purportedly "sanctifying" those practices. This was represented by the golden cup that she was holding, "full of abominations and filthiness of her fornication" (Rev. 17:4). Just as Israel was guilty of mingling with the pagan nations surrounding her and rightly deserving God's condemnation, so has the harlot Rome been guilty of this same kind of spiritual whoredom.

The description of the figurative city—the spiritual state—continues. All of the nations of the world "have drunk of the wine of the wrath of her fornication, and the kings of the earth have committed fornication with her" (v. 3). This is figurative language which speaks of the spiritual mingling that she has fostered and seduced the entire world with. As discussed earlier, the fornication is not limited to the spiritual either since she has been involved in the politics of the world (Rev. 17:18), as shown by her riding the beast (Rev. 17:3), and has led the world into material idolatry: "And the merchants of the earth are waxed rich through the abundance of her delicacies" (v. 3). This is represented by the costly attire, gold, precious stones, and pearls that she is wearing (Rev. 17:4).

This brief passage presents a picture of the spiritual state of Babylon, which speaks of all ungodly worship, religious idolatry, political meddling, and material idolatry. It is God's wrath that has been

---

8   Hislop, *Two Babylons*, 91–198, chaps. 3–6; Hunt, *Occult Invasion*, 407–431.

stirred up as a result of these abominations, and we will see that he will render judgment upon her for her iniquities (vv. 5–6). While this Babylon accurately describes the Church of Rome, it is not limited to only Rome. In addition, it also speaks of a worldwide condition of false worship and placing material gain above God, thus the reason for the broader understanding of Babylon the Great presented earlier. This broader "Babylon" will continue after the destruction of Rome by the ten kings and is what God's final vial of wrath will put an end to.

> [4]And I heard another voice from heaven, saying, Come out of her, my people, that ye be not partakers of her sins, and that ye receive not of her plagues. [5]For her sins have reached unto heaven, and God hath remembered her iniquities. [6]Reward her even as she rewarded you, and double unto her double according to her works: in the cup which she hath filled fill to her double. [7]How much she hath glorified herself, and lived deliciously, so much torment and sorrow give her: for she saith in her heart, I sit a queen, and am no widow, and shall see no sorrow. [8]Therefore shall her plagues come in one day, death, and mourning, and famine; and she shall be utterly burned with fire: for strong is the Lord God who judgeth her. (Rev. 18:4–8)

Next, we see the figurative city of Babylon—the people—being addressed (v. 4). After Rome is destroyed and the formal religion put to an end, those who have been partakers of the idolatries must now repent and leave those practices and convictions or be subject to the wrath of God at the seventh vial. She will come into "remembrance" of God (v. 5; c.f Rev. 16:19) and he will "reward her" (v. 6) for her sins. All of her self-glorification will be rewarded with torment (v. 7). Verse 8 speaks of her demise coming in one day. There will be two fulfill-ments of this demise. The first will be when Rome and Roman Catholi-cism are destroyed by the ten kings. The second will be when God pours out his wrath on all remaining vestiges of Babylon at the end of the Seventieth Week (Rev. 16:19). Each will occur in one day.

There is some good news in this passage for Catholics and all others of Babylon. God is addressing people in this figurative city as "my people" and imploring them to "come out" of it (v. 4). This means that those who heed this advice will be forgiven and not subject to his wrath at the end of this world or at the great white throne judgment. Unfortunately, it also makes it clear that God will not be mocked, and those who are unwilling to repent and part with the sins of Babylon will suffer God's wrath on the last day. What follows is a lament for the city:

> [9]And the kings of the earth, who have committed fornication and lived deliciously with her, shall bewail her, and lament for her, when they shall see the smoke of her burning, [10]Standing afar off for the fear of her torment, saying, Alas, alas, that great city Babylon, that mighty city! for in one hour is thy judgment come. [11]And the merchants of the earth shall weep and mourn over her; for no man buyeth their merchandise any more: [12]The merchandise of gold, and silver, and precious stones, and of pearls, and fine linen, and purple, and silk, and scarlet, and all thyine wood, and all manner vessels of ivory, and all manner vessels of most precious wood, and of brass, and iron, and marble, [13]And cinnamon, and odours, and ointments, and frankincense, and wine, and oil, and fine flour, and wheat, and beasts, and sheep, and horses, and chariots, and slaves, and souls of men. [14]And the fruits that thy soul lusted after are departed from thee, and all things which were dainty and goodly are departed from thee, and thou shalt find them no more at all. [15]The merchants of these things, which were made rich by her, shall stand afar off for the fear of her torment, weeping and wailing, [16]And saying, Alas, alas, that great city, that was clothed in fine linen, and purple, and scarlet, and decked with gold, and precious stones, and pearls! [17]For in one hour so great riches is come to nought. And every shipmaster, and all the company in ships, and sailors, and as many as trade by sea, stood afar off, [18]And cried when they saw the smoke of her burning, saying, What city is like unto this great city! [19]And they cast dust on their heads, and cried, weeping and wailing, saying, Alas, alas, that great city, wherein were made rich all that had ships in the sea by reason of her costliness! for in one hour is she made desolate. [20]Rejoice over her, thou heaven, and ye holy apostles and prophets; for God hath avenged you on her.

²¹And a mighty angel took up a stone like a great millstone, and cast it into the sea, saying, Thus with violence shall that great city Babylon be thrown down, and shall be found no more at all. ²²And the voice of harpers, and musicians, and of pipers, and trumpeters, shall be heard no more at all in thee; and no craftsman, of whatsoever craft he be, shall be found any more in thee; and the sound of a millstone shall be heard no more at all in thee; ²³And the light of a candle shall shine no more at all in thee; and the voice of the bridegroom and of the bride shall be heard no more at all in thee: for thy merchants were the great men of the earth; for by thy sorceries were all nations deceived. ²⁴And in her was found the blood of prophets, and of saints, and of all that were slain upon the earth. (Rev. 18:9–24)

There is an Old Testament parallel to this in the lament for the city of Tyre. Ezekiel prophesied the destruction of Tyre (Ezek. 26) and followed with a lament (Ezek. 27), which is very similar to the one here (Rev. 18:9–24). Also, there is a narrow definition of "kings" and a broad definition. The narrow (Rev. 17:12), refers to the ten kings of future Rome, the broad (Rev. 16:12, 14; 17:2, 18; 18:3, 9), refers to the many leaders of the nations of the world. It will be the ten kings of future Rome that conspire to destroy Rome; however, v. 9 shows the broad definition of kings, meaning the many kings of all the nations of the world, will mourn the loss of Babylon. Not only they, but the merchants of the world will join this lament as well. This is not only speaking of the destruction of Rome but of the entire worldwide "city" of spiritual and material idolatry. The way of life that has propped up the leaders of the world and made the businessmen wealthy will come to an end when the Antichrist consolidates all religious worship to himself (Rev. 13:4, 8, 15) and takes control of the economic systems of the world (Rev. 13:16–17). This lament also makes it evident that the material excess that has been a characteristic of Babylon will no longer exist under the Antichrist, mark of the beast, economic system.

There are four separate "demises" in sight in this brief passage. Roman Catholicism, the city of Rome, and global materialism will come to an end at the midpoint of the Seventieth Week. The final destruction of the remaining spiritual state of Babylon (religious and material) will occur at the seventh vial when God pours out his judgment on the people who still hold those idols in their hearts at that time.

This lament contains seven references to the "city" of Babylon and thirteen to "her." Throughout the passage, the woman is equated with the city, as we saw previously (Rev. 17:18). By doing this, there is a blending together of the destruction of the religious system with the destruction of the worldwide figurative cities. This means that there can be multiple interpretations of what is being spoken of at any point. In broad terms, it appears that vv. 9–20 have the destruction at the midpoint of the Seventieth Week in mind, and vv. 21–24 appear to jump ahead to the final destruction at the seventh vial. The lament also seems to alternate between the destruction of Catholicism and Rome (vv. 10, 16, 20, 24) and the end of global materialism (vv. 9, 11–15, 17–19, 21–23), with possibly both in mind in v. 18.

The only element of Babylon the Great that is not specifically lamented in this passage is the end of all false religions and worship. We know that the formal practice of these religions will come to an end at the midpoint of the Seventieth Week when the Antichrist makes the official religion of the world Antichrist worship and uses the death penalty to enforce it. However, these practices will remain in the hearts and minds of the people who have participated in them, thus the need for God's judgment at the seventh vial on those who fail to repent.

It appears that the Antichrist will amass enormous wealth for himself (Dan. 11:43). However, the economic system that he puts into place will be highly coercive for the people of the world, requiring a mark to even buy food. Material idolatry is clearly a characteristic of the harlot system, but it doesn't seem to be a part of the Antichrist system. His religious system will be equally coercive since all who do not worship his image will be put to death (Rev. 13:15).

Concluding Thoughts

In this vision, the woman is the primary symbol and was also said to be a city. The visual imagery and spiritual name—Babylon—associated with the woman teach us about her nature: drunken, murderous, idolatrous, and rebellious. Since she was equated with the city, it was said that in totality, what was being spoken of is a religious system, its

213

people, a global spiritual state consisting of all religious and material idolatry, as well as a literal city, Rome.

The all-encompassing ungodliness of Babylon the Great is juxtaposed against New Jerusalem in Revelation 21 and 22. We will see the same combination of symbolism (a woman—the bride) and figurative language (a city—New Jerusalem) used to represent God's holy religious system, its people, all godly worship, and a physical city in the new heaven and earth, making New Jerusalem the polar opposite of Babylon the Great.

We are told nothing more about the Antichrist killing three of the ten kings of future Rome in these chapters (c.f. Dan. 7:8, 20, 24). We are, however, told that ten will hand the kingdom over to him. It appears that the killing of the three must occur after that, sometime during the great tribulation.

At this point in our studies, we have identified all of the factors that result in the final rise of the Antichrist. They are unbelieving Israel, Roman Catholicism, worldwide Babylon, the apostate church, the world system, future political/governmental Rome, the false prophet, and Satan.

15

The End of This World

Up to this point in the book of Revelation, we have been prophetically brought up to the Day of the Lord on seven occasions. Each of the series of seven judgments (seals, trumpets, vials) concludes with a different picture of the events on that day. The parenthetical sections between the sixth and seventh seals and trumpets showed us the glorified tribulation church in heaven after the Day of the Lord (Rev. 7:9–17) and the resurrection of the two great tribulation witnesses on that day (Rev. 11:12–13). The Day of the Lord was symbolically shown to be the final fulfillment of the Feast of Ingathering (Rev. 14:14–20). And finally, the destruction of spiritual Babylon and all of its material and religious idolatry was shown (Rev. 18:21–24).

We have been told exactly how the believer is expected to contend with the circumstances of the great tribulation in each of the three interludes of Revelation 12–14 (Rev. 12:10–11; 13:10; 14:12–13). These brief passages make it clear that it is the believer's continuing faith that the Lord calls for. Broadly speaking, this is called "the patience and the faith of the saints" (Rev. 13:10).

Eschatological promises that were prefaced by "to him that overcometh" were made to each of the seven churches of Revelation 2 and 3—promises that look forward to this day in the future. These promises have been extended to *all* church-age believers by the statement in each epistle, "Hear what the Spirit saith unto the churches."

Daniel teaches of this day, when the Lord will return in the clouds (Dan. 7:13–14) and give the kingdom of God to the saints (Dan. 7:27). The book of Revelation opens with a similar statement: "Behold, he cometh with clouds; and every eye shall see him, and they also which pierced him: and all kindreds of the earth shall wail because of him" (Rev. 1:7). The Lord reminds us of this day in the brief parenthetical aside between the sixth and seventh vial judgments: "Behold, I come as a thief. Blessed is he that watcheth, and keepeth his garments, lest he walk naked, and they see his shame" (Rev. 16:15). And now here we are, presented with the fullest account of this day in Revelation.

The Day of the Lord

Revelation 19 opens with a new vision given to John. This will be the day that the entire Seventieth Week has been leading up to. Old Testament prophecies of this day had a primary focus on Israel and its eventual redemption. In this New Testament presentation, the church takes the central role. Israel is not prominently featured, as it was earlier, but we know that the promises that were made to the Jews will be fulfilled on this day as well. The Day of the Lord is covered in its entirety in Revelation 19:1–20:6. This is now the time when dead believers will be raised incorruptible and the living gathered together with them. Preparations for the marriage supper of the Lamb will be made since the bride will have made herself ready, and the Lord will begin his reign on earth. But before Christ's millennial reign can begin, the Lord will return in "power and great glory" (Matt. 24:30) to defeat the Antichrist and the armies arrayed against Jerusalem and render destructive judgment on the unbelieving world (Rev. 6:16–17).

The Day Begins

> [1]And after these things I heard a great voice of much people in heaven, saying, Alleluia; Salvation, and glory, and honour, and power, unto the Lord our God: [2]For true and righteous are his judgments: for he hath judged the great whore, which did corrupt the earth with her fornication, and hath avenged the blood of his servants at her hand. [3]And again they said, Alleluia. And her smoke rose up for ever and ever. [4]And the four and twenty elders and the four beasts fell down and worshipped God that sat on the throne, saying, Amen; Alleluia. [5]And a voice came out of the throne, saying, Praise our God, all ye his servants, and ye that fear him, both small and great. (Rev. 19:1–5)

This vision begins with a fourfold praise of God in heaven for his judgment of the harlot Babylon. His judgments are described as righteous, and now the deaths of true believers that were martyred by the Church of Rome will be avenged (v. 2). John describes what he heard as "a great voice of much people in heaven" (v. 1). Notice the difference between this description and the one that follows (v. 6).

The Dead Raised, the Living Raptured

> [6]And I heard as it were the voice of a great multitude, and as the voice of many waters, and as the voice of mighty thunderings, saying, Alleluia: for the Lord God omnipotent reigneth. [7]Let us be glad and rejoice, and give honour to him: for the marriage of the Lamb is come, and his wife hath made herself ready. [8]And to her was granted that she should be arrayed in fine linen, clean and white: for the fine linen is the righteousness of saints. [9]And he saith unto me, Write, Blessed are they which are called unto the marriage supper of the Lamb. And he saith unto me, These are the true sayings of God. [10]And I fell at his feet to worship him. And he said unto me, See thou do it not: I am thy fellowservant, and of thy brethren that have the testimony of Jesus: worship God: for the testimony of Jesus is the spirit of prophecy. (Rev. 19:6–10)

The voice that John heard in v. 6, following the brief introduction in vv. 1–5, is given considerably greater prominence in the text and appears to be the voice of a larger multitude. I contend that the difference between these descriptions is that the first voice is that of the souls of dead believers in heaven, and the second is the voice of the glorified church after the resurrection and rapture. Revelation 20:4–6 will provide an overlay (recapitulation) to this prophecy, and the resurrection/rapture will be much more clearly stated. This is the moment at which believers will be given their immortal bodies.

Continuing, the voice of this great multitude in heaven is further distinguished from the first voice by a threefold description: "the voice of a great multitude, and as the voice of many waters, and as the voice of mighty thunderings." They make the statement that the Lord now reigns (v. 6). They announce the marriage supper and declare that the "bride"—all church-age believers—has made herself ready (v. 7).

This is the moment that the admonitions to endure and the promises to preserve have been leading up to—believers have now been given their rewards (c.f. Matt. 16:27). The dead have been raised, and the living have been caught up with them in the clouds (1 Thess. 4:16–17; c.f. 1 Cor. 15:51–54). The end of this age has arrived, believers have been clothed in the righteousness of Christ (v. 8), and the invitations to the marriage supper have been sent out (v. 9, c.f. Matt. 25:1–13).

The voice that John heard in vv. 6–8 is that of the great multitude. In vv. 9–10, the angel spoke to him and pronounced a blessing on those who have been invited to the marriage supper and affirmed that what he had heard is God's truth. John fell at the angel's feet to worship him but was told not to since he is a fellow servant of God. This may well be the "sweet" part of the prophecy contained in the little book that John was told to eat earlier (Rev. 10:8–10). If that is the case, then what follows would understandably be the "bitter" part of that prophecy:

The Wrath of the Lamb

> [11]And I saw heaven opened, and behold a white horse; and he that sat upon him was called Faithful and True, and in righteousness he doth judge and make war. [12]His eyes were as a flame of fire, and on his head were many crowns; and he had a name written, that no man knew, but he himself. [13]And he was clothed with a vesture dipped in blood: and his name is called The Word of God. [14]And the armies which were in heaven followed him upon white horses, clothed in fine linen, white and clean. (Rev. 19:11–14)

Next, John was given this vision of the Lord appearing in the heavens in glory (c.f. Matt. 24:30; Dan. 7:13). This is Christ's return to render judgment on the unbelieving world, put an end to the reign of the Antichrist, and usher in the kingdom of God on earth. He is given the titles "Faithful and True" and "The Word of God." Jesus was faithful to death on the cross in his first incarnation. He appears now, the second time, not as a sacrificial lamb riding into Jerusalem on a donkey (John 12:12–14) but as a victorious king.

Several verses earlier we saw that he was faithful to his promises to believers; now, he will be faithful to the promises of rendering destructive judgment on all evil in the world and in the hearts of unbelievers. The titles given Jesus throughout Scripture provide descriptions of his nature and character. He is given the title "the Word" in the epistle penned by John (John 1:1, 14). In v. 16, he is called the "King of Kings, and Lord of Lords." These make it clear that it is the Lord that John has been shown returning at his Second Coming.

The blood on the Lord's clothing (v. 13) is not from his crucifixion. It is the blood of battle (Isa. 63:1–4; 34:5–8). The armies that are with him, "clothed in fine linen, white and clean" (v. 14), are none other than believers who have just been given their immortal bodies in the resurrection/rapture (v. 8; c.f. 1 Thess. 2:19, 3:13; Col. 3:4; Jude 14).

The Antichrist and the Armies of the World Destroyed

> [15]And out of his mouth goeth a sharp sword, that with it he should smite the nations: and he shall rule them with a rod of iron: and he treadeth the winepress of the fierceness and wrath of Almighty God. [16]And he hath on his vesture and on his thigh a name written, KING OF KINGS, AND LORD OF LORDS. [17]And I saw an angel standing in the sun; and he cried with a loud voice, saying to all the fowls that fly in the midst of heaven, Come and gather yourselves together unto the supper of the great God; [18]That ye may eat the flesh of kings, and the flesh of captains, and the flesh of mighty men, and the flesh of horses, and of them that sit on them, and the flesh of all men, both free and bond, both small and great. (Rev. 19:15–18)

The vision continues with John being shown the fulfillment of all of the Old Testament prophecies of the Lord returning and destroying unbelievers at his Second Coming (c.f. Isa. 11:4; 34:3; 66:16). This will be the near-term fulfillment of the judgment of nations taught in the parable of the sheep and goats (Matt. 25:31–46). Jesus will destroy the armies of the world, which will be arrayed against Jerusalem (Zech. 14:1–7), while God's final vial of wrath will be poured out on the entire world (Rev. 16:17–21).

> ¹⁹And I saw the beast, and the kings of the earth, and their armies, gathered together to make war against him that sat on the horse, and against his army. ²⁰And the beast was taken, and with him the false prophet that wrought miracles before him, with which he deceived them that had received the mark of the beast, and them that worshipped his image. These both were cast alive into a lake of fire burning with brimstone. ²¹And the remnant were slain with the sword of him that sat upon the horse, which sword proceeded out of his mouth: and all the fowls were filled with their flesh. (Rev. 19:19–21)

Verse 19 describes the battle that will be facilitated by the pouring out of the sixth vial (Rev. 16:12–16). The Euphrates River will be dried up for the land forces to gather in the area of Mount Megiddo, and the three demon spirits will work miracles to deceive all the nations to join against Jerusalem (c.f. Zech. 12:1–9).

Verse 20 introduces us to the "lake of fire." This will be the final state of hell for all eternity. The beast of v. 20 is the man—the Antichrist. He and the false prophet will be the first to be thrown into this burning fire (c.f. Isa. 24:18). This will be the fulfillment of the prophecies of the Antichrist being "broken without hand" (Dan. 8:25), "that determined" being "poured out upon the desolate" (Dan. 9:27), and coming "to his end, and none shall help him" (Dan. 11:45). Paul speaks of the Antichrist ("that Wicked") as being the one "whom the Lord shall consume with the spirit of his mouth, and shall destroy with the brightness of his coming" (2 Thess. 2:8). This will be "the day of wrath and revelation of the righteous judgment of God" (Rom. 2:5; c.f. 2 Thess. 1:6–10).

After the Antichrist and false prophet have been eliminated, the Lord will do battle with the armies that have been gathered against him and Jerusalem (v. 19). Jerusalem will fall (Zech. 14:2), the Lord will set foot on the Mount of Olives (Zech. 14:4), and he will destroy the armies in the battle of Armageddon (v. 21; Rev. 16:14, 16; c.f. Zech. 12:9). At that moment, the Lord will pour out the Holy Spirit upon the Jews (Zech. 12:10), they will begin their period of mourning (Zech. 12:11), and he will be king over all of the earth (Zech. 14:9).

Satan Bound

> ¹And I saw an angel come down from heaven, having the key of the bottomless pit and a great chain in his hand. ²And he laid hold on the dragon, that old serpent, which is the Devil, and Satan, and bound him a thousand years, ³And cast him into the bottomless pit, and shut him up, and set a seal upon him, that he should deceive the nations no more, till the thousand years should be fulfilled: and after that he must be loosed a little season. (Rev. 20:1–3)

The prophecy continues with additional details of the events that will transpire on the Day of the Lord. Satan and his demons will be bound in the pit for one thousand years (v. 2): "And they shall be gathered together, as prisoners are gathered in the pit, and shall be shut up in the prison, and after many days shall they be visited" (Isa. 24:22). This is the same pit that the Antichrist will be raised from (Rev. 11:7; 17:8). This is not the lake of fire that the Antichrist and false prophet will be thrown into on the last day. Satan and his demons will be bound in the pit for almost the entire duration of Christ's reign on earth. They will only be allowed out at the end for a very short time, "and after that he must be loosed a little season" (v. 3).

This teaches that the kingdom of God on earth will be free from the deceptions and temptations of the devil for nearly its entire duration. This passage also provides the first two of six references to the duration of the kingdom of God on earth—one thousand years. This is the reason for the designation millennial kingdom.

The Millennial Kingdom Begins

The Resurrection, Rapture Revisited

> ⁴And I saw thrones, and they sat upon them, and judgment was given unto them: and I saw the souls of them that were beheaded for the witness of Jesus, and for the word of God, and which had not worshipped the beast, neither his image, neither had received his mark upon their foreheads, or in their hands; and they lived and reigned with Christ a thousand years. ⁵But the rest of the dead lived not again until the thousand years were finished. This is the first resurrection. ⁶Blessed and holy is he that hath part in the

> first resurrection: on such the second death hath no power,
> but they shall be priests of God and of Christ, and shall
> reign with him a thousand years. (Rev. 20:4–6)

The prophecy now continues with the greatest details of the resurrection that can be found in the Bible. In the first half of v. 4, John saw thrones and those that sat upon them. This speaks of all church-age believers and Old Testament saints. Thrones are a symbol of judgment, and we know that all of the faithful will be given this authority in the kingdom of God (Luke 22:28–30; Matt. 19:28; 1 Cor. 6:2; Dan. 7:22). John confirms this understanding of the thrones symbol by stating that "judgment was given unto them" (v. 4).

Following this broad description of all believers, John continues by describing a specific subset of this group—the great tribulation martyrs. These are believers who have been faithful unto death (Rev. 2:10). Please note John initially describes this group as "souls" (v. 4). At the end of v. 4, he indicates that "they lived," meaning that he had just witnessed the resurrection of the dead and rapture of the church, the moment of transformation of all believers into their immortal bodies. Many modern Bible translations render this, "and they came to life." This is an overlay to the prophecy that we studied in Revelation 19:6–9, providing additional details to the description of the bride having "made herself ready." The significance of specifically identifying this group of martyrs as being included in the resurrection will become apparent shortly.

Verse 4 concludes by saying that the resurrected believers "lived and reigned with Christ." Once again we know this to be one of the promises given to believers (Rev. 2:26–27; 3:21; 5:9–10; 2 Tim. 2:12; Rom. 5:17). There are also ample prophecies to support the understanding that Old Testament saints will be included in this resurrection as well (Ezek. 37:12–14; Dan. 12:1–3; Isa. 26:19; Rom. 11:15).

Passages like Daniel 12:2, John 5:28–29, and Acts 24:15 make it clear that there will be those who will be resurrected to eternal life and those who will be resurrected to eternal damnation. However, it is only now that we are taught that these are two separate resurrections, occurring one thousand years apart. Verse 5 indicates that what John had just witnessed was the first of these resurrections, the "resurrection of life" (John 5:29). Those who are not in this resurrection will not be raised from the dead until the thousand-year reign of Christ has ended: "But the rest of the dead lived not again until the thousand years were finished." Verse 6 provides a brief statement that this first resurrection will initiate the millennial reign of Christ on earth and that those who are in it—all believers—will live and reign with him.

We were introduced to the term "second death" in the eschatological promises to the seven churches (Rev. 2:11), and here we see the term again (v. 6). Later, it will be explained that the second death will occur at the second resurrection when unbelievers will be given their immortal bodies and thrown into the lake of fire for all eternity (Rev. 20:14–15; 21:8). Considerable prophetic foreshortening occurs between this verse and the one that follows.

Satan's Final Rebellion

> [7]And when the thousand years are expired, Satan shall be loosed out of his prison, [8]And shall go out to deceive the nations which are in the four quarters of the earth, Gog and Magog, to gather them together to battle: the number of whom is as the sand of the sea. [9]And they went up on the breadth of the earth, and compassed the camp of the saints about, and the beloved city: and fire came down from God out of heaven, and devoured them. [10]And the devil that deceived them was cast into the lake of fire and brimstone, where the beast and the false prophet are, and shall be tormented day and night for ever and ever. (Rev. 20:7–10)

The prophecy continues with a very brief description of how the millennial kingdom will come to a close. Satan and his demons will be allowed out of the pit to deceive the people of the world one final time (vv. 7–8). The armies of the world will surround Jerusalem again, and this time they will be destroyed by fire from heaven (v. 9). Satan and his demons will now be thrown into the lake of fire where the Antichrist and false prophet have been for the entire one thousand years (v. 10). "Gog and Magog" (v. 8) should probably be thought of as symbolic names since this is not depicting the same battle as that prophesied in Ezekiel 38–39.

The Great White Throne Judgment

> [11]And I saw a great white throne, and him that sat on it, from whose face the earth and the heaven fled away; and there was found no place for them. [12]And I saw the dead, small and great, stand before God; and the books were opened: and another book was opened, which is the book of life: and the dead were judged out of those things which were written in the books, according to their works. [13]And the sea gave up the dead which were in it; and death and hell delivered up the dead which were in them: and they were judged every man according to their works. [14]And death and hell were cast into the lake of fire. This is the second death. [15]And whosoever was not found written in the book of life was cast into the lake of fire. (Rev. 20:11–15)

Next, John saw a great white throne with God seated on it (v. 11). The earth and heaven "fled" away from him "and there was found no place for them." This is describing the final destruction of this universe, the moment that Peter prophesied as follows:

> [7]But the heavens and the earth, which are now, by the same word are kept in store, reserved unto fire against the day of judgment and perdition of ungodly men. [10]In which the heavens shall pass away with a great noise, and the elements shall melt with fervent heat, the earth also and the works that are therein shall be burned up. (2 Pet. 3:7, 10)

This will be the moment when this earth comes to an end—the time of judgment of the "ungodly." John saw the dead stand before God for judgment (v. 12). It is important to understand who will be included in this group. First will be all unbelievers that lived before the Second Coming of Christ. This includes the church age and all before that as well. The souls of these people will have been in hell the entire time from their deaths up to this judgment at the end of the millennium. Second will be all people who died during the millennium. This will include those who entered in their natural bodies at the end of this world and those who were born in the millennium and died during the millennium. This second group will be comprised of both believers and unbelievers. Church-age believers who died before the Second Coming and those raptured on the last day will not be in this group since they will have already been given their immortal bodies and judged at the judgment seat of Christ (2 Cor. 5:10; Rom. 14:10–12; 2 Tim. 4:1).

John describes "books" that people will be judged out of and "another book," which is clearly stated to be the "book of life" (v. 12). The "books" referred to can only be speaking of books of works that have been done throughout individuals' lives since it is stated that they will be judged out of these books "according to their works" (vv. 12, 13). The "book of life" is the book in which all believers have their names written (c.f. Rev. 3:5; 13:8; 17:8; 20:15; 21:27). This is the book that determines where a person will spend all eternity, either with God or in the lake of fire.

This passage is not teaching that there will be works-based salvation during the millennium. All people will be judged on their works (1 Pet. 1:17; Rom. 2:6, 10, 11; Rev. 2:23). Christians will be judged to determine their rewards (1 Cor. 3:12–15; Rev. 22:12), and unbelievers, presumably, to determine punishment (Rev. 20:12–13; 18:6; Matt. 11:24).

Verse 14 shows that the temporary place "hell" will be replaced with the permanent state, "the lake of fire." This will also be the time that death will be "swallowed up in victory" (1 Cor. 15:54). It was stated earlier that "the rest of the dead lived not again until the thousand years were finished" (v. 5). Remember, all church-age believers, including great tribulation martyrs, will be given their immortal bodies at the Second Coming (v. 4). Verse 5 tells us exactly what will happen to all unbelievers at the end of the millennium; they will "live again," be given immortal bodies as well.

This second resurrection will be the "resurrection of damnation" (John 5:29), the "resurrection of the unjust" (Acts 24:15). The particularly ominous news for unbelievers is that they will be given an immortal body that will be able to endure the lake of fire forever. After they are given this body and found not to have their name in the book of life, they will be judged according to their works and thrown into the lake of fire (v. 15). This is what is meant by the "second death" (vv. 6, 14; c.f. Rev. 2:11).

Also, v. 15 provides the definitive teaching on the "book of life." Anyone whose name is not in this book will be thrown into the lake of fire. This book contains only the names of believers, and it is not the book that anyone would want their name "blotted out" of (Rev. 3:5).

Concluding Thoughts

If any readers find themselves in a conversation with someone who is asserting a pretribulation rapture, the passage studied earlier (Rev. 20:4–6) is the best text to start the discussion with. It must be affirmed that what John had just witnessed is clearly described as the *first* resurrection, and great tribulation martyrs are expressly stated to be in that group. There is no other time in this world but in the great tribulation when a believer can be described as having not worshipped the beast or not taken his mark.

John initially saw them in their pre-resurrection state, "souls," and then directly after as "living." This is the group described by Paul as "they that are Christ's at his coming" (1 Cor. 15:23) when he addressed the order of the resurrection. And since the living will not precede the dead in the resurrection (1 Thess. 4:16–17), there is no possible way that the living could have been raptured at any time prior to Christ's Second Coming.

This passage also teaches that the first resurrection is not merely a "spiritual resurrection" but a physical one. If it were only spiritual, the Word of God would not have stated that they transitioned from souls to living. They would have just remained as souls. And there would be no need to juxtapose those who were just resurrected against those who were not (the unbelievers) by stating that the "rest of the dead lived not again until the thousand years were finished."

Revelation 20 also teaches us about the kingdom of God that is to follow this world. It will be a thousand-year reign of Christ on this earth. Following that manifestation of the kingdom, there will be the eternal manifestation (Rev. 21–22). This is not a contradiction to what was taught in Daniel 7:14 and 27, where it was said that upon Christ's return, he would establish an "everlasting kingdom." Instead, the later prophecy has provided additional details of how this everlasting kingdom will come to pass, first with the millennial reign and then in the eternal state, with God himself present, on a new earth with a new heaven.

So why go through an entire one thousand years on this earth just to have it all end with another rebellion? First, God made unconditional promises to Israel of a kingdom on earth with Christ seated on the throne of David. This will be given to the Jews at that time. Also, there will be a partial lifting of the Edenic curse, but not complete. This is because there will be people who enter the millennium in their natural bodies and their children who will also be in natural bodies. Even with Satan bound, this natural body and its sin nature, referred to as "the flesh" (Gal. 5:16–17; Rom. 7:5, 7:15–8:8), will still be the cause of sin and death (Isa. 65:20). For these people, the millennium will be a time of testing, just as this world is for us. And just as in this world, no one will enter into the eternal state with God without passing the test first.

Satan will not be allowed to entice man to sin for almost the entire one thousand years. However, at the end, he will be released and allowed to do so. The consequence of which will be a massive rebellion against the Lord. The unfortunate reality is that even with the Lord reigning from Jerusalem, many, "the number of whom is as the sand of the sea" (v. 8), will choose to deny the Lord and rebel against him. God will put down this final rebellion and put an end to this earth, fulfilling this prophecy:

> 24Then cometh the end, when he shall have delivered up the kingdom to God, even the Father; when he shall have put down all rule and all authority and power. 25For he must reign, till he hath put all enemies under his feet. 26The last enemy that shall be destroyed is death. (1 Cor. 15:24–26)

After this final rebellion and Christ putting down all his enemies, the kingdom will be delivered to God (v. 24). This will occur at the end of the millennial reign of Christ and will usher in the eternal state with God (Rev. 21–22).

There was an interesting passage in Daniel that I called attention to: "As concerning the rest of the beasts, they had their dominion taken away: yet their lives were prolonged for a season and time" (Dan. 7:12). It is only now that it can be understood. Daniel 7:11 teaches that the Lord will come and destroy the Antichrist, exactly as we just saw with the beast that will be thrown into the lake of fire (Rev. 19:20). However, the disposition of the other "beasts" (Dan. 7:12) is different. They will have their dominion taken from them but their lives will be prolonged for a while ("a season and time"). This is exactly what we just saw in these chapters of Revelation. Christ will return and destroy the Gentile kingdoms of the world and he will kill the people of those "beasts" (Rev. 19:21). Yet, their lives will be "prolonged" for the duration of the millennium—in hell—until the great white throne judgment (Rev. 20:5), at which time they will suffer the second death (Rev. 20:14–15).

This passage looks ahead to the one thousand year separation between the resurrection of the just and the resurrection of the unjust (Acts 24:15; c.f. John 5:29). The following passage also looks ahead to the time of Christ's millennial reign: "And they shall be gathered together, as prisoners are gathered in the pit, and shall be shut up in the prison, and after many days shall they be visited" (Isa. 24:22). As mentioned previously, this passage speaks of Satan and his demons being bound for nearly the entire duration of the millennial kingdom, only to be released for a short while at the end to deceive the people one final time (Rev. 20:7–8). Once again, this is an issue that only now we can have complete clarity on.

16

The Eternal State

We have been shown the end of this world as well as the manifestation of the kingdom of God that is to follow—the millennial kingdom. We have also been shown how the millennial kingdom will come to an end—a satanically led rebellion, which God will quash. At that time, this entire universe will be dissolved (Rev. 21:1; c.f. Rev. 20:11; Matt. 24:35; 2 Pet. 3:7, 10–11), and a new heaven and new earth will be formed by God (Rev. 21:1; c.f. Isa. 65:17; 66:22; 2 Pet. 3:13). All believers from the beginning of this world to the end of the millennial kingdom will have been given their glorified bodies, those who lived in this world at the first resurrection (Rev. 20:4–6) and those who lived during the millennial kingdom at the second resurrection (Rev. 20:12–15). There will be no more grief, and the final enemy—death—will have been destroyed (Rev. 21:4; c.f. 1 Cor. 15:26). God himself will be with his people for all eternity. This will not be some kind of a nebulous state where believers will be floating in heaven playing harps. Instead, it will be what Paul wrote of when he said, "But as it is written, Eye hath not seen, nor ear heard, neither have entered into the heart of man, the things which God hath prepared for them that love him" (1 Cor. 2:9).

With that said, there is no way that we can fully understand what this time will be like. However, God provides highly symbolic visual imagery for us to contemplate in the final two chapters of Revelation. Before proceeding, we must briefly review some aspects of the prophecies presented up to this point. Just as previous visions in Revelation have been highly symbolic in their presentation, this vision should be understood in the same way. We know not to expect four riders on horseback (Rev. 6:1-8), a woman to appear in heaven (Rev. 12:1), or a hideous beast to arise from the sea (Rev. 13:1). Likewise, we know that the imagery of the drunken, blasphemous harlot (Rev. 17:3–5) is intended to teach us symbolically. I believe that it is appropriate to consider the prophecies in the vision that follows to be equally symbolic and not to read them in an absolute, literal sense.

It will also now be apparent why the presentation of Babylon the Great was given as it was several chapters earlier in Revelation. To recap, the woman was the primary symbol in the prophecy and she was said to also be a city. The visual imagery and the spiritual name—Babylon—associated with the harlot taught of her nature: drunken, murderous, idolatrous, and rebellious. And since she was equated with the city, it was said that in totality, what was being spoken of was a religious system, its people, a spiritual state, as well as a literal city, Rome.

In this vision, the city is the primary symbol, and it is said to also be a woman, the Lamb's wife (Rev. 21:9–10). The visual imagery and spiritual name—New Jerusalem—associated with the city teach us about its nature: glorious, godly, faithful, and true. In this case, the religious system is Christianity, and its people are all Christians. The spiritual state is true godliness, and the literal city will be our eternal home with God—New Jerusalem. New Jerusalem symbolizes all godliness, the polar opposite of Babylon the Great.

A New Heaven and a New Earth

¹And I saw a new heaven and a new earth: for the first heaven and the first earth were passed away; and there was no more sea. ²And I John saw the holy city, new Jerusalem, coming down from God out of heaven, prepared as a bride adorned for her husband. ³And I heard a great voice out of heaven saying, Behold, the tabernacle of God is with men, and he will dwell with them, and they shall be his people, and God himself shall be with them, and be their God. ⁴And God shall wipe away all tears from their eyes; and there shall be no more death, neither sorrow, nor crying, neither shall there be any more pain: for the former things are passed away. (Rev. 21:1–4)

This vision begins with John describing a new heaven and a new earth. The old will be completely destroyed and a new created, free from the defilement of sin (c.f. Isa. 24:5; Jer. 3:9). This is what Peter meant when he said that "the works that are therein shall be burned up" (2 Pet. 3:10). Since this vision should be understood to be highly symbolic, I believe that the "sea," which will no longer exist, refers to Gentile, unbelieving nations of the world (v. 1). The New Jerusalem that John saw coming down from heaven was prepared as a bride (v. 2). Later, this city is said to be the bride (vv. 9–10). This means that the city is a figurative reference (metonym) to all believers—the people of the city. During the millennium, Christ was on earth to rule with a rod of iron (c.f. Rev. 2:27; 12:5; 19:15). There were both believers and unbelievers on earth at that time. In the eternal state, God will finally be with his people and there will only be believers present.

The Overcomer Will Inherit All Things

> [5]And he that sat upon the throne said, Behold, I make all things new. And he said unto me, Write: for these words are true and faithful. [6]And he said unto me, It is done. I am Alpha and Omega, the beginning and the end. I will give unto him that is athirst of the fountain of the water of life freely. [7]He that overcometh shall inherit all things; and I will be his God, and he shall be my son. [8]But the fearful, and unbelieving, and the abominable, and murderers, and whoremongers, and sorcerers, and idolaters, and all liars, shall have their part in the lake which burneth with fire and brimstone: which is the second death. (Rev. 21:5–8)

God will make "all things new," and there will no longer be any suffering of any kind. The "fountain of the water of life" (v. 6) is a figurative reference to eternal life (c.f. John 4:13–14). Verse 7 promises that the "overcomer" will "inherit all things." This is consistent with everything that we have studied to this point. Regardless of when a believer lives, they will encounter countless attempts by Satan and his demons to get them to depart from the faith or to believe some false doctrine (2 Cor. 11:3–4). To overcome means to remain in the faith and in the truth. All others (v. 8) will be in the lake of fire for all eternity.

The Religious System and Its People

> ⁹And there came unto me one of the seven angels which had the seven vials full of the seven last plagues, and talked with me, saying, Come hither, I will shew thee the bride, the Lamb's wife. ¹⁰And he carried me away in the spirit to a great and high mountain, and shewed me that great city, the holy Jerusalem, descending out of heaven from God, ¹¹Having the glory of God: and her light was like unto a stone most precious, even like a jasper stone, clear as crystal; ¹²And had a wall great and high, and had twelve gates, and at the gates twelve angels, and names written thereon, which are the names of the twelve tribes of the children of Israel: ¹³On the east three gates; on the north three gates; on the south three gates; and on the west three gates. ¹⁴And the wall of the city had twelve foundations, and in them the names of the twelve apostles of the Lamb. (Rev. 21:9–14)

One of the angels continues with John by showing him the bride of Christ (v. 9). As before, a woman symbolizes the religious system, in this case, Christianity. We know the bride is a reference to all believers —the church (Eph. 5:25–27; 2 Cor. 11:2). This bride has been faithful to her betrothed, unlike the unfaithful wife of God, Israel (Jer. 3; Ezek. 16; Hos. 2), or the harlot Babylon.

After telling John that he would show him the bride, the angel carried John away to a high mountain and showed him New Jerusalem descending from heaven, confirming our understanding of the figurative meaning of the city being the people of that city. In this case, the people are all Christians, contrasted to the people of Babylon the Great, the ungodly.

The Spiritual State–All Godliness

The remainder of the description of the city conveys its spiritual state (vv. 11–14), in this case, all godliness. Please recall the spiritual state of Babylon the Great was conveyed by the imagery of the woman; here, it is conveyed by the imagery of the city. The city is said to have the glory of God (v. 11). Its light is akin to that of precious stones. Entrance into this city is through twelve gates, named after the twelve tribes of Israel. And it is built on the foundation of the twelve apostles. The picture is of Jews and Christians being united as the one people of God—believers in Christ (c.f. Eph. 2:11–22; Gal. 3:26–29).

> ¹⁵And he that talked with me had a golden reed to measure the city, and the gates thereof, and the wall thereof. ¹⁶And the city lieth foursquare, and the length is as large as the breadth: and he measured the city with the reed, twelve thousand furlongs. The length and the breadth and the height of it are equal. ¹⁷And he measured the wall thereof, an hundred and forty and four cubits, according to the measure of a man, that is, of the angel. ¹⁸And the building of the wall of it was of jasper: and the city was pure gold, like unto clear glass. ¹⁹And the foundations of the wall of the city were garnished with all manner of precious stones. The first foundation was jasper; the second, sapphire; the third, a chalcedony; the fourth, an emerald; ²⁰The fifth, sardonyx; the sixth, sardius; the seventh, chrysolite; the eighth, beryl; the ninth, a topaz; the tenth, a chrysoprasus; the eleventh, a jacinth; the twelfth, an amethyst. ²¹And the twelve gates were twelve pearls; every several gate was of one pearl: and the street of the city was pure gold, as it were transparent glass. (Rev. 21:15–21)

The angel continues by instructing John to measure the city. This indicates ownership by God (c.f. Ezek. 40–42; Rev. 11:1–2). The city is a perfect cube, which follows the design of the Most Holy Place of the temple (1 Kings 6:19–20). The remainder of the description of the city, its wall, gates, and all that pertains to it speaks of absolute perfection and godliness, adding to the symbolism presented in vv. 11–14. Many of the precious stones are part of the high priest's breastplate (Ex. 28:15–21). And the gates are pearls, just as the Lord is referred to as the "pearl of great price" (Matt. 13:45–46); he *is* the entrance to this city (John 14:6).

The Literal City–God Resides With His People

> ²²And I saw no temple therein: for the Lord God Almighty and the Lamb are the temple of it. ²³And the city had no need of the sun, neither of the moon, to shine in it: for the glory of God did lighten it, and the Lamb is the light

thereof. [24]And the nations of them which are saved shall walk in the light of it: and the kings of the earth do bring their glory and honour into it. [25]And the gates of it shall not be shut at all by day: for there shall be no night there. [26]And they shall bring the glory and honour of the nations into it. [27]And there shall in no wise enter into it any thing that defileth, neither whatsoever worketh abomination, or maketh a lie: but they which are written in the Lamb's book of life. (Rev. 21:22–27)

[1]And he shewed me a pure river of water of life, clear as crystal, proceeding out of the throne of God and of the Lamb. [2]In the midst of the street of it, and on either side of the river, was there the tree of life, which bare twelve manner of fruits, and yielded her fruit every month: and the leaves of the tree were for the healing of the nations. [3]And there shall be no more curse: but the throne of God and of the Lamb shall be in it; and his servants shall serve him: [4]And they shall see his face; and his name shall be in their foreheads. [5]And there shall be no night there; and they need no candle, neither light of the sun; for the Lord God giveth them light: and they shall reign for ever and ever. (Rev. 22:1–5)

God and Jesus will be the temple of this city (v. 22). Their thrones will be in this city (vv. 1, 3). There will be no need for any light from the sun or moon since God's glory will be its light (v. 23). I believe that statements like this are intended to teach us much more than their literal meaning. In this case, that God will be present with his people, and there will be no evil (figurative darkness) in this place whatsoever —only the pure light of God's holiness (c.f. 1 John 1:5; Isa. 60:19–20). It is confirmed that nothing abominable will be allowed to enter (v. 27).

Verse 24 speaks of the people of the city also being there with God. They will serve him (v. 3), they will see his face (v. 4), and they will reign with him (v. 5). All of these statements point to New Jerusalem being a literal city as well. We also have confirmation that entrance into this city is based on faith in Jesus Christ: "They which are written in the Lamb's book of life" (v. 27; c.f. Rev. 20:15; 22:19).

Please notice something interesting. In this brief passage (Rev. 21:9–22:5) the description of this city has symbolically conveyed that it is referring to a people, a spiritual state, and a literal city. Also, the city has been equated to a woman—symbolically a religious system. In this case, that woman is the faithful bride—Christianity. Similarly, Babylon the Great was depicted in this fourfold manner as well. In the case of Babylon, the figurative cities spoke of the people and the spiritual state (all ungodly worship and materialism); and the literal city spoke of Rome. The woman, depicted as a harlot, was a reference to the religious system—Roman Catholicism.

The Gift of Eternal Life

Beginning in Revelation 22, the symbolism also transitions to a picture of the eternal life that will be given to the believer. Certain elements of this vision should be familiar to us, such as the "water of life" (v. 1; c.f. John 4:13–14; Rev. 7:17; Zech. 14:8) and the "tree of life" (v. 2; c.f. Gen. 2:9; Rev. 2:7; 22:14). These are figurative references to eternal life. It is also clear that this passage is still highly symbolic since the fruits from the tree of life are said to be for the "healing of the nations," something that will not be needed in the eternal state since there will be no death, illness, or grief of any kind (c.f. Rev. 21:4).

Be in a State of Watchful Preparedness

6And he said unto me, These sayings are faithful and true: and the Lord God of the holy prophets sent his angel to shew unto his servants the things which must shortly be done. 7Behold, I come quickly: blessed is he that keepeth the sayings of the prophecy of this book. 8And I John saw these things, and heard them. And when I had heard and seen, I fell down to worship before the feet of the angel which shewed me these things. 9Then saith he unto me, See thou do it not: for I am thy fellowservant, and of thy brethren the prophets, and of them which keep the sayings of this book: worship God. 10And he saith unto me, Seal not the sayings of the prophecy of this book: for the time is at hand. 11He that is unjust, let him be unjust still: and he which is filthy, let him be filthy still: and he that is righteous, let him be

235

> righteous still: and he that is holy, let him be holy still. (Rev. 22:6–11)

In the Olivet Discourse, Jesus said, "For all these things must come to pass" (Matt. 24:6). This was repeated at the beginning of Revelation in the statement, "Things which must shortly come to pass" (Rev. 1:1; c.f. Rev. 4:1). Here, the angel reminds John again that these events *must* occur (v. 6).

Further, the book of Revelation opens with the statements that the events described will occur "shortly" (Rev. 1:1) and that the time is "at hand" (Rev. 1:3). Here, the angel restates that these events will occur "shortly" (v. 6) and that the time is "at hand" (v. 10). And Jesus tells us that he will come "quickly" (Rev. 22:7, 12, 20). Do these statements mean that the events of Revelation should have already happened?

The Greek *tachu*,[1] translated "quickly" (vv. 7, 12, 20), can mean suddenly and by surprise (c.f. Rev. 2:5, 16; 3:11), corroborating his unexpected return, "like a thief" (Rev. 16:15). And the Greek *en tachos*,[2] translated "shortly," means "in a brief space" or "in haste." This means that the events will not be spread out over many years but will rather all occur within a short period of time.

Please recall the tribulations of the entire church age are foreshadowings of the great tribulation (Matt. 24:4–6), all of which "must come to pass" to serve God's purposes. The statements that the events will come "shortly," are "at hand," and that Christ will return "quickly," combined with the teaching that the book is for church-age believers (v. 16), serve to reinforce the message from the Olivet Discourse that believers must, at all times, be in a state of watchful preparedness (Matt. 24:32–25:13). Even though the prophecies of Revelation pertain to a future Seventieth Week, the expectation is for all believers to maintain spiritual preparedness regardless of when they live.

To counter the idea that his Second Coming would be coming soon, the Lord did imply that it would be a long time before his return. In the parable of the virgins, it was said that the "bridegroom tarried" (Matt. 25:5). In the parable of the talents, the master was said to be "traveling into a far country" (Matt. 25:14). And in the parable of the pounds (Luke 19:11–27), the Lord spoke of a nobleman traveling to a "far

---

1   Strong, *Concordance*, G5035.
2   Strong, *Concordance*, G1722, G5034.

country" to receive a kingdom specifically to dispel the notion that the kingdom of God would be coming soon (Luke 19:11).

Sheep and Goats Judgment–the Final Fulfillment

> [12]And, behold, I come quickly; and my reward is with me, to give every man according as his work shall be. [13]I am Alpha and Omega, the beginning and the end, the first and the last. [14]Blessed are they that do his commandments, that they may have right to the tree of life, and may enter in through the gates into the city. [15]For without are dogs, and sorcerers, and whoremongers, and murderers, and idolaters, and whosoever loveth and maketh a lie. (Rev. 22:12–15)

Earlier in these studies, it was stated that the sheep and goats judgment (Matt. 25:31–46) will have a near-term fulfillment and a distant, final fulfillment. The near-term will occur at Christ's Second Coming and will be a judgment of wrath. The final will occur at the end of the millennial kingdom and will be the permanent separation of believers from unbelievers. We have seen this final fulfillment described as the great white throne judgment (Rev. 20:11–15). Now, we have three more references to this final judgment (Rev. 21:8, 27; 22:15). In each case, unbelievers are described in vivid terms, and it is clear they will spend all eternity in the lake of fire—the second death (Rev. 21:8). They will not have any part of God's holy city (Rev. 21:27; 22:15).

In each case, the unbelievers are juxtaposed against believers. Believers are those who "overcome" (Rev. 21:7) and have their names in the book of life (Rev. 21:27; c.f. Rev. 20:15). They are said to be allowed to enter through the gates of the city (Rev. 22:14). The gates are symbolic of Jesus Christ, and only believers will be allowed to enter. It is important to understand the one characteristic that differentiates these two groups—faith in Jesus Christ.

Once again, works (v. 12) will be the basis for determining rewards. Similarly, the statement "Blessed are they that do his commandments" (v. 14; c.f. v. 7) is not teaching a different salvation from faith. Instead, it is consistent with other New Testament teachings. John teaches, "And hereby we do know that we know him, if we keep his commandments" (1 John 2:3). He further says, "And the world passeth away, and the lust thereof: but he that doeth the will of God abideth for ever"

(1 John 2:17). And, "For this is the love of God, that we keep his commandments: and his commandments are not grievous" (1 John 5:3). James teaches us to be "doers of the word, and not hearers only" (James 1:22, 25). We are told to pursue holiness (Heb. 12:14; 1 Pet. 1:15). We are to "put ye on the Lord Jesus Christ, and make not provision for the flesh, to fulfill the lusts thereof" (Rom. 13:14). And the Lord said, "Blessed are they that hear the word of God, and keep it" (Luke 11:28). Consequently, in v. 14 above, it should be understood that the statement "Blessed are they that do his commandments" is descriptive of true believers and not prescriptive for salvation since we know that salvation is entirely a gift of God through faith and not of works (Eph. 2:8–9).

Prophecy for the Churches–the Gift Is Free

> ¹⁶I Jesus have sent mine angel to testify unto you these things in the churches. I am the root and the offspring of David, and the bright and morning star. ¹⁷And the Spirit and the bride say, Come. And let him that heareth say, Come. And let him that is athirst come. And whosoever will, let him take the water of life freely. (Rev. 22:16–17)

The book of Revelation opens with the statement that it was given to John by an angel (Rev. 1:1), and now it closes similarly (v. 16). The prophecies contained here are for the churches so that we can be aware of what is coming, hold fast to our faith (Rev. 3:11), and be prepared to stay faithful unto death (Rev. 2:10) if called upon to do so. There is a "crown of life" (Rev. 2:10) waiting for all who "hear the words of this prophecy, and keep those things which are written therein" (Rev. 1:3; c.f. Rev. 22:7).

Jesus is both the root that David sprung from (c.f. Isa. 11:1, 10) and the physical offspring as well (v. 16; c.f. Matt. 1:1; Luke 1:32). The eternal life that he offers, which has been most gloriously depicted in these final two chapters of Revelation, is available to all. Anyone who thirsts can come and "take the water of life freely" (v. 17; c.f. John 3:16). All that a person has to do is believe that Jesus died for their sins and have faith in his atoning sacrifice.

The Lord's Final Warning

> [18]For I testify unto every man that heareth the words of the prophecy of this book, If any man shall add unto these things, God shall add unto him the plagues that are written in this book: [19]And if any man shall take away from the words of the book of this prophecy, God shall take away his part out of the book of life, and out of the holy city, and from the things which are written in this book. [20]He which testifieth these things saith, Surely I come quickly. Amen. Even so, come, Lord Jesus. [21]The grace of our Lord Jesus Christ be with you all. Amen. (Rev. 22:18–21)

There is general agreement that when differentiating between essential and non-essential Christian doctrine that eschatology falls into the non-essential category. I would tend to agree if that means that differing views should not constitute a reason for separation from other believers or imply that salvation is dependent on one's view.

However, vv. 18–19 above present an incredibly serious warning. It is to all that hear (can be applied to reading as well) the words of Revelation. Adding to or taking from these words will be met with the most serious consequences. There can be no question that being taken out of the book of life means eternity in the lake of fire (Rev. 20:15). There can also be no question that being taken out of the holy city means not being a part of the bride of Christ and not partaking of the gift of eternal life with God. Further, receiving the "plagues that are written in this book" means suffering the torments of unbelievers during the great tribulation.

Are these warnings only for teachers? That could be since the person has to "add to" or "take away," which may imply teaching. In any case, there can be no question that it will end up being an "essential" doctrine for those guilty of either of these transgressions. These final two chapters of Revelation contain the most beautiful promises to believers but also some of the most severe warnings, demonstrating what can only be described as the "goodness and severity of God" (Rom. 11:22).

"But ye, brethren, are not in darkness, that that day should overtake you as a thief" (1 Thess. 5:4). Come, Lord Jesus.

Bibliography

Bullinger, E. W. *Number in Scripture: Its Supernatural Design and Spiritual Significance*. 1921. Reprint, n.p.: Alacrity Press, 2014.

Gundry, Robert H. *The Church and the Tribulation*. Grand Rapids: Zondervan, 1973.

Hislop, Alexander. *The Two Babylons*. 1858.

Hunt, Dave. *Occult Invasion*. Eugene: Harvest House, 1998.

Hunt, Dave. *A Woman Rides the Beast*. Eugene: Harvest House, 1994.

Ladd, George Eldon. *The Blessed Hope: A Biblical Study of the Second Advent and the Rapture*. Grand Rapids: Eerdmans, 1956.

Longman, Tremper, David E. Garland, eds. *The Expositor's Bible Commentary*, vol. 13, Hebrews–Revelation. Grand Rapids: Zondervan, 2006.

McCarthy, James G. *The Gospel According to Rome*. Eugene: Harvest House, 1995.

Miller, Stephen R. *The New American Commentary: vol. 18 Daniel*. Nashville: B&H, 1994.

Rose Publishing. *Rose Book of Bible Charts, Maps & Time Lines*. 10th anniv. ed. Carson: Rose, 2015.

Strong, James. *The New Strong's: Expanded Exhaustive Concordance of the Bible*. Nashville: Nelson, 2001.

Tregelles, Samuel P. *The Hope of Christ's Second Coming.* 1864. Reprint, Bellefonte, PA: Strong Tower, 2006.

Tregelles, S. P. *Tregelles on Daniel: Remarks on the Prophetic Visions in the Book of Daniel.* 1852. Reprint, Eugene: Wipf & Stock, 2007.

Walvoord, John F. *Revelation.* Edited by Philip E. Rawley & Mark Hitchcock. Chicago: Moody, 2011.

West, Nathaniel. *Daniel's Great Prophecy: The Eastern Question. The Kingdom.* 1898. Reprint, University of Michigan Library, 2019.

Wenham, G. J., J. A. Motyer, D. A. Carson, R. T. France, eds. *New Bible Commentary.* 21st Cent. ed. Downers Grove, IL: InterVarsity, 1994.

Zuck, Roy B. *Basic Bible Interpretation: A Practical Guide to Discovering Biblical Truth.* Colorado Springs: Cook, 1991.